Karl Rahner

THEOLOGICAL INVESTIGATIONS

Volume VII: Further Theology of the Spiritual Life I

CONTENTS:

THEOLOGICAL
INVESTIGATIONS

Volume VIII

Also in this series

THEOLOGICAL INVESTIGATIONS

THEOLOGICAL
INVESTIGATIONS

VOLUME VIII
FURTHER THEOLOGY OF THE SPIRITUAL LIFE 2

by
KARL RAHNER

Translated by
DAVID BOURKE

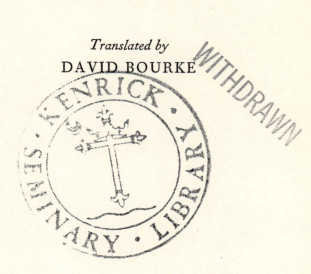

LONDON
DARTON, LONGMAN & TODD
NEW YORK
HERDER AND HERDER

DARTON, LONGMAN & TODD LTD
85 Gloucester Road, London, S.W.7

HERDER AND HERDER INC
232 Madison Avenue, New York, N.Y. 10016

A Translation of the second part of
SCHRIFTEN ZUR THEOLOGIE, VII
published by Verlagsanstalt Benziger & Co. A G., Einsiedeln

Printed in Great Britain by Cox & Wyman Ltd., London,
Fakenham and Reading. Nihil Obstat: John M. T. Barton, S.T.D., L.S.S., *Censor*.
Imprimatur: ✠ Victor Guazzelli, V.G. Westminster, 18th June, 1971.

CONTENTS

PART ONE

Patterns of Christianity

I

WHY AND HOW CAN WE VENERATE THE SAINTS?

THE seventh chapter of the Dogmatic Constitution on the Church lays down certain points which are additional and supplementary to what is usually called, in the current theological parlance, 'the veneration of the saints'. These are concerned with the eschatological character of the pilgrim Church and with the 'last things'. On the whole, however, this chapter remains in its definitive form as it was originally planned, a chapter on the veneration of the saints, and (without going into details) it presents a comprehensive view of what manifestly belongs to the Church's tenets and convictions on this point as upheld in her faith and life.

Over and above this certain considerations must here be presented which affect our attitudes as men and Christians of *today* towards the veneration of the saints.[1]

I. THE VENERATION OF THE SAINTS AS AN EXISTENTIAL AND THEOLOGICAL PROBLEM

On closer examination this chapter of the conciliar constitution appears to be devoid of any answer to a question which appears to us of today to be more pressing than it did to those of former generations. This is not intended as a criticism, or to suggest that there is a deficiency in the document which could have been avoided. What we feel to be missing here could not in any sense have been put forward as a conciliar statement, at

[1] In addition to the articles on this subject in the lexicons cf. M. Lackmann: *Verehrung der Heiligen* (Stuttgart, 1958); B. Kötting, 'Heiligenverehrung' in *Handbuch theologischer Grundbegriffe* I (Munich, 1962), pp. 633–641; P.-Y. Emery, 'L'unité des croyants au ciel et sur la terre. La communion des Saints et son expression dans la prière de l'Eglise' in *Verbum Caro* 16 (1962), No. 63, pp. 1–240; P. Molinari, *Die Heiligen und ihre Verehrung* (Freiburg, 1964).

any rate not at present, because virtually speaking it has not yet attained any *conscious* position in the Church's explicit awareness of her faith. Expression is given to the objective reality of the communion of saints, their existence in blessedness, their exemplary status, the fact that they are worthy of veneration, their ability to intercede for us with God. Attention is drawn to the fact that in all ages the Church has venerated the saints. By these statements – this is the message of the decree whether explicitly or implicitly expressed – the situation is made clear. We can and should venerate the saints. The only thing left for us to do is to respond to the reality with which we have been presented in the appropriate manner, and in fact to venerate the saints. At this point, however, it may appear to the man of our own times that one factor of decisive importance has been overlooked, namely himself. In other words the question has not been answered as to why and how he, in view of his own special peculiarities, can achieve any kind of relationship with the world of the saints even though the objective reality of this world is not denied. Presumably when faced with the Council's teaching on this point he feels like a young man (if the somewhat startling analogy may be forgiven) to whom a mother is describing the good qualities of her daughter, whom she is seeking to recommend to him as a future wife. He hears the message and does not dispute its accuracy, and yet no love is aroused in him. The fact that the girl is worthy of love does not mean that there is any corresponding ability to love on the part of the young man. 'Can' we of today venerate the saints? What has to be present in us as persons? What has to be brought out into the open, roused from its state of inertia, in order that we can manage effectively to respond to the reality which the Church brings to our notice? What are the basic conditions, subjectively speaking and from our side, in order that we can achieve anything approximating to a veneration of the saints?

How little the constitution is concerned with these difficult and obscure questions appears still more clearly from two small points in particular, to which attention may be drawn. The Evangelical Christian will perhaps admit the validity of all the objective statements contained in this chapter, and still not feel himself moved to actually venerating the saints in practice. In a certain sense it could be said that there is nothing in his own religious experience to correspond to this objective reality as stated in the constitution (and *for this very reason* and on these grounds alone he will find himself tempted to contest the objective accuracy of these statements).

And further: there is no doubt that an approach to the veneration of the saints might be worked out on 'existential' lines, or at least the ground might be prepared for such an approach. It might be pointed out that a Christian who believes in the truth that the dead are hidden in Christ with God now regards those whom he himself has loved in his own lifetime as already with God, whither they have gone before him. But the constitution contains no mention of any need for such an approach to be worked out, any need to try to appeal to religious experience of this kind at the human level, which is more readily responded to than the adulation of the Church's 'official' saints. Instead the constitution launches itself straightway into the world of the saints, quite unaffected by these considerations, and in this sense seems to envisage a kind of Christian who, with a kind of naïve religious realism, takes the objective reality of this world for granted as though it were obvious right from the outset, the kind of Christian who needs only to be told of the fact itself that the saints are worthy of veneration in order to respond, and does not need to be told how and why he should respond in the concrete.

The Decline of the Veneration of the Saints in Our Own Time

The present situation, however, is such that at least in the 'Cisalpine' countries of Europe veneration of the saints has suffered an extraordinary decline even among Catholics, so that the ability to practise such veneration seems to have undergone some kind of process of atrophy and decay. This assertion cannot, of course, be proved statistically, especially since the official cult of the Church has continued unchanged. But the fact itself should not be contested on this account. Rather it should be frankly recognised, and the causes of it should be enquired into. Nor should it be presumed from the outset that these causes must necessarily and in all cases be regrettable. This is not to say that we should no longer concern ourselves with the saints. The literature of the last few decades is probably neither smaller in volume nor worse in quality, but on the contrary, has become better than in former ages. But the interest which this literature presupposes and stimulates in the readers is still far from implying any attitude of veneration in the truly theological sense. We may have the greatest admiration for Francis of Assisi, and feel whole-heartedly that he is the very pattern and prototype of Christian living, yet at the same time not have 'said any prayers to him'. In this religious interest in Christians whose lives are impressive, exemplary or powerfully inspiring we Catholics are not fundamentally different from the Evangelical Christians who also have their saints in this sense (even to the point of martyrdom). Whether one venerates Bodelschwingh or Charles de Foucauld in this sense is a secondary question. The real question is whether the modern Catholic, when he has read the life of de Foucauld or his letters, really manages to enter into prayerful communication precisely with *him* as person, to 'call upon' him, to venerate him in a 'cult', as the language of tradition optimistically dares to call it. Now from this point of view it cannot be contested that modern man has to a large extent lost his capacity to venerate the saints. Admittedly a thousand examples to the contrary can be pointed to in the complex community of the Church, in which many ages live side by side with one another. Of course there is much to be found which seems to contradict this assertion in religious houses with their stable customs and their holy eagerness to see new saints from among their own members raised to their altars, as also in the practice of novenas and pilgrimages. But what we are concerned with here is the member of the Church precisely as conditioned in a special way by the atmosphere of the present world and of contemporary life. Even though he obviously intends to be a Christian and a Catholic he maintains an attitude of aloofness towards religious tradition and its usages, an attitude which is sometimes explicitly declared, but sometimes too only implicit and beneath the surface of his conscious life. And the real question is whether this decline in the veneration of the saints applies in the case of *this* kind of Christian. It is a question which in all sincerity must be answered in the affirmative. The fact that modern churches are, to so large an extent, bereft of images and pictures is in itself a sign of this. The statues and pictures of the saints are not missed or at the most are only missed because their absence makes the churches seem too cold and bare.

The Experience of the Silent God in Our Own Time

The reasons for this decline are manifold and far-reaching. Most contemporary Christians have already ceased to have any sense of being actively in communication with their own dead, the members of their family and the relations whom they have lost. Though there are exceptions to this the general attitude is that they have departed and vanished from this life. They are forgotten, and in so far as they are thought of at all attention is focused upon their lives while they were still among us and not in any true sense upon the fact that they are still living. It is not that we contest the fact that they are, in principle, living on in the presence of the God of the living, but so far as we are concerned they are not alive. They have been, so to say, completely and totally removed from our sphere of existence. Do we really believe that the city dweller still feels any need to visit the graves of his departed on Sunday after Mass as does the countryman? Is not the custom of placing lights upon the graves on All Souls' Day, at Christmas, etc., confined to one quite well-defined group which cannot possibly be regarded as 'representative' of contemporary life, a group which is slowly but relentlessly being squeezed out of modern society? But if a man thinks even of his own 'nearest and dearest' as disappearing at death into that darkness which surrounds the meagre light of our existence with its silent infinitude how can he then find it in himself to take up an attitude of veneration towards other dead persons during his life merely on the grounds that they were holier?

But there is a further and more radical reason. The capacity of modern man is essentially dependent upon an experience of God which is 'epochal', that is conditioned by the special circumstances of his own particular time. Thus special factors do arise even within the one 'final age' of the Church because the climate of thought and the situation of the world has a profound effect upon the Church also, its destiny and the quality of its faith. Now today it is precisely the man who really and genuinely believes who feels that God has become incomprehensible and 'remote' from him (even if the Christian knows that this incomprehensible and remote God is at the same time infinitely close as the mystery which freely imparts itself to him). Naturally this is something which has always been known and recognised. But modern man experiences it with a new and radical keenness because the world has become so inescapably vast and at the same time so profane, and also because, not surprisingly, God does not appear as one factor 'along with' others which are given in the everyday experience of this world. God is, to a large extent, experienced as the silent mystery, infinite in his ineffability and inconceivability. And the more man advances in his religious life the more *these* aspects of God come consistently to the fore (instead of diminishing). Into this silent, unfathomable and ineffable mystery the dead disappear. They depart. They no longer make themselves felt. They cease any further to belong to the world of our experience. When spirit and heart seek them, when our gaze follows them into the distance, and precisely when this quest is made in the religious sense (which has nothing to do with a 'spiritualist' kind of communication that remains within the dimension of this present world) then manifestly this gaze of ours meets only with the darkness of the divinity in which nothing can be distinguished any longer. Even if we say that for all this we 'know' by faith that the dead have not been dissolved into this unfathomable and ineffable darkness of the divine, but still live on, then it is always possible to reply: 'But they are no longer distinguishable *so far as we are concerned.*'

In other words it is possible to put the objection that the veneration of the saints considered precisely as a *religious* act cannot be thought of as a further projection of our ordinary connection with other media within this world, for this would be a kind of spiritualism. It must be specifically religious, i.e. the exercise of it must be directed towards God, and must bear upon the dead or the saints only in general terms in the attainment of this end. But ultimately speaking this must be reduced to an act of falling down in dumb adoration before the ineffability of God, and in that case how can it put us in touch with the saints? How can an act of this kind fail to be totally absorbed in and taken up with the inconceivability of God and his will? How can there still be any interest in the individual finite reality of this or that saint? When even petitionary prayer to God constitutes a difficult and obscure chapter in the religious life of modern man how can he still turn to a specific saint with a specific prayer for precisely *his* help? Will a man of our own times find it easy to believe, supposing that his prayer is heard, that it has been heard precisely because he turned for help to this specific saint? How many men of our own times will have the courage (leaving out of account the possibility that it is simply the mechanics of ancient religious custom that are at work) to choose one particular saint rather than another as a matter of personal inclination to be their patron? When the official Church, even today, still designates specific saints as 'patrons' for particular 'concerns' does any *genuine* religious interest still survive in this fact? Is not the fact that the veneration of the saints is in practice concentrated upon Mary, however wonderful this Marian devotion may be, in itself an indication of how slight the distinctions have become, so far as our personal feelings are concerned, between the individual saints in our veneration of them?

The Problem of How the Veneration of the Saints Is Reconcilable with the Adoration of God
It is only with great difficulty that modern man can achieve any clear

conception of what is meant by the intercession of the saints in heaven such as can be reconciled with his own 'rationalism' (which is, however, a justified rationalism) and with a kind of theological thinking that is realistic and not overweighted with fantasy. The questions which the modern Christian has to put (and he asks them either explicitly or as implied in his basic outlook on life, which is an extremely potent factor in his religion) are these: What sort of idea of the intercessory activity of the saints should I have? Is this intercessory activity on the part of the saints intensified or diminished according to the extremely varied ways in which those still on earth have recourse to them for their intercession? How is their intercessory activity to be conceived of in view of the absolute and immutable decrees laid down from all eternity in the mind of God, by which all things are controlled, and which themselves cannot be determined by any creature? In view of this can this intercession of the saints be anything else than the unconditional adoration of God, whose ways are unsearchable, to whom no-one gives counsel and who has no counsellor? But if this is the case then can we still say that the intercession of the saints is what we normally conceive it to be? And is it still dependent upon whether we who are still on earth supplicate the saints for their intercession? Is it not simply imparted to us according to the degree of our union with God, whether we explicitly ask them for it or not? For instance were Mary or figures such as Augustine less favoured with this intercessory activity since certainly they did not ask for it so much as a devotee of the Middle Ages? Now can it really be said that to all these questions the standard theology of the day has ready to hand an answer that is simple, clear and easy to understand?

Merely as an afterthought it may be pointed out that the distinction which is drawn between mere veneration and invocation of the saints (*dulia*) and the adoration of God (*latria*) is important and certainly correct in itself. But it rather obscures than solves the important problem involved. For while we think that we have arrived at a clear and valid distinction we overlook the fact that the *unity* of the two kinds of veneration represents just as great a problem, and indeed one that is even more important. Unless we can find a clear answer to this second problem it will be impossible to explain what is specifically Christian and *religious* in the nature of our veneration of the saints, and equally impossible to find out whether the veneration of the saints is in fact a Christian activity *or* a sort of mitigated spiritualism, magic, or a watered-down form of polytheism. We cannot simply assert that the veneration of the saints does not derogate from our adoration of God or of Christ as the unique mediator. We cannot simply regard the veneration of the saints (*dulia*) and adoration (*latria*) as basically united in virtue of the fact that there is unity in the object of these acts, in other words that the saints are united with God through grace and glory. We must also make it clear that there is unity in the subjective acts themselves, that they both pertain to one and the same basic act of 'religion'. In the theology of love of neighbour as a supernatural 'infused' virtue (of charity) an attempt is made at least to explain why and how such an act can and must at the same time be an act of the love of God himself. We should do the same with regard to the connection between veneration and adoration. It will have to be shown why and how the act of venerating the saints is really and intrinsically included, made valid and upheld by that of adoring God, because only in this way can it be a specifically *religious* activity, that is an act proceeding from our immediate union with God and empowered by the grace of God. Otherwise it would actually remain worthless, and even dangerous, from a religious point of view. The (correct) distinction mentioned above actually conceals something essential. It can be taken in the same sense as the statement 'Love of neighbour is not love of God', a statement which even though formally speaking it is correct, obscures the deeper truth of the unity which exists between these two kinds of love.

II. SOME PRELIMINARY THEOLOGICAL CONSIDERATIONS

But enough of problems. What can now be said in positive terms to explain the veneration of the saints, especially with regard to its 'subjective' aspects? In answering such a question it must always be borne in mind that the analysis of an act which is essential for our nature as human to be brought to its fullness, does not in itself effect this fullness in the concrete but rather presupposes it, and is ultimately comprehensible only in terms of it. For instance it is impossible to explain what love is in terms of a philosophy and theology of love to one who has never actually loved in any sense in the concrete. In the investigation which follows no claim is made to provide a comprehensive answer to the problem. Moreover other questions, connected with this central problem, will not be explored here, such as the question of what the saints in the Church are. They are not merely the happy 'fruit' of the Church considered as an official salvific institution, but rather the creators of new ways of Christian living, i.e. those specific kinds of holiness which have been required of the Church at particular epochs in her history. In the same way we shall not be treating of the question of the imitation of the saints, and why their life represents not simply a constructive model for others to copy but also a dangerous adventure which cannot simply be entered upon without qualification as a 'rule of life' (quite apart from the question of how far their personal limitations and weaknesses may have been conditioning factors in the total image of their lives). Furthermore the reader cannot be excused from having his attention drawn to certain prior considerations which may not be entirely familiar to him in all cases. In every department of theology the whole of theology must in some sense be present if it really is to be a department of theology in any genuine sense at all. But this inevitably increases the difficulty entailed in discussing specific points in theology.[2]

Christ Our Mediator With the Father
We may commence with the simple statement that for the Christian the connection with Jesus Christ the crucified and risen Lord is the basic and decisive act of religion, in which he attains to God who is *his* God and the God of grace, i.e. the absolute proximity of the mystery which imparts itself in the mode which makes it most effectively and most personally present. Two points are implied here.

The Significance of the Humanity of Jesus for Our Relationship with God
The specifically Christian connection with God is in its very immediacy mediated by the connection with Jesus, in other words through a creaturely reality. Naturally it is not possible here to develop this statement in its full significance and depths. Certain brief remarks must suffice at this point. First it has to be recognised that the risen and glorified Lord is and remains truly man. This fact of itself raises the same problem at this point as the one which we touched upon with regard to the veneration of the saints. So far as the exercise of *our personal* religion is concerned, why does Jesus as man not disappear into the silence and darkness of the divinity? This real and creaturely humanity of Jesus – why does it not become, in a certain sense, uninteresting and indifferent when we try,

[2] On this cf. K. Rahner, 'The Church of the Saints', *Theological Investigations* III, pp. 91–104.

with all the resources of our spirit, absolutely to transcend all that is finite, and in grace (which, in the last analysis, is the very presence of God himself to us), to find a way of entering into an absolute immediacy with God? Or is the position that we of today have arrived at such that we actually 'bypass' Jesus? And in that case are we really still Christians, or is Jesus, so far as we are concerned, simply an episode in saving history enacted here below upon earth, so that once he has attained to God himself at the resurrection, and once we have attained to God by the gift of uncreated grace, he simply disappears from view? There can be no doubt that many Christians, so far as any clear and explicit awareness of their religious life is concerned, remain, strictly speaking, at the level of an abstract monotheism. Certainly they recognise that they have been brought into God's mercy and into a direct relationship with him through the redemption wrought by Christ. But precisely on that account they suppose that they no longer have to deal with anything except with God himself purely in his divine nature and abstracting from the incarnation.

There is no doubt that the theology explicitly worked out by teachers and preachers has paid far too little attention to this question,[3] so that it almost appears as though the connection with the risen *humanity* of Jesus is a sort of adjunct within the total vision of the heavenly glory, supplementary to the vision of the triune God. And the experience of being brought into contact with mythological ideas has only had the effect of making it still more difficult to maintain this idea. If the teaching of the Church on this point is to have a genuine and non-mythological significance then it must simply be the case that the humanity of Jesus is the medium through which our immediate relationship with God is achieved. Of course if we 'picture' the 'figure' of Jesus to ourselves and use as a model for this purpose our external relationships with another man here in this life this statement is untenable. But in that case we have falsified our basic presuppositions. The immediacy of our relationship with God is certainly not invalidated by the fact that we achieve this relationship as our own ultimate act, and at the same time in this act achieve a special relationship with ourselves, find ourselves, as it were, anew. Rather both relationships must be thought of as essential and mutually complementary factors within one and the same act. We shall

[3] On this cf. K. Rahner, 'The Eternal Significance of the Humanity of Jesus for Our Relationship with God', *Theological Investigations* III, pp. 35–46. J. Alfaro, 'Christo glorioso, revelador del Padre', *Gregorianum* 39 (1958), pp. 220–270.

have something more to say on this point at a later stage, but for the moment let us notice in this connection that man is, from the very first moment of his existence and throughout, the being that achieves a relationship with itself precisely by achieving a relationship with the 'other', in the first instance the other creature, the 'thou', whether this latter relationship be one of love or hate. He is the being that can only achieve its true mode of existence, its own truth and the fullness of its own personhood precisely in this state of communication with the 'other'. In the light of this truth, this process by which our immediate relationship with God is achieved through the medium of Jesus the man becomes intelligible. We obscure the truth of this process of mediation if we think of it too much in the concrete. It must never be forgotten that the most real factor in the spirit is its cognition, its freedom, its love. In thinking of the spirit we must not take material entities as our conceptual model. We must not think of the spirit as a sort of 'support' on which the cognitive powers are then superimposed, and in relation to which they are merely secondary and supplementary, less 'real' than that which 'supports' them. It is only in its activities that the spirit achieves its own reality, and it is only in love that it comes alive in that twofold relationship which is essential to it right from the outset. When I love Jesus I perform that act which effectively achieves direct relationship with God. Why the mediating factor in this case should be precisely Jesus, why it should be that even in the case of one who does not explicitly recognise Jesus (in 'historical' terms) there is still a 'quest' for Jesus, albeit a blind one, in order that the immediate relationship with God may be achieved by grace and may be achieved through him as the mediator – all this cannot be gone into any further at this point. But in any case one fundamental principle is indicated here as to how the Christian experience of the sheer and absolute transcendence of God is achieved: not by rising above and leaving behind the finite, but precisely by being mediated through the finite, the 'world'. It attains to this 'absoluteness' of God as inserted into the world itself (at any rate in the case of Jesus), and recognises it as that which is most proper to itself, the 'supernatural state of being' bestowed upon it by God's grace. At this point the concepts break down. But we need only to remind ourselves of the teaching of the God-Man to realise as a doctrine indispensable to the Christian faith that God bestows himself in such a way that while remaining utterly unaffected in his own transcendence and grace he nevertheless becomes, in the most immediate sense, the *suppositum* of a created nature (and that too, in a mode which essentially goes beyond the ordinary 'Creator-creature' relationship). And what takes place in Jesus Christ with a pre-eminent fullness applies essentially, though in a minor and modified degree, to the world in general which God takes into his grace. But if this is so, then it follows that a right and full relationship with the world (which is, above all, a world of persons communicating in love and freedom) is in itself a relationship of immediate contact with God himself. This is not because of any logical necessity inherent in the conception of the world as created, but rather because, of his own free grace, God has, in this way, inserted himself into his own world. As a result this grace-given 'fact' is a permanent and essential factor in the life of every spiritual creature, one which it has to respond to whether implicitly or explicitly with either assent or denial if it is genuinely to arrive at a discovery of itself in a free act of self-comprehension (and by that very fact discover also the 'this-worldly' and creaturely 'thou' which corresponds to it).

Excursus: The Proximity of the Silent God in Jesus Christ
It may be permitted to insert at this point a brief consideration of certain aspects of saving history. Since the essential characteristics of the individual acquire their definitive form in his own history it follows that the historical situation in which he is placed, the spirit of an epoch, plays its part in determining the mode of his formation, and changes the mode in which these characteristics find expression. But now there is only one direction in which the history of man's discovery of himself can run its course; the eschatological situation brought about by Jesus, in which this history must unfold, cannot be reversed. And because of this the task of the Christian, the task which the message of Jesus Christ forces him to face up to, cannot consist simply in establishing for himself that God is silent and absent from his life (whether this is true or only a misinterpretation to be ascribed to his own subjective thought-processes), or in enduring this state of affairs as something to which he has been subjected. It is required of him to make real to himself the immediacy of God as the mystery which in Jesus is *near* to him and forgiving. He has to do this in the conscious effort of a faith which is capable of growing. The contemporary historical situation which was touched upon at the outset can play its part in determining the form which this effort of faith takes. As an effort of faith it may bear the 'signs of Jesus' in itself, and bring with

it the experience of his own desolation on the Cross. But in making this
effort man is promised that by grace he will achieve a sufficient degree of
success. But now, among the factors present in this special situation of the
age we live in, there is one in particular which belongs to it in a quite new
and radical manner, one which is still growing and the full benefits of
which may perhaps only be felt in the future. This is the fact that man finds
himself only in his fellow man, that it is in love for his fellow that man
realises himself, and this love is not simply one task or duty among many
others, but rather the fulfilment of the 'law', i.e. of his own nature (and
if there is a true sense in which a man's 'heaven' must be his fellow man as
beloved by him, then Sartre's aphorism to the effect that 'Hell signifies
other people' cannot be true). But if this is the case then it follows that
our contemporary situation, viewed precisely from a Christian point of
view, cannot be characterised as the absence of God as thus conceived of at
all. It cannot be that which makes it impossible to discover him in Jesus for
what he is in himself, in his immediacy. Someone may reply that the
terrible thing about the present is precisely that we cannot love our
'neighbour', that he is precisely hell for us. But one who in a spirit of
faith and love never permits himself to doubt the fact that he is able to
love cannot truly dare to say that in this particular contemporary situation
of the spirit of Jesus one cannot love. How man can do this and what the
implications are of the fact that Jesus is not simply another word, a
mythological cypher for God, but rather is himself the crucified and
risen Lord, and how and why God himself is attained to precisely in this
(not through this) and attained to in himself alone – these are questions
which cannot be entered into further at this point. For the purpose of our
considerations it is sufficient to take our stand upon the fact that it is
possible for Christ to be our mediator in bringing us to the immediacy
of God through the 'thou' of another as accepted in love, because this
loving mediation in Jesus is the basic doctrine of our Christian faith.
Indeed 'faith in Christ' should not be misinterpreted as mere faith in a
state of affairs, or supposed to be faith in God himself which is merely
'stirred up' and encouraged by our encounter with the historical Jesus. This
faith means a true and essential personal connection 'in Christ' with God.

The 'Presence' of the Historical Lord

This act which is basic to the Christian religion, in which Jesus the crucified and risen man becomes the mediator who brings us to the immediacy

of God, is also and no less essentially an '*anamnesis*', the recalling and rendering present of his history in the Eucharist and in the tradition of the Church. The subject of this act is the risen Lord as now living. But it is of decisive importance to understand that the act bears upon him precisely in so far as he once had a history of his own, a history which he has now left behind him as that which has passed away, and yet, insofar as he *has* his own history, still remains present and effective precisely as something which is no longer in process of development, but as something completed and existing in his 'eternity'. The connection with the risen Lord and with the 'historical Jesus' is not achieved by two distinct acts of religion, but by one and the same act. Eternity is not a further projection of history into another dimension of time, but the sheer reality of the history itself as accomplished and complete. And thus the connection with the glorified Lord is the *anamnesis* of the crucified and dead Lord not merely in the sense that we 'know' that he whom we love 'once' had this history, but in the sense that he is loved in the eternal and enduring reality of his *history*, and, precisely as the one who has lived through this history, is the mediator who brings us into the immediate presence of God.

The Love of God and the Love of Neighbour is One and the Same Love
Now it might be objected that the considerations set forth above with regard to our relationship to Jesus do not advance us any further in what is for us the real question, first on the grounds that because of the uniqueness of Christ's mediatorship it is illegitimate for us to apply our findings on this to the saints and our veneration of them, and also on the grounds that in our observations up to this point the possibility of venerating the saints from the *subjective* point of view has not been made clear. In other words the problem which we are really seeking to solve still remains outstanding. Certainly these christological considerations do throw light upon one point at least, namely the value of a religious act in which a creaturely entity endowed with personality and a personal history becomes a mediator, and so provides access to God himself, so that this act really does become an act of religion. But to enter more deeply into both of these ideas let us make use of a consideration which can serve to make two points more comprehensible: first how rightly to transfer the specifically christological ideas to the relationship between us and the saints, second the subjective aspects of the possibility of venerating the saints. We refer

to the relationship between love of neighbour and love of God within one and the same grace-given power of charity.

Personal Love as a Basic Human Act

First it must clearly be recognised that the relationship of love between a spiritual 'I' and a similarly constituted 'Thou' is not simply one kind of achievement among many others of equal value, but rather *the* true and all-embracing act which is fundamental to human living. The very fact that the human environment in the true and authentic sense is constituted by the *persons* with whom one lives is in itself sufficient to establish this. It is the environment of *personal relationships* in this sense that provides the world in and through which man discovers himself and realises himself, and . . . comes forth from himself. Knowledge must be integrated and elevated through this love in order to have a completely human meaning. The world of facts is, in the last analysis, significant only as one element in the life of man or in the world of personal relationships which is his. Personal love of one's fellows is the basic act, the truly and fully moral good (*bonum honestum*).

Now against this thesis it might immediately be objected that it is rather love of *God* which is *the* basic act, or which is at least as important in its claims upon man, if indeed it does not stand higher in the scale of values by comparison with the act of loving personal communication. But abstracting for the moment from the question of how we can determine more precisely how the two acts are interrelated (a point which we shall shortly have to enlarge upon) it must not be overlooked, in the first place, that in himself and so far as the created spirit is concerned, God is not one 'object' *among* others. Man cannot orientate himself to God in the same way in which he orientates himself to the multiplicity of objects and persons in his 'this worldly' experience, that is with a divided and partially distracted mind. In the original and basic act in which God impinges upon man (and this act precedes all conscious awareness of him) he is always given simply as the ultimate *basis* of experience, that which is beyond the world, upholding it in being and so making the experience possible. In other words God is present here not as a direct object of knowledge or experience but only 'indirectly' as that which is on the horizon of our experience. And even in those cases in which God is taken as the 'subject' of our religious thought, and so, in a true sense, as an 'object', where he himself speaks to us and becomes a 'partner', this always takes place in a

man who is already 'worldly', i.e. has committed himself by loving intercourse with his fellow men to personal encounter and communication
with the 'thou' in his 'this-worldly' experience. And conversely this
communication in love on man's part with the persons with whom he lives
is in itself (at least implicitly) a coming to God and into his presence,
because the self-commitment of a love which totally accepts the 'thou' of
the other being is always in itself, and in an implicit manner, love of God
as well. Thus when God addresses man in saving history, and so makes it
possible for man to realise and reflect upon his relationship with God, this
always presupposes as an essential prior condition that man has already
committed himself to a relationship of love in the 'this-worldly' context,
and this human love of his has in itself and of its very nature an implicit
tendency towards an immediate relationship with God. Impelled by the
dynamism of the spirit and by grace it carries man towards God, and only
in doing so fulfils its own nature.

Love of Neighbour as Love of God

Our meaning will be made clearer if we consider the more concrete
assertions of traditional theology. Theology firmly maintains that there is
a love of neighbour which is itself a 'divine virtue', such that its 'formal
object' is God himself, i.e. a virtue which is exercised and achieved in a
relationship of immediate contact with God in himself. Now however
traditional this thesis may be in theology it is an astonishing one. For what
it implies, if it is taken seriously, is that the neighbour is not only loved
because God wills it and so any violation of this commandment would also
constitute a denial of the love of God. What this thesis implies is that the
exercise of love of neighbour (as charity) is *ipso facto* and in itself the love
of God. But as true love it is a love that is supported by grace. In other
words it is a love that is made open by God to attain to God. Now this is
achieved not merely here and there but always and in all cases, where the
neighbour is truly loved. For there is no need (at least in any absolute
sense) for us to think of the grace necessary for this as though it were
merely offered at random and now and then. On the contrary this grace
is bestowed upon man, certainly as an act of God's free favour, but in *all*
cases, regardless of whether it is accepted by him (to his sanctification) or
refused (in which case it inevitably becomes a judgment upon him). This
love of neighbour is really *love* in a sense which conforms to the genuine
and most basic experience of man in the actual cases in which he loves. It

is not, therefore, merely the fulfilment of one commandment which is intended to protect man by shielding him from the effects of the brutish egoism involved in another. Where it is only the rights of another that are respected, where man keeps himself to himself, there is no love in the true sense, and in this situation the absolute essence of love cannot be achieved. It is for *this* reason that love of neighbour can be of supreme value, and can in itself be the fulfilment of the law. And it is for this reason that in Jesus' description of the judgment the judge only enquires into the one point of whether in our acts or our omissions we have loved our neighbour, seeming in this to be judging by norms which are quite atheistic in character.[4]

The Experience of God as Transcendental and as an Object of Enquiry in Itself

But how is this possible? In order to see clearly on this point certain distinctions must be recognised from the first. Knowledge that is developed and *reflexive* (and the decision corresponding to this) bears directly upon the *concept* of a given reality, whereas the *original* act of knowledge and freedom (however much this may also entail an element of the conceptual) bears upon *the actual reality itself*. This is made present to the knower either directly as an *object*: the flower and the man whom we love, or indirectly and in a manner which does *not* make it present as an object, in that dimension in which the spirit of man is infinitely removed from, and elevated above everything in the human environment and in human relationships which could be rendered present to it as an object, and comes to that state which we call one of 'elevation', the transcendental state.[5] In this state God's self-bestowal in grace is experienced with an immediacy in which the 'object' is precisely not brought into line with the other objects of the first-named experience, is not assignable to any particular 'category'. Thus the process by which we make conceptually present to ourselves both God himself and our connection with him in knowledge and love, so that both he and it become 'objects of enquiry' to us, however important and necessary this process may be, is ultimately *secondary*. Of course in this too it is precisely the reality of God himself

[4] For fuller details on this cf. 'Reflections on the Unity of the Love of Neighbour and the Love of God', *Theological Investigations* VI, pp. 231–249.

[5] cf. K. Rahner, 'Reflections on the Experience of Grace', *Theological Investigations* III, pp. 86–90.

that we are explicitly directing our attention to. But in the last analysis this
is in fact because in this act, which bears upon a concept, a still more basic
and more elemental act takes place, one which has been elevated by grace
to a state of transcendence in which it bears upon the reality of God himself and is upheld and sustained by it. The act achieved by our explicit
consciousness always rests upon and presupposes the basic act, without
being able to 'take it in' or thematise it in any exhaustive or comprehensive
sense in each case.

The original transcendental experience of God in grace, however, is
necessarily mediated by personal communication within the 'this-worldly'
sphere. For even an act of this kind, and precisely this, needs an object
presented in terms of the particular categories, in other words ultimately a
'this-worldly' 'thou'. The original relationship with God is love of neigh-
bout, the ultimate value of which is, of course, dependent upon this grace-
given connection with God implicit in it. The thematic act which refers
to God in conceptual (symbolic, cultic, etc.) terms always bears the sign
of its origins and the fact that it proceeds from that act of love of God
which is love of neighbour. Without this reference to one's fellow men it is
not genuine. Certainly this theological character of love of neighbour is
only present in it through grace, and this itself cannot fully be the object
of reflection. But the theological character of love of neighbour is, nevertheless, something that we can experience, even though inadequately,
and even though we certainly cannot recognise it by investigating it in
isolation and without reference to the history of salvation and revelation.
For it is in this history that this character of love of neighbour has acquired
objective status and becomes assignable to a particular category. For in
the free decision of love, in the total and earnest acceptance of our neighbour, we assent to God in an act which, upheld as it is by the grace of
God, signifies our immediate relationship with God. And even though
man cannot be certain that he has achieved this assent, cannot 'take any
credit' for it, still he can have some awareness of it in a non-objective
sense; for even though it has been bestowed upon him in grace it is, nevertheless, the assent which he himself utters to God in his heart.

To sum up: Love of neighbour is the unique categorical and original
act in which man attains his full creaturely reality, and thereby achieves
the transcendental and direct experience of God through grace. This
experience represents the highest aspect and the ultimate value of love of
neighbour, and it is objectified in our explicitly religious acts. In this

sense it is the ultimate and *basic* act of love of God *and* of neighbour, which the *explicit* acts presuppose, but among all those acts of personal fulfilment which can be objectified to ourselves the religious act derives its special value from that which the agent explicitly formulates to himself as its object, and is therefore higher in degree than an act in which the agent takes a creature as the object which he makes conceptually present to himself.

In conformity with this the love of Jesus Christ represents the unique and the highest act of love of neighbour, because when he becomes the 'thou' which is the object of this act the absolute fullness is given irrevocably of that which all love of neighbour presupposes and gives its assent to in the 'thou' to which this love is directed: a unity of God and man which is the basis for that unity which exists between the divine and human aspects in love of neighbour.

III. THE VENERATION OF THE SAINTS AS ADORATION OF GOD

We are now in a position briefly to apply what has been said to the saints. The 'saints' – in common with all who have died in Christ[1] – belong to Christ Jesus. They are a part of his Body, are included in the *anamnesis* in which the Church becomes a further projection of the Body of Christ, and therein maintains herself as well as their history now become definitive and complete.

The saints can be loved with a true and grace-given love, and in such love just as immediate a relationship with God is attained as is achieved in other situations through a Christian love of neighbour. This latter, indeed, becomes a specifically *religious* act precisely in virtue of the fact that it brings us into an immediate relationship with God in this way. But in our love of the saints the unity with Christ which is present in this love and which is presupposed in the beloved is not (as in love of neighbour in the ordinary sense) simply an implicit unity, and one which is in danger of being lost (because the unity of the neighbour with Christ has not yet been 'made manifest' in its definitive fulness). The unity with Christ achieved in love of the saints is rather something that is explicit and definitively complete and is the object of faith. This means that it has one advantage over love of neighbour in the ordinary sense: the theological

---

[1] cf. K. Rahner, *On the Theology of Death*, 'Quaestiones Disputatae' 2, 2nd ed. (London and New York 1965).

and christological character of love of neighbour here comes clearly to
the fore. Now we can only effectively realise such love when it has first
been given to us to come to the act of love in the concrete for the man
who confronts us in the body here and now, and only in virtue of this.
And because of this fact, even in the most sublime act of love for Jesus
and those who have been definitively united with him, the ordinary love
which we bear to the 'thou' of our everyday lives is the basis and prior
condition for this (and, as has been said, this 'down-to-earth' love in
itself constitutes us in an immediate relationship with God in Jesus). To
put it in biblical terms, only he who has encountered the Christ whom he
does not yet recognise in his brother and sister can then go on to encounter
him in manifest and explicit form, at latest in the judgment.

Now abstracting from the veneration of the saints as practised by the
Church as a whole and in her 'official' life (she *must* venerate the saints
in order thereby to preach the victory of God's compassion), the outcome
of these considerations is that the veneration of the saints is not in itself
laid as an absolute duty upon the individual Christian. He already achieves
the essence of this act in his love of neighbour. Of course he should not
radically and explicitly disassociate himself from the exercise of this
veneration in the liturgy, in which the Church bears concrete witness to
the fact that the grace of God does achieve its redemptive purpose in
actual fact in the world taken as a whole. From what has been said it can
also be understood that in order to bring the individual to any living
understanding of what veneration of the saints should mean we must
begin by making him understand that his absolute love, which he bears
towards the men involved in his own personal life, remains and undergoes
further development into what truly is a veneration of the saints, provided
only that this love has in it the courage of the Christian hope that those
who are loved have been saved by God's grace. We must begin by making
the individual understand not only this but also the reasons for this. Even
though we of today leave the dead in what seems to be the silence of
neglect this still has a wholly positive side, which can serve as a recommendation to achieve genuine discretion and quietness in the official
veneration of the saints too. In the silence of death, in the silent presence
of God precisely as the inexpressible mystery, God is actually closer and
more 'present' than in much talking. This must be allowed to apply
equally to the private and the 'public' or 'official' veneration of the saints.
Moreover this latter does not only celebrate the saints as they were on the

day of their death, but envisages their actual home-coming. In view of this it can be said that even the evangelical Christian does, in a certain sense, venerate the saints, for he loves his dead, whom he believes to have gone home to the Redeemer. Now the further step of 'invocation' is at basis only the courage of that love which utters a 'thou' that extends beyond all death, and the courage to believe that no-one lives alone, but that the life of each individual in Christ had a value in God's eyes which makes it efficacious for all. But the 'intercession' of the saints does not in any sense signify some kind of agency of intermediaries or 'court of second instance', but rather this: that every life lived in faith and love is of permanent value and significance for all, and that the redeemed man in the state of blessedness receives and lives this significance of his life. And because it is a spiritual world that is in question here, to which God has imparted himself, and in which each is responsible for all, in which one can have a significance for others, the invocation of an 'official' saint whether explicit or implicit, or of one of the individual Christians whom we believe and hope to have gone home to God, and whom we still love, is always the invocation of *all* the saints, i.e. an act by which we take refuge in faith in the all-enfolding community of all the redeemed.

The basic mystery of Christianity is not that God has created a world different from himself, in which he must be served as Lord, which gives him greater honour in proportion as it disappears, but rather that the grace which in the last analysis is identical with God himself, has permeated the world with God's own presence. And when the world runs its course in this sense it is progressively glorified and redeemed. God himself celebrates the increase of his glory, and causes man to come into a direct relationship with himself in and through this divinised world. All this in and through Christ; but nevertheless through Christ he does achieve this as a real and effective relationship. Hence the doctrine of the veneration of the saints is not merely a demand for us to learn what Christianity means. We of today find this part of Christianity difficult, for in the present situation the practice of Christianity is not easy. We must not make it still more difficult by acting as though it were so. But the saints whom the Church venerates will help us precisely here in our current practice of Christianity. They are our brothers who have already attained their perfection, and they entreat the God of the living to let that light shine upon us too which is the manifestation of his own love and the blessed eternity of his own life.

2

ALL SAINTS

This festival at the end of the ecclesiastical year, which is consecrated to the memory of all saints and celebrated with such solemnity and joy in the liturgy, does not seem to represent any very effective or living force in the awareness of the Christian of today. This may be due in no small part to the fact that it coincides so closely with All Souls' Day, and therefore derives its character to a large extent from this latter festival in our religious practices. On All Souls' Day we are accustomed to make pilgrimages to the graves of our dead, to those final memorials which signify that one who was beloved is still not forgotten. When we consider the matter from the theological point of view it is by no means so far-fetched to regard All Saints and All Souls as connected by the fact that a single common meaning is to be found in both. In fact we do not know precisely where the dividing line falls between All Saints and All Souls. In the deepest sense, indeed, it is not of any great significance, and is in any case provisional. Certainly on All Souls' Day we pray for those who are still in an imperfect state, those already beyond the grave who are still in process of coming to their final perfection. But at the same time these are the ones who have departed in God's grace, who, as the liturgy puts it, have gone before us in the sign of faith and now rest in the sleep of peace. We are praying, therefore, for those upon whom God has finally and definitively bestowed his grace, never more to withdraw it from them. And when we celebrate All Saints we have in mind chiefly those saints who are anonymous, the unknown saints who have not made any general impact in the Church and are not mentioned in her praises.

From one point of view, therefore, the distinction between All Saints and All Souls is only slight. But at the same time it must be recognised that each of these days has a special mystery of its own which distinguishes it from the other, a mystery which deserves to be pondered and prayed in its own right, a word peculiar to itself which has been spoken by God into the Church and is intended through it to reach into our hearts. What mystery, then, does this word stand for which is addressed to us on the festival of All Saints? By way of preliminary it might be answered: The fact that men have attained to their ultimate and definitive goal – that in itself constitutes something that is wonderful. Anyone capable of feeling a spirit of fraternal solidarity with others, anyone who can mentally project himself into others, who is not so terribly isolated from others that when anyone else is mentioned he asks either explicitly or implicitly what that other is to him – anyone of this kind must or should in a very real sense celebrate a festival of rejoicing in his heart because he can say to himself: there are some who actually have arrived, who are perfected, who are already in a state of blessedness, who have attained their due measure of perfection and have not wasted their lives, men to whom something improbable has happened: to be drawn out of and beyond themselves in love, men in whom one does not find emptiness and hidden egoism when they are stripped bare and exposed to view, men who have not wept in vain, who have found life through death and the eternal kingdom through loss, men who by the everyday conduct of their ordinary lives have achieved a dimension of life which is to an undreamt of extent absolute and of such value th 'once for all', andat it is worthy never more to perish for all eternity. To this it might be added that we have the right to hope that we can find all those whom our hearts have loved among these who have won and been favoured with the happiness of eternal bliss. Our forebears, the friends who have already gone home, our dead comrades, the nameless soldiers who have died, those who suffered so much while they were upon this earth, the noble spirits whom we have known, all – all who have impressed us as having hearts that were far too full of goodness and human greatness for the eternal God to allow them to perish, for them to have been lost to him who sought them upon his own way of the Cross, who was looking to them even as his darkened eyes gazed upon the void of that death which he had taken upon himself in order to save sinners. We might add that a further implication of this is that *all* human life is so precious and so noble that it can be brought to this final outcome, that it is only to our short-sightedness, our hardness of heart, our pride, that it seems as though there were far too many human lives, as though there were a sort of mass-production of humanity and a frightful waste of human material in the mass. We might add, therefore, as a further message which this festival has for us, that God can make all

into saints, into miracles and masterpieces so full of unexpected blessedness that one's heart can be transfixed with delight at them a whole eternity
through. What this festival is saying to us is: Where there is not actually
the most profound guilt, where there is not diabolical evil, there, ultimately speaking, there are no minor or intermediary degrees of goodness
at the end, but only saints. Then we shall be in a position analogous to that
of connoisseurs of art quietly going about their business. We shall seem
to go into the junk-shops of world history and wearily rummage about
in them with the feeling that in fact all the great works of art have been
discovered long since, and given an honourable place in the museums and
in the history of art, only to discover under the dust of the altar new and
brilliant masterpieces captivating and delightful as on the day when they
were painted.

But we must dig deeper in order to discover the theological meaning of
the festival of All Saints in its entirety, in order to penetrate to the depths
of God's message for this day. Certainly we celebrate All Saints *sub una
veneratione*, and therefore the unknown saints as well, those who lived
queitly in the land, the poor and the little ones who were great only in
God's eyes, those who go unacclaimed in any of the rolls of honour
belonging to the Church or to world history. But in celebrating these
anonymous ones we precisely group them together with those whom we
can call upon by name, those upon whom the Church calls when the
holy community is assembled and she raises her eyes to the thrice-holy
God. Now this is something that is indispensable, that in some sense we
should celebrate not only the saints who are canonical because they have
been canonised, but also, in addition to these, those nameless saints
who are consecrated in silence and upon the private altars of our own
hearts.

But in order to understand this we must first ask: What does it mean for
the Church to canonise saints? What precisely is it which takes place in
this act? This is by no means all that easy to define. Whence does the
Church have the right to act in this manner at all? Is it not written that
we should not judge our fellows until the Day of the Lord comes? Can
it then be that the Church can see into the hidden depths, the impenetrable
recesses of the human heart? In other contexts does she not take great
pains to guard against making judgments about the ultimate subjective
state of the individual in God's sight? How can she dare to make such a
judgment in this unique instance? Is she in any sense justified in this

merely on the grounds that in this case she is not condemning but rather pronouncing individuals blessed? We can only rightly reply to these questions when we understand what the Church herself is. She is not, in the first instance, the proclaimer of that law which makes demands and indeed exhorbitant demands upon men. She is not a sort of institute of salvation which seeks to draw the utmost out of men in all departments of their lives, and then, not knowing herself what the result of her labours may be, leaves it to the judgment of God. Rather she is herself the holy Church. And this holiness of hers consists not exclusively, and not first and last in the holiness of her truth, her laws, her institutions and her sacraments, but in the holiness of her members. It is *as* the Church of the Incarnation of the divine compassion that she is the holy and the holy in a visible sense. Her mission is not, properly speaking, to proclaim the demands of God's law in such a way that it remains open to question what the outcome of this will be. Rather she is the compassion of God as eschatologically victorious. She is the victory of that grace which has not merely *sought* to save men, but actually *has* saved them. The reason that there is a Church at all is that God's grace can no longer be defeated in its effects taken as a whole, and in its impact upon the history of mankind as a whole; because the grace of God is more powerful and has the last word no matter how men may seek to contradict it; because the world has been received into this grace definitively and irrevocably in the dead and glorified flesh of Christ; because the drama of world history, however much longer it may still have to run, however much it may still seem to advance amid blood, tears and despair, has already been brought to its end in Christ with the definitive victory of God as the triumph of holiness and blessedness. And it is of this truth that the Church is witness and representative. It is for this reason that she has the right to be bold enough – bold to an absolutely frightening extent – to make a definitive and unreserved declaration about some at least, referring to them unambiguously by name, and not simply in vague and uncommitted generalities, saying: 'These specific individuals have been redeemed, have been saved for all eternity. These are men who even now have been pronounced free for all eternity, men of whom we know that fact which is the most unascertainable of all, and even though it is the mystery of divine and human freedom, namely that God has received them into his heart for all eternity.' It is because the grace of God is present in the world as eschatologically victorious, because this grace is attainable in the Church, which is the salvation of God actually come into the world – it is because of this that there are canonised saints.

And now – certainly these saints were saints in an heroic degree. But for all this they lived in the midst of their own brothers and sisters, among us, among those who, as we hope, are in heaven. They themselves did not seem so very wonderful and blessed to themselves – certainly not as the elect in any special sense. They trod our ways, the habitual ways of our lives, in which we hope against all hope, the ways which led, so to say, by a whole series of stations of the Cross to that state of final helplessness in which everything seemed to end in emptiness and ultimate futility. And if they had one advantage over us then it was this: that they suffered especially acutely from that which, as we feel, makes our lives petty, pitiful and humdrum. The geniuses among men come to the fore of themselves. Their brilliance speaks for itself. In the case of the Church's saints, she often has to examine with great care in order to discover what she is seeking for: the divine greatness present in a life lived in the pitiful circumstances of tears, suffering and in the monotony of routine. When, therefore, the Church singles out by name those who are the blessed saints, who represent the Church herself in her function of being the presence of the victorious compassion of God as made accessible in the world, then in a real and justifiable sense the brilliance of these saints falls upon the unknown saints, and can truly bring the consolations of eternity to the heart that is willing to receive them. In the praise of All Saints, however, we are celebrating the Church herself, who, even though she is made up of ourselves, and therefore remains the Church of the sinners, of the poor and insignificant, of the despondent and exasperated sinners, is still the Church of the saints, the Church which is so beloved by Christ with a love unto death – almost, one might say, a fierce love – that she can no longer escape this love. In all the saints we praise the power of that grace which, so to say, makes use of men in order to bring about our salvation, which gives what it demands, which sets us free for that liberty in which we are the freed and the blessed.

If therefore, this is the mystery of this day, to make present and accessible to us, to those who are still imperfect, still toiling, still forever stumbling, those who are in despair and who cry out for help, to make available for these the consummation of grace and of its victory over the weakness and lowliness of man, then the festival of All Saints is not only the festival of the blessed in heaven, but our festival day too, on which we make a fresh start and set out anew on our course with rejoicing. All Saints is the festival of our blessed hope that what they already possess may be imparted to us too. Hope in the new and eternal age is not only an attitude which one adopts or entertains on the grounds that to hope is always better and more pleasant than to despair. The very nature of hope itself has been transformed, since Christ is present where we are, and is present there in a definitive sense. Hope is hope in the victory of Christ. It is not so much a moral requirement which demands something from us, but something which is bestowed, which one should practise and which one possesses simply because God *is* already bestowing his grace. Such is the hope that is proclaimed on the festival of All Saints, for this is the festival of the victory of grace, the grace which is what it is not because we are the ones who first and last make it victorious, but because the grace itself brings about its own acceptance on our part. We hope because God has acted, not because we have the intention to act. We hope because there are saints.

All Saints is a festival of love. We should pray that God may touch our hearts in order that for once we may be able to forget ourselves, in order that for once we may find another word than merely the word of self-accusation. We should praise God for his power and mercy in a love which can be extended to others too, and actually bring happiness to them. We should bend our ears to the quiet of eternity, which, if only we are willing to hear it, speaks louder than all the tumult of noise in the world. We should hear it when it says: 'Therefore the Spirit says "Blessed are the dead who die in the Lord; they shall rest from their labours for their works follow them".' We should realise that in the course of the world's history an innumerable multitude has already been drawn into the eternity of God before us, so that we are the late-comers. And the realisation of this should generate hope and consolation in us, courage and trust. And in this spirit we should speak with *our* saints. We should greet them, call upon them for their help on the way which is bringing us to where they are, before the face of Our Lord.

PART TWO

Positions and Callings in the Church

3

IDEAS FOR A THEOLOGY OF CHILDHOOD

O<small>UR</small> purpose in offering a few ideas on the theology of childhood at this point is not, in any direct sense, to be of assistance to those who, in some way or other, whether as parents or teachers, are engaged in looking after children. We have no intention of offering any guidance of this kind to such people. For this cannot be the aim of a theologian. Certainly he too has responsibilities in the 'field of pedagogy', and not least where this applies to children. He has to proclaim the gospel to the children too. But in this priestly task he has many collaborators. The subject of the discussion which follows, however, is one which goes beyond the immediate sphere of pedagogy, for here we shall be considering what the divinely revealed word has to say about childhood. In the intention of the Creator and Redeemer of children what meaning does childhood have, and what task does it lay upon us for the perfecting and saving of humanity? That is the question before us. It may be that in the course of answering it we shall be able to throw fresh light not only upon our own lives but also such as will be of assistance to those whose daily lives are spent in working for children, loving them, watching over them, estimating their progress and always and in all circumstances loving them. Admittedly in so brief a sketch as this there can be no question of developing more than a few fragmentary aspects of the theology of childhood.

I. THE UNSURPASSABLE VALUE OF CHILDHOOD

The first point of which we intend to treat can perhaps be expressed as the direct relationship to God which is achieved at each of the stages in human development and growth, and so in childhood too, and, arising from this, the unique and unrepeatable value attached to childhood in particular. What is meant by this? In virtue of the fact that we are naturally orientated outwards to the world about us we men are extremely liable to the

33

temptation of interpreting ourselves according to the categories, models and prototypes which confront us from the purely physical or merely biological environment in which we live. And we do the same thing with time too. We interpret the time which belongs to the specifically human dimension, the dimension of man's personal history, in terms of the laws of physical time as these have been worked out and established. Now this means that we think of ourselves in terms that are unphilosophical, unhuman and un-Christian. We conceive of our personal lifespan as the sum total of a series of phases in life, each of which as it is exhausted leads on to the next, the very meaning of which is to disappear into the next, to be a preparation for it, to 'exist' for the further stages beyond itself. Above all we conceive of youth and childhood in this sense. For at this stage above all most of our life has still to come. In relation to the future stages of life which still await us when we are children, therefore, this subordinate and preparatory function is at its most intense in childhood itself. And when that for which childhood is a preparation arrives, then – such is our conception – childhood itself disappears. Now it is precisely the Christian above all who seems to lay special emphasis on the merely subordinate role of childhood, this character which it bears as preparation for the life that is to come, by comparison with the stage of adult life, which in consequence seems to be understood as life in the true sense, as the goal and measure of life. Of course it cannot be disputed that this kind of time, which unfolds uniformly in a single direction, is to be found in man as his history too. On this understanding of time the earlier stages of life are indeed rightly conceived of when they are regarded as subordinate to and preparatory for what is still to come, as practice for what follows, as giving place to a predetermined future. Woe to anyone at any stage of life, and so at that of childhood too, if he seeks simply to remain fixed at that particular stage, living it for its own sake as though idealising it, and making himself as he exists at that particular stage into his own god! Woe to him if he is not ready to relinquish that stage and to enter the coming one! If the present is not ready to bow down before the holiness and majesty of the future!

And yet this is only one part of the truth with regard to the sort of time involved in man's personal history. Man is not a thing that is simply pushed through the space-time dimension as though it were only in possession of the transient moment which is called the present. Man is a subject. He possesses himself. He is at all stages capable of taking himself as a whole. And for this reason, in spite of the continuous process of change and the alternation of action and passion in the time to which he is subject, he has before him his time *as a whole*. As his life advances he *retains* the past and goes forward into a future *that he has already worked out* beforehand. By the exercise of his freedom he makes the time allotted to him present to himself as a whole, past and future together. Now because of this the totality of man's existence as saved and redeemed in its complete and consummated state, in other words the eternity towards which man is advancing in his time, does not constitute a further period appended to, and following upon his life in any true sense, as a further projection of it which could be conceived of in linear terms as extending into an unending future. Rather this eternity is the enduring validity of man's existence before God as lived in freedom. It is the abiding fruit, the sheer definitive consummation of man's time and of man's time as a whole. What confronts man as the goal towards which he advances in his historical existence, in his saving history, is not a further prolongation of incalculable extent added on to his present life. Rather he gathers up the totality of his life as freely lived, he achieves himself *in the fulness of his subjectivity and freedom as determined by the content of his life*, just as at every moment of his temporal life he has already obtained a degree of self-possession such that it embraces *the totality of his* own life-span considered formally as an empty space to be filled out with content. He gathers himself up in his completed state. He finds himself. His temporal existence is not something which, so to say, he brings behind him, but something which he makes present to himself. He does not bring his temporal mode of existence to an end by quitting it, but by compressing it, so to say, and bringing it with him in its totality into his eternity which is his time as summed up and completed. His future is the making present of his own past as freely lived.

Now all this is every bit as true of childhood as it is of all the other individual phases of human life. Indeed it has to be asserted of childhood more clearly and more emphatically than of any other phase precisely because this one most of all suffers from the impression that it is a mere provisional conditioning for the shaping of adult life in its fulness, and, this being its only function, should be left behind as quickly and completely as possible and vanish into unreality. Childhood endures as that which is given and abiding, the time that has been accepted and lived through freely. Childhood does not constitute past time, time that has eroded away, but rather that which remains, that which is coming to meet us as an intrinsic element in the single and enduring completeness of the time of our existence considered as a unity, that which we call the eternity of man as saved and redeemed. We do not lose childhood as that which recedes ever further into our past, that which remains behind as we advance forward in time, but rather we go towards it as that which has been achieved in time and redeemed forever in time. We only *become* the children whom we *were* because we gather up time – and in this our childhood too – into our eternity. Throughout our entire life-span, and because of the decision which is required of us and which bears upon our life as a whole, childhood may always remain open. And we may still have to go on living through our own childhood in our life taken as a whole because it always remains an open question for us. But all this does not alter the fact that we do not move away from childhood in any definitive sense, but rather move towards the eternity of this childhood, to its definitive and enduring validity in God's sight. Childhood is not only of eternal significance for man's destiny to the extent that in childhood the foundations are laid for decisions which have an eternal significance. It is important not only as a point of departure for the adult man, having an influence beforehand on what actually takes place later and thereby on that which will finally takes place when the individual's life comes to its close. More than this it is important in itself also, as a stage of man's personal history in which that takes place which can only take place in childhood itself, a field which bears fair flowers and ripe fruits such as can only grow in *this* field and in no other, and which will themselves be carried into the storehouses of eternity.

All this is to put the matter in a very abstract and formal way. But if it is understood, then it imparts to childhood a value and an importance which are beyond all conception. Childhood itself has a direct relationship with God. It touches upon the absolute divinity of God not only as maturity, adulthood and the later phases of life touch upon this, but rather in a special way of its own. The special character of childhood may always be fading away so far as *we* are concerned, and may also disappear into that which comes afterwards in point of time, so that it seems only to derive its justification and its value from this, but this is not so. *This* morning does not derive its life simply from the afternoon which follows. This playtime with its beauty is not important simply as a prelude to life as lived in full earnest. It is unique. It has a value in itself (admittedly precisely as that which contributes unreservedly to that which is to come). It is precious not merely because it seeks the riches of life in its maturity. The strange and wonderful flowers of childhood are already fruits in themselves, and do not merely rely for their justification on the fruit that is to come afterwards. The grace of childhood is not merely the pledge of the grace of adulthood. The values of imperishability and eternity are attached to childhood in its unique properties even in those points in which it differs from life in its broader phases. The fact that it contributes to the later stages of life is not the sole criterion of its own intrinsic rightness. It must be the case that childhood is valuable in itself, that it is to be discovered anew in the ineffable future which is coming to meet us.

II. THE CHRISTIAN AWARENESS OF CHILDHOOD

What understanding of childhood is to be found in the Christian scriptures and tradition? That is the second question which we wish to put in this modest and fragmentary approach to a theology of childhood. Here there can be no question of supplementing the observations which follow with an exhaustive documentation or substantiation from scripture, still less from the innumerable witnesses of tradition. Even so I believe that it will be acknowledged that what is said here has the value of an authentic witness to the Christian awareness of what childhood means.

First and foremost the child is the *man*. Probably there is no religion and no philosophic anthropology which insists so manifestly and so strongly upon this point as one of its basic presuppositions as does Christianity; the point namely that the child is already the man, that right from the beginning he is already in possession of that value and those depths which are implied in the name of man. It is not simply that he gradually grows into a man. He *is* a man. As his personal history unfolds he merely realises what he already *is*. He does not seek about in a void of indefinite possibilities ranging from all to nothing, to see what he can achieve by chance. He is equipped as a man, given his allotted task and endowed with grace to perform it right from the very outset with all the inexpressible value and all the burden of responsibility which this entails. And this, because it comes from God and because his personal history, in spite of being inextricably bound up with the history of the cosmos and of the life principle as a whole, is related with absolute immediacy to God himself, to his original creative and inalienable design for him. The child is the man whom God has called by a name of *his own*, who is fresh and unique in each individual instance, never merely a 'case', a particular application in the concrete of a general idea, *always* having a personal value of his own and therefore worthy to endure for ever. He is not an element in a process advancing and receding incalculably like the tides, but the unique explosion in which something final and definitive is constituted. The child is the man who is, right from the first, the partner of God; he who opens his eyes only to keep that vision before him in which an incomprehensible mystery is regarding him; he who cannot halt at any point in his course because infinity is calling him; who can love the smallest thing because for him it is always filled with the all; he who does not feel the ineffable as lethal to him, because he experiences the fact that when he entrusts himself to it without reserve he falls into the inconceivable depths of love and blessedness. The child is the man, he, therefore, who is familiar with death and loves life, does not comprehend himself but knows this, and precisely *in* this (provided only that he commits himself to the incomprehensible one in trust and love) has precisely understood all, because thereby he has come into God's presence. The child is the man; the one, therefore, who always lives in a spirit of fraternity, leads a life of infinite complexity, knows no law other than that of endlessly journeying on and of great love and of that adventure which he can only recognise that he has come to the end of when he stands before God in his absolute infinitude. This is how Christianity views man and it sees all this already present in the child. And for this reason it protects the child while it is still in its mother's womb. It takes pains to ensure that the sources of life are not poured away upon the trifles of the lowlands of mere lust and desire. It has reverence for the child, for the child is a man.

The child is a man *right at the very outset*. Christianity is aware of the mystery of that beginning which already contains all present within itself, and yet still has to become all; the beginning which is the basis and foundation of all that is to come, its horizon and its law, and yet at the same time cannot even come to its own fulness except in what has still to come in the future. Thus the state of childhood too, is regarded as the beginning of the state of manhood. The child is already spirit and body united in a single entity. It is already nature and grace, nature and person, possessing itself yet exposed to the influence of the world and of history, and for all this it has still to become all things in the future. What is already present in the child has still to be realised, to become actual in experience. And this unity which exists between the beginning and the stage of full development is itself in its turn a mystery which man lives and to which he is subject, but which he does not preside over or control by his own power. It is only when his final completion has been attained that this origin of his is revealed to him; the origin in which he was set on his course. For he began as a child and as a child of God. It is not until evening that the morning has completely passed away.

Childhood is a beginning in *two different senses*. The assertions of Christianity do not make reality in general, and above all the reality of man, any simpler than it in fact is. Thus Christianity has the courage to recognise the duality which man experiences in his existence even in the very beginnings of that existence. Now man's existence as an individual is historically conditioned, and viewed in this light he is not simply *pure* beginning, unaffected by anything that has gone before. In spite of the immediacy to God which is his right from his origins as that unique and particular creature, fresh from the hands of God, he is the beginning which springs up in the midst of a pre-existing context, a history already wrought out by man before this particular individual arrived on the scene. And this history is, right from the outset, also a history of guilt, of gracelessness, of a refusal to respond to the call of the living God. The history of the guilt of mankind taken as an unity right from the beginning of that history regarded as a single whole is also a factor in the history of the individual. The love which brings grace to man, the love in which God himself with the fulness of his life gives himself to the individual is not simply, or in any obvious sense, an intrinsic element in a love which God might have born right from the beginning towards an humanity which did not fall into sin. Rather it is a love which endures despite the fact that sin rose to power in history right at the origins of the human race. In terms of the history of human existence this is the situation which the language of tradition calls original sin. It is a situation which radically and interiorly affects the individual, and in consequence of which the individual can count upon the grace which he needs, on the sheer proximity of God to shelter and sanctify him, not right from the beginning and in the very nature of humanity as such, but only in virtue of the redemption wrought by Christ. And for this reason Christianity knows that the child and his origins are indeed encompassed by the love of God through the pledge of that grace which, in God's will to save all mankind, comes in all cases and to every man from God in Christ Jesus. But

Christianity cannot on this account regard the origins of childhood as a sort of innocent arcadia, as a pure source which only becomes muddied at a later stage and *within* the sphere of human cares in which man can control and guide his own course. It cannot view childhood as though prior to this stage it was simply the same as when it came from God as its eternal source, or as though for this reason, even in the context of the actual personal history of the individual and of mankind childhood might once more be wholly purified of every kind of blemish. No, Christianity views even childhood as already and inevitably the origin precisely of that man to whom guilt, death, suffering and all the forces of bitterness in human life belong as conditions of his very existence. But since all this remains within the compass of God, of his greater grace and his greater compassion, therefore this realism with which Christianity reacts to the very origins of man in the child and its beginnings is far from being any kind of implicit cynicism. Christianity's awareness of the guilt and tragedy which belong even to the beginning is, on the contrary, the necessary outcome of its awareness of the blessedness of grace and the redemption which overcomes this guilt and tragedy, and which comes both before and after it. For this is precisely the grace and redemption which the Christian experiences and to which he submits himself.

The child is a *child*. As soon as we look more closely into what is said about the child, especially in scripture, we notice that in reality it is almost always *presupposed* that we already know what a child is, so that no explicit information on this point is given to us. Thus the word of God itself indicates that we should rely upon the infinitely complex experiences of our own lives and our contacts with children in those lives as well as on the experience of our own childhood. It is the totality of this experience as summed up in the word 'child' that holy scripture draws upon when it tells us that we must become as children, that we are 'children' of God by grace, that even the children can come to the messiah, and that they both need and are capable of attaining to the kingdom of heaven, that they can believe in Jesus, that to give scandal to them is a crime to be punished by a terrible death. Thus scripture and tradition alike presuppose that we already know precisely *what* a child really is far more than they tell us this explicitly or treat of it as a distinct question. They leave it to our experience to determine what a child is, and what it means to be a child. But when we consider this experience of ours is it not dark, complex and conflicting in character? Most certainly it is. But even as such it is sanctioned by scripture and tradition, and in this sense we are obliged to put up with the obscurity and complexity of our experience of childhood, not to try to iron out the complexities, but to endure them and still manage to be true to our own experience of children in arriving at an idea of what a child is. This is, in fact, only in conformity with the basic principles of which we have already spoken, namely that the child is the man himself in his incipient stages, and, what is more, man as divided within himself right at the beginning of his life and from the beginning onwards. In accordance with this the genuinely Christian understanding and the Christian experience of the child is both idealistic *and* realistic at the same time. The New Testament, no less than antiquity, the Old Testament and Judaism, shows itself aware of the factors of immaturity and weakness in the child (*TWNT* V 641, 41–48; 644, 46–645, 8), as can plainly be sensed not only in the writings of Paul (1 Cor 3:1; 13:11; 14:28; Gal 4:1–3; Eph 4:14; Heb 5:13), but also in the words of Jesus himself in the parable of the children in the market-place who are sulky in their play (Mt 11:16f.) But this does not mean that the 'little ones' are lightly estimated by Jesus in accordance with the attitude prevailing among his people and at his time. The children can serve him as examples of lack of false ambition, of not seeking for dignities or honours, of modesty and lack of artificiality in contrast to their elders, who are unwilling to learn anything from them (Mt 12:2 ff.; 19:13 ff.) When Jesus holds up the child to us as the prototype of those for whom the kingdom of heaven is there it cannot be said, even in a relative sense (much less in an absolute one), that what he is thinking of is its innocence. What is implied in this saying in which he holds up the child to us as an example is something far more important: that we can be like children in being receivers and as such care-free in relation to God, those who *know* that they have nothing of themselves on which to base any claim to his help, and yet who trust that his kindness and protection will be extended to them and so will bestow what they need upon them. And thus without glorifying children or failing to recognise the radical insufficiency of their natures Jesus does see in children those whom he can receive lovingly into his heart. This is what he means when he says 'Of such is the kingdom of heaven' (Mt 19:14). They are those with whom he identifies himself. The woes he pronounces are designed to protect them against scandal, and as he sees it there is an angel who watches over their salvation and who continuously beholds the countenance of the Father in heaven.

For these reasons childhood is, in the last analysis, a *mystery*. It has the force of a beginning and a twofold beginning at that. It is a beginning in the sense of the absolute origin of the individual, and also the beginning which plunges its roots into a history over which the individual himself has no control. Childhood has the force of a beginning such that the future which corresponds to it is not simply the unfolding of some latent interior force, but something freely sent and something which actually comes to meet one. And it is not until this future is actually attained to that the beginning itself is unveiled in its significance, that it is actually given and comes to its own realisation, as a beginning which is open to the absolute beginning of God who is utter mystery, the ineffable and eternal, nameless and precisely as such accepted with love in his divine nature as he who presides over all things. Such a beginning as this cannot be otherwise than mysterious. And because it is a mystery, and because as a beginning it bears all one's future life within itself, therefore life itself is mysterious, something which is already endowed with a certain autonomy, albeit in a hidden manner, and freed from external control. Hence too, provided we reverently and lovingly preserve this state of being delivered over to the mystery, life becomes for us a state in which our original childhood is preserved for ever; a state in which we are open to expect the unexpected, to commit ourselves to the incalculable, a state which endows us with the power still to be able to play, to recognise that the powers presiding over existence are greater than our own designs, and to submit to their control as our deepest good. In this state we become guileless and serene – serene in a Mozartian sense even in those cases in which we weep and are overcome by dejection, because even these tears we accept as they are sent to us, recognising that the sadness which they express is ultimately a redeemed sadness. And when our powers are at an end we realise in a childlike spirit that our task too is at an end, since no-one is tried beyond his own strength. When we take up this attitude we make the mystery the protection and defence of our lives. We are content to commit them to the ineffable as sheltering and forgiving, to that which is unspeakably close to us with the closeness of love. It is not as though the child as such has already achieved this in any fully developed sense. But this is how we see the man who, in spite of the perilous state in which he stands, is open to such self-commitment to the protection of the mystery of existence, recognising that the duality of his nature is always more than compensated for by the deed of God wrought upon him. And therefore the kingdom of heaven is for those who are children in this sense when, on the basis of this attitude of openness, and not without a certain *metanoia*, they become what they are – precisely children. Now this also implies, however paradoxical it may appear, that we do not really know what childhood means at the beginning of our lives until we know what that childhood means which comes at the end of them; that childhood, namely, in which, by God-given repentance and conversion, we receive the kingdom of God and so become children. It is in this sense that we only recognise the child at the beginning of life from the child of the future. And in the light of this, once more, we can understand that childhood invokes a mystery, the mystery of our whole existence, the ineffable element in which is God himself.

III. THE FULNESS OF CHILDHOOD CONSISTS IN BEING CHILDREN OF GOD

We have now reached a stage at which we can take a third point as the object of our enquiry. In a theology of children something must also be said about what it means to be a *child of God*. At first this may appear strange. The idea of being God's child stands for a reality which seems to be associated with the first phase in human life only through a meta-phorical, i.e. inappropriate, application of the concepts of 'child' and 'childhood' to our relationship with God, and therefore to be wholly excluded from the area in which these concepts of child and childhood can be applied in their proper sense. What is correct in this objection is that in a consideration of the theology of childhood as such we cannot under-take the task of pursuing the Christian message of what it means to be a child of God as such. A theological discourse on justification and the grace of childhood in this sense, and as understood theologically, would certainly not be appropriate at this point. But for all this it may be per-mitted to draw attention to this topic in connection with the subject we are investigating here, because to do so will serve to bring home to us more forcibly the significance and value of childhood in the human sense of the term. The real situation here is not simply that we already possess concepts of child and childhood in the purely human and natural sense, which are then applied in a secondary and metaphorical sense in order to express a religious reality. Rather the primary meaning in itself, which, because it is primary seems to be merely human, is in its turn illuminated and deepened by the fact of being applied in the theological sense. In other words it is only through the revelatory usage of the terms 'child' and 'childhood' that the depths and fulness of the human concepts as such can be realised and appreciated in their entirety. For this reason it is surely justifiable to say something of what it means to be a child of God, even in a context in which we are strictly speaking concerned only to say something about the ideas of child and childhood in a human sense. This is, in fact, the situation at this point, and this for a twofold reason. It will be valuable to consider this, and in this way, by including the human and theological concepts of childhood in one and the same treatment, we can ensure that they will constantly reflect and throw light upon each other.

First it is generally recognised what a decisive influence the *experience of a secure childhood* can have in the majority of cases for that attitude of commiting oneself to trust in the radical and metaphysical sense, which has a vital and basic function to perform in religion, considered as that which unites us to God as our Father. Certainly this cannot be exaggerated. One must not conceive in terms that are too absolute of the connection between the child's actual experience of his father on the one hand, and the possibility of achieving a relationship to God as Father in the absolute sense by faith on the other. It is perfectly possible that a lack of protection, a lack of that sheltering solicitude and security which comes from the love of one's parents, may actually serve to spur us on to the metaphysical quest for one who will provide us with our ultimate support, who will sustain us and protect us. Otherwise it would in fact be rather difficult to meet the objection that religion in general is only the projection of the father image into the dimension of the infiite, and as such a sort of colossal infantilism. We must, then, observe due caution in deciding where the connection lies between the experience of a childhood that is protected and secure and religious experience. But even allowing for this there is a further point that cannot be contested. We may take the case of one who has never been able to realise in this way what a close relationship with his father means, one which he has felt that he could absolutely rely upon to provide him with love, protection and security. It is precisely such a one as this who can only succeed with difficulty in achieving that idea of God's Fatherhood which he needs, at the level of conscious thought, so that he can express this idea and objectify it to himself in terms of the ordinary categories of thought and action which he uses in his life. Yet it is only so that he can attain to that attitude of radical trust in the very basis of existence, that submissive and trustful self-commitment to the mystery which permeates and presides over the whole of existence, the mystery of God's protective and forgiving love and absolute nearness to him.

In the majority of cases it is true to say that only one who has been able to learn that the names 'father' and 'mother' stand for a protecting love to which he can unquestioningly trust himself — only he will find the courage trustfully to give the name 'father' to that ineffable and nameless source which upholds him in being (and yet this is the primary concept of true religion), to recognise that he has not been swallowed up by it, but that he has found the very source of his own existence in it and has been empowered by it to be really and authentically himself. And conversely: in those cases in which the individual, while he is a child, feels himself to be bereft of protection and abandoned, he will almost inevitably interpret this as the experience of lack of protection in an ultimate and metaphysical sense, as abandonment to absurdity and meaninglessness, to his own personal deprivation of God. He will not overcome the subsequent experiences of life's hardships, and sometimes psychological traumas, by having recourse to the experience of a secure childhood which was able to assent to meaning and to life without reserve. Rather he will interpret this as the logical further projection of that experience of insecurity, of a childhood devoid of love and protection, which was his in the beginning, when life for him was so empty and so devoid of promise. Now this reference to a fact which is recognised by, and a major preoccupation to those engaged in religious pedagogy and depth psychology only serves to emphasise still more the further fact that the human circumstances and the human concept of child and childhood is of the utmost importance for the way in which we understand and apply in religious terms those realities which are expressed by the transferred concepts of child of God, God the Father, etc. However it has still not been made clear that what has been said so far has brought to light a further point, namely that the relationship between the two contexts, the human and the divine, works in the opposite direction. Now this is precisely what is of interest to us at this point.

In order to develop this point the following consideration has to be borne in mind (and here we come to the second stage of our investigation). By way of preliminary it might be asked in a more formal and logical manner what, in view of what has been said, the situation is with regard to the co-called 'transference' of concepts at least in specific instances: Whether in all cases a concept, a word, is only 'transferred' to another context *after* the particular characteristics of *both* contexts are already known independently one of another, and after certain points in common have in this way been established from among these characteristics, which make this process of 'transference' natural; *or*, on the other hand, whether there are *also* cases, at least in addition to the first-named, in which the so-called 'transference' is precisely the original mode in which the second state of affairs is known, and in which the knowledge of the first comes to its true fulness. Let us take the case of one who, from his knowledge of the Christian approach to ontology in general, knows what the position is with regard to the concept of being, and how he should express the idea of God as the being who is in absolute possession of being as such. Such an one knows what is meant by this second of the two alternatives we have presented. We do not know that a given object which is presented to our experience is a being, and only then go on to infer that God too is a being, only one of particular power and depths, so that this predicate of being can be applied to him too in a more particular manner. Rather the very fact that man recognises a being is in itself something that takes place within a general sphere governed by the transcendental, non-objective knowledge of being. Our non-objective awareness of this sphere in itself always includes – even though in a non-objective and unexplicit manner – the being in the absolute who possesses all being, namely God. The very fact that we recognise a being means that we have this awareness of God at least implicitly. And when this initially implicit awareness is turned into objective knowledge, then we also achieve a better and deeper awareness of what is really meant by calling that object which we directly experienced a being. In this case at least the process of 'transference' is not a subsequent poetic invention, but rather throws light upon the basic movement of the spirit itself, which only grasps something in that it first moves into the sphere of this 'something', grasps it in that it draws it back to the knower himself in *his* sphere, and so 'transfers' it. In other words it is only by being transferred that that which is transferred to the knower's own ground is brought to its true status, the status of intelligibility. Now it is at least possible that this may also be the case when we 'transfer' the experience of a child-parent relationship in the earthly and human sense to a relationship with God, and then speak in a 'transferred' or metaphorical sense of God as Father. For only thus can we know how to call upon the nameless by name. We repeat: it is at least *possible* that this is the case. But that it actually is so in fact, in other words that the human concept of childhood and parenthood is only fully realised when it is transferred to God, because the transference involved here is at a sublime level – this is a point that must be made clear by approaching the question from a quite different angle.

By way of preparation let us recall (and in fact this means harking back to the first point in our considerations as a whole) that childhood is not a state which only applies to the first phase of our lives in the biological sense. Rather it is a basic condition which is always appropriate to a life that is lived aright. For in the last analysis all the stages of life have an equally immediate relationship to God and to the individual's own ultimate perfection, even though in saying this we must fully recognise the fact that man's life advances towards God precisely through a time-sequence consisting of a series of stages following one upon another. But if childhood as a basic condition were not applicable to a rightly orientated life at all times the principle stated above could no longer be upheld. And there is a further point that everyone understands, namely that for our existence to be sound and redeemed at all, childhood must be an intrinsic element in it. It must be a living and effective force at the roots of our being if that being is to be able to endure even in the depths of the mystery. Childhood as an inherent factor in our lives must take the form of trust, of openness, of expectation, of readiness to be controlled by another, of interior harmony with the unpredictable forces with which the individual finds himself confronted. It must manifest itself as freedom in contrast to that which is merely the outcome of a predetermining design, as receptivity, as hope which is still not disillusioned. This is the childhood that must be present and active as an effective force at the very roots of our being. Everyone understands too that the childhood which belongs to the child in the biological sense is only the beginning, the prelude, the foretaste and the promise of this other childhood, which is the childhood proved and tested and at the same time assailed, which is present in the mature man. In other words we must take childhood in this *latter* sense as the true and proper childhood, the fulness of that *former* childhood, the childhood of immaturity.

But once we perceive the unity which exists between the childhood that comes at the beginning of our lives and the mature childhood, and once we realise the light which each throws upon the other, then it easily becomes clear that childhood in itself, and even at the human level, entails an *orientation to God*, that it achieves perfection in that relationship which we call being a child of God, that it is not merely a question of a metaphor, the transference of a *word* from one objective situation to another similar one, in which the comparison is merely secondary and incidental. Here it is rather the *reality* of childhood in the human sense that is 'transferred' into childhood in the divine sense. For if childhood (and this applies to childhood in the human sense as well) is openness, is trustful submission to control by another, the courage to allow fresh horizons, ever new and ever wider, to be opened up before one, a readiness to journey into the untried and the untested (and all this with that deep elemental and ultimate trust which seems inexhaustible in its endurance, the trust which the sceptics and those who have made shipwreck of their lives bitterly describe as 'naïve') then in all this that transcendence of faith, hope and love in which the ultimate essence of the basic act of religion precisely consists is already *ipso facto* an achieved and present fact. It is a transcendence in which the act of encountering and coming to terms with the world can be elevated to a religious act, the ideas in which we apprehend the world can be elevated to the level of prayer, and the active control which we exercise over our worldly affairs can be elevated to a point at which we are moved and inspired. In this religious act our first intimations of God are attained, although we do not presume to have acquired any kind of comprehensive knowledge of him. Now it belongs to the essence of such an act that it should not hold back at any point, that its outward movement into the boundlessness of God should proceed without restraint or inhibition, that it should not come to rest at any other point except that of total self-abandonment to the incomprehensible infinitude of the ineffable mystery. And it follows from this that it can be asserted truly and without reserve that man remains religious when he experiences the childhood which is an elemental factor in his nature, when he adopts this and maintains it as his basic attitude and outlook, and allows it to develop to the full and without limitation.

Childhood is openness. Human childhood is infinite openness. The mature childhood of the adult is the attitude in which we bravely and trustfully maintain an infinite openness in all circumstances and despite the experiences of life which seem to invite us to close ourselves. Such openness, infinite and maintained in all circumstances, yet put into practice in the actual manner in which we live our lives, is the expression of man's religious existence. Now this infinite openness of existence which we maintain, and which is childhood in the developed sense, can have its counterpart in our experience in the form of an infinite and loving self-bestowal on God's part. We can experience the fact that it is because of this self-bestowal of God that we do maintain our basic openness. And this openness of ours as men is an infinite openness, which we accept from God, which is upheld by his act of self-bestowal and basically made possible by him. Now it is this openness that constitutes the very essence of childhood in the mature sense, and it is nothing else than what is called in theological language childhood of God, the grace of divine sonship in the *Son*. When, therefore, human childhood finds the courage to be true to its absolute essence, when it realises its own nature as an openness that is unconditional and infinite, then it moves on to a further stage, projects itself by a process of 'transference' to the ultimate consummation of its own nature, to the childhood of man before God as orientated to him and proceeding from him.

We are told in Eph 3:15 that all Fatherhood in heaven and on earth derives its name from the one and eternal Father who is God. We can go on from this to say also that all childhood in heaven and on earth derives its name and its origin from that one childhood in which the Logos itself receives its own nature in the act of eternal generation by the Father, in which we ourselves are admitted by grace to become participants in this self-bestowal of the Father upon the Logos and so have a share in the divine nature. In the last analysis, therefore, human childhood is not transferred by some dubious process of metaphorical or poetic transference to a quite different reality which we call childhood of God, but rather has its ultimate basis in this itself, so that the latter is always and right from the first contained in the former, and finds expression in it. What a mystery a child is! So writes the poet. Yes indeed! Childhood is only truly understood, only realises the ultimate depths of its own nature, when it is seen as based upon the foundation of childhood of God. And when we really want to know what the real connection is between human childhood and childhood of God, then we need to commit ourselves to the infinite depths and power of that transcendental movement which is latent in human childhood itself, and allow ourselves to be projected from this into that which is enjoined upon us in the Christian teaching about the Father in heaven, and about men who have received the grace from the life of God himself to be children of God and brothers and sisters of one another.

From this view we can then turn our gaze back once more to the child in a biological and social sense as well. In the child a man begins who must undergo the wonderful adventure of remaining a child forever, becoming a child to an ever-increasing extent, making his childhood of God real and effective in this childhood of his, for this is the task of his maturity. It is only in the child that the child in the simple and absolute sense of the term really begins. And that is the dignity of the child, his task and his claim upon us all that we can and must help him in this task. In serving the child in this way, therefore, there can be no question of any petty sentimentality. Rather it is the eternal value and dignity of man, who must become a child, that we are concerned with, the man who only becomes a sharer in God's interior life in that he becomes that child which he only begins to be in his own childhood.

About fifteen years ago I met a well-known positivist philosopher of the Jewish race, one upon whom the fate of his people had left its mark, and who was oppressed by all the agonising questions which his calling and the responsibility of his mission in life raised for him. He asked himself whether he believed in God. And the answer he gave to himself and to others was 'I do not know'. But in saying this he added, 'That we are children of God – that I do believe.' Now perhaps we understand what is sought to be expressed here in a paradox. He who has the courage to accept and to preserve the pure spirit of childhood within him, and to carry it with him throughout his life – he it is who finds God. And he who accepts *in this sense* the childhood that is in his brothers and sisters has already found God. This is a truth which is present in a very real sense in the text of scripture itself. For what we find written there (though here, it is true, we are turning a negative formulation into an affirmative one) is: 'If you become as children you will enter the kingdom of heaven', and 'He who receives a child such as this in my name receives *me*' (Mt 18:5).

4

THE SACRAMENTAL BASIS FOR THE ROLE OF THE LAYMAN IN THE CHURCH

THE subject on which I have been called to speak is entitled 'The Sacramental Basis for the Role of the Layman in the Church'. The topic to be treated of here, therefore, is one which belongs to the realm of Catholic dogmatic theology. In the very nature of the case, therefore, as also with regard to those to whom this paper is addressed, the acceptance of the Christian faith is presupposed. This does not of itself mean, however, that it is a theme which should evidently be treated of only in the pulpit, or one which could only be conceived of as a kind of parenesis, an exhortation addressed to the Christian to do that very thing which, as a matter of faith, he has already committed himself to long since. For there are enough subjects to be found in the field of dogmatics which are certainly not matters of dispute, which in a certain sense every Christian holds to be true as a matter of faith, which even become present to him in the awareness of his faith as manifest truths when explicit reference is made to them, but which, nevertheless, remain for the most part far too much at the implicit level in this awareness of his faith, are far too little thought out, play far too little part in the normal outlook and attitude which the average Christian strives to bring to bear on the realities of his faith, for them to be able to constitute an effective, formative or decisive force in the concrete practice of Christian living. In this sense we can point to a phenomenon which might be called the heresy of forgetfulness, of inadvertence, of inertia, and which is possible even within the Church's fold, and that to a very advanced degree. Now to speak of such truths and realities of faith explicitly, to express them with all due conceptual exactitude, is a function not merely of preaching but also, and primarily, of speculative theology itself. And such theology is not merely the preserve of the theologians, but is also of concern to every Christian whose general intellectual awareness is such that he must either allow his faith to become an active force in his thinking, or else incur the danger of losing this faith as an effective force in his existence. Now the reality to which expression has been given in the title to this paper is to be numbered so it seems to me, among truths and realities of his kind.

Let us be honest and clear-headed. Certainly much has already been said during the past four decades of the necessity of the Church becoming a living force in the spirit and heart of the faithful; of the fact that the Christians *are* the Church and should not merely be regarded as subject to her directives and the object of her solicitude and protection. Movements have indeed arisen in the fields of Catholic action and liturgy and work upon these is still progressing. But for these to be significant and effective at all a necessary prior condition is that the average understanding of the relationship between Church and layman shall be reappraised. Nevertheless the fact must be faced that ever since the end of the patristic age of the Church has become, not indeed in theory, not in her innermost understanding of her faith, but certainly to a large extent in average and everyday conception and practice, a Church of mere institutionalism, a clericalised Church. For her all those not included in the ranks of the clergy, the laymen, are the object of her direction and care, of instruction and leadership, to whom grace and salvation must be applied in each individual case. But they have not, properly speaking, themselves taken an active part in the constructive work of the Church or in helping to support her. In view of this we must not expect that in the space of four decades (in other words since the end of the First World War) a radical alteration has already been brought about in a mentality which is the outcome of a history now one-and-a-half millennia old. In the centuries of the great shifts of population the Church came to the barbarian peoples as the representative of a cultural force higher than their own. But her members were not in a position to make actual in any way at all their basic function as constitutive elements in the Church. In the Investiture Controversy and similar episodes the Church had definitively to dissociate herself as an hierarchical entity from the secular and civic community, so as to overcome the danger which had arisen from circumstances reaching far back into the past of the emperor usurping the prerogatives of the Pope. In the time of the Reformation the Church was compelled to set bounds to the demands of the laity, which arose with the onset of the new age and which in themselves were due and timely, that the universal priesthood of all Christians should be actualised in the Church, and to confine this demand within those limits which are, as a matter of divine law, inherent in the hierarchical structure of the Church. These limits are thrown still more clearly into relief when the forces of democracy and social reform first begin to make their impact at the beginning of the new age in movements such as that of the renaissance, the Peasants' Revolt, the Anabaptist movement, etc., which must not be confused with that other tendency, similar in appearance indeed, and occurring about the same time but nevertheless essentially different, for the laity in the Church consciously to assume an active role in helping to discharge her responsibilities.

All this should cause us neither disappointment nor surprise. So far as concerns the awakening awareness, in any concrete or effective sense, that all Christians have this active function to perform in the Church we are still in the initial stages. The Spirit of God in the Church palpably presses us on to giving practical effect to this new awareness. But God grant of his providence that it may not turn out that the only way of achieving this will be for the Church so to be reduced to the 'little flock' that those belonging to her come spontaneously to be united in the closest possible spirit of fraternity, when each individual – and this includes each individual member of the clergy as well – realises that now all and each must play their part! For in such a case, those who aspire to the honour and dignity of making an active contribution to the work of the Church will have to realise that this can only mean toil and danger for them, and that they must be ready for the ultimate sacrifice. And we must not wait until we are only too glad to provide opportunities for them to play an active part in this way on the grounds that there are all too few individuals left in the Church to lay claim to such an honour. For when we take a sober and unromantic view of the real, average, day-to-day outlook and attitude of the individual members of the Church what do we see? We are compelled to reply: 1. That the Church still persists in being an institution supported exclusively by the clergy, an institution catering for the eternal salvation of the rest of men, the so-called laity, by mediating the truth of divine revelation and sacramental grace to them, and 2. That the layman in the Church is still regarded as the 'layman' in the sense of the non-expert, the non-specialist in ecclesiastical matters. In other words the term carries no further implication than the purely negative assertion that such an individual is precisely excluded from the official administration of the Church, the dignities and functions which are the prerogative of those who, in contrast to the laity, exercise a formative and representative function in the Church.

Of course this everyday and average outlook does not amount to a conscious and clear declaration in so many words that this is in fact the situation. Such an assertion would be heretical. But what still remains to be said about the layman over and above this merely negative estimate of his function is left vague and unexplicitated. It does not constitute any real or effective force in the awareness of the faithful in general or of the clergy in particular. It is not until urgent and pressing reasons arise for actually needing the layman that the *other* and more positive truths are recalled, which, on any adequate conception of what the Church means in terms of the Catholic faith, must apply to the layman too. In such a situation the layman is suddenly confronted with these truths, and then we are surprised when he does not respond as swiftly and vigorously as we had really expected, and make a practical application of them in situations in which it is really the strains imposed on the clergy that are at stake. But we should not be surprised at this, in view of the fact that the moment the threat to the Church becomes less palpably evident than it is precisely at the present moment, we so supinely (though certainly without any deliberate ill-will) allow ourselves to sink back into our former attitudes and let these truths with regard to the vocation of the layman to contribute actively in the work of the Church to recede into the background. In view of this there is one principle which needs to be stated, explained and proved not because it is new and unheard of, but because the long-established truth which it embodies is still far from having penetrated into the hearts and minds of us all sufficiently deeply. It is this: by sacramental consecration every Christian in the Church has been authorised and empowered for the task of actively co-operating in the work of the Church both interiorly and exteriorly. This task is laid upon every Christian as a duty, and he has been equipped to discharge it. Thus our immediate purpose here is simply to explain and to justify this one principle alone – nothing more than this. There are two points to be considered here: first, *what this task is*, which the Christian – every individual Christian in the Church – has laid upon him for which he is equipped; second, *the means by which* he is effectively called and equipped for this task, namely the sacraments which he receives. But it will be simplest to take both these points simultaneously and to develop them in a single line of argument. On any other approach we could not avoid being excessively repetitious.

It is through baptism that one becomes a Christian and a member of the Church. Baptism is the first sacrament of the forgiveness of sins, that in which which the grace of divine glory is mediated, that by means of which we are admitted to a share in the divine nature and equipped interiorly and permanently with faith, hope and love for God and man. But how is this interior and permanent grace imparted to the individual man in baptism, transforming him from a sinner into one who is justified? It takes effect in him in virtue of the fact that through this initiation rite he is received into the people of God constituted as an hierarchical society, that is into the community of the believers and of those who acknowledge salvation from God in Christ. It is in virtue of the fact that God incorporates man into the *Church* in baptism that he gives him the grace he needs for his own individual salvation. The state of belonging to the Church, of being incorporated as a member of the Church, is the first and most immediate effect of this sacrament of initiation, which every Christian receives. For all Christians it is this that constitutes the basis for their being Christians at all, and so for each and every function, whether it derives from hierarchical office or sacramental power or rank, with which the individual Christian can be invested in his life. For if he is not baptised then he can no longer validly receive any other sacrament, nor lawfully be invested with any official power in the Church. It is in virtue of the fact that baptism makes man a member of the Church that it gives him the grace to attain to his own salvation. Are we to conclude, then, that the sole and exclusive purpose of this membership of the Church which is imparted through baptism is precisely that the baptized individual may then go on to receive these further benefits, namely his own individual sanctification and justification? To suppose this would precisely be to deprive the principle we have just enunciated of its real force, and this must at all costs be avoided. How utterly false such a supposition would be appears simply from the fact that this purely individual justification and sanctification can, in cases of need, be attained to through faith and charity alone without the sacrament, and that this does certainly take place in the case of many unbelievers. It follows that over and above these particular effects of the salvation of the individual baptism must have a further significance in terms of its positive effects, one which cannot be reduced to this effect of individual salvation. Membership of the Church is not simply a means of attaining to the goal of one's own private salvation, but rather has a meaning of its own which it derives from baptism itself. This is something which follows necessarily from the meaning and function of the Church in general. And if we ask what this meaning may be, we can only reiterate the point which we have just made.

The significance and purpose of the Church is not merely or exclusively to make possible or to facilitate the attainment of salvation in the sum total of many individual cases. For while the Church could be regarded as making a useful and significant contribution to this end, her existence is not absolutely necessary for it in view of the fact that this purpose is in fact often achieved even without any evident intervention on the Church's part. This is not, of course, to deny that since salvation is to be achieved through obedience to God's commandments and a readiness to receive his prescribed sacraments this too is normally to be attained to within the Church. But in the concrete there is one thing that is absolutely impossible without the Church (even if in the abstract it might be possible to conceive of this Church as constantly varying in the forms and constitutional structures which she assumes). This single factor is that the grace of God in Christ is present in the world as an event, and an event which is manifest and enduring in history and incarnate in a physical body. It should be remembered that God has willed to bestow himself as salvation and forgiveness, and to permeate the world with his divinity in an act of supernatural 'pan*en*theism' (if we may make so bold as to express it in this way) only in the incarnation of his Logos, and presumably he could only will to achieve it in this way. And because of this it is of the essence of this particular grace, and belongs to the innermost nature of this self-bestowal of God which penetrates with its 'divinising' influence into the very depths of man's heart in his ultimate free decision as an individual, that it should be actually manifested in the dimension of space and time, that it should have a place in history in the here and now, that it should be projected beyond all mere interiority of the conscience and extended to all the dimensions of human life including the history, the social and political living, the laws, the science and the art which belong to it. Because salvation comes in the flesh of Christ, and because man has to be made whole in and throughout all the dimensions of his existence in their mutual interdependence and influence one upon another, it follows that grace must be embodied, must be an historical and social reality. That grace, as made immanent in these dimensions is called the Church. He, therefore, who is endowed with faith through baptism in that he is incorporated into this Church as an historical and social embodiment of the grace of Christ in the world necessarily obtains, together with this grace of the Church, the right, the task and the necessary equipment to become an active participator in this function of the Church, that namely of *being* the historical concretisation of the grace of God in the world. To express the matter in another way: grace has a force that actively constitutes the Church in virtue of the fact that it is conformed to Christ in the sense that it is 'incarnational'. From this it follows that even though the actualisation of this essential property of grace may remain at a completely rudimentary stage in many cases, still it must be constitutive of the Church in this sense wherever it is found. When, therefore, this grace is actually present as *essentially belonging to the Church herself*, in other words as sacramental, its function as constituting the Church must attain a higher degree of actualisation, and must equip those who receive it still more fully. In other words it must so incorporate the individual into the Church that in very truth he does become a member, in other words an actively functioning unit in this community, and an active participant in the basic functions of this community.

Now given that the Church is of this nature, that it is the historical concretisation of the grace of God in the world in which every baptised individual obtains an active share through baptism what are the implications of this in the concrete? What is it that causes grace to create for itself a quasi-sacramental embodiment in the world in this way? It does this in virtue of the fact that it derives from Christ the incarnate word of God. It is because in this way it stands revealed most clearly and unmistakably in its true nature as a free act of God deriving not from forces intrinsic in the creation and coming from below, but rather directly from God's own sovereign initiative. In this way it can be accepted in its true nature. For it makes its impact not simply by diffusing itself constantly and all-pervasively throughout everything in the world, and therefore in a manner which makes it indistinguishable from the world. Rather it has a distinct historicity of its own. And the final reason for grace being accorded a quasi-sacramental embodiment in the world is that it must confront man as a free and embodied, and therefore historical person as such. In other words it must itself be historical in this sense. Thus the Church has not simply the function of mediating grace, such that strictly speaking the Church would be superfluous if this grace of God were, so to say, designed of itself to penetrate and percolate into man's innermost soul. The function of the Church is rather to provide an outlet by which grace breaks out into the world, into history, into the social and communal life of man. She has the function of giving grace a concrete embodiment in the word, in the sacrament, in ecclesiastical law, in the concrete visible lives of those endowed with grace, simply in order to ensure that this grace may be extended into these spheres also, that these spheres also may be drawn into the kingdom of God, may become the body of the Logos. The Church is the quasi-sacramental word in which the all-pervasive activity of this grace becomes effective, in which it is made present in history with an exhibitive force, in which the fact that it has come and come victoriously is publicly proclaimed. And every individual who has been baptised has a share in this function. When we view the phenomenon of Christianity from this aspect the actual fact itself indeed remains unaltered, but the perspective in which it can be viewed surely does alter in certain notable respects, for now the Christian is no longer so much one who possesses grace (as though it were more or less *certain* that this is not the case with non-Christians) as one in whom grace is meant to be made manifest in the dimension of history. In fact can we say with certainty of any individual, even if he is unbaptised, that he certainly is not endowed with the grace of God, the forgiveness of sins? No. And in that case what precisely is the difference between those who are Christians *ex professo* and those who are so in an unacknowledged sense (if I may so refer to the unbaptised who are, nevertheless, justified)? The difference consists precisely in the fact that baptised Christians appear visibly in the dimension of history and before their fellows as those who have embraced the word and the sacrament, whereas the others are Christians only in the hidden dimension of their own interior consciences, informed by a faith that is only implicit and of which they may not necessarily be conscious in any explicit sense. And the explicit, i.e. baptised Christians have an absolute *obligation* to be what they are in this dimension of the historical and the social. The task is laid upon them to be true to this state which they have entered upon, to be upholders of the Church's function as the visible and social embodiment of grace, and they have really to embrace this state as a matter of personal decision, to undertake it and act upon it in every department of their lives. What applies to the Church applies also to the individual baptised Christian. By baptism he is deputed to be a bearer of the word, a witness of truth, a representative of the grace of Christ in the world. The unbaptised man is the object of the Church's solicitude, on whom she brings to bear the force of her sanctification, her forgiveness and her grace. At the very moment when this takes place he who has hitherto been the object of the Church's solicitude is transformed into a member of the Church, into an element in the Church's subjective life and activity. He is no longer 'over against' the Church, but rather stands with the Church 'over against' the world. He is one who has been called, chosen, separated from the world. He must shine like the stars in heaven in the midst of a generation that is dark and desolate.

Of course even when the individual has been baptised the Church still continues to maintain her role in his regard. In relation to him she is the subject from whom he receives benefits, and to whose guidance he submits, while conversely in relation to her he is in the position of a recipient of favours. But with regard to one who is a *member* of her own self, subordinate to her, paying heed to her and led by her, and to whom she is related as subject to object, the Church exercises this function of hers *in a particular way*, and, moreover, a way that is *different* from the way in which she acts towards one who is not baptised, although in fact she has claims over him too. But she would be quite *incapable* of acting in this particular way towards the baptised individual if he were not precisely also a member of her own self, one who shares in her own position as subject, and assists her in sustaining her active function. Moreover it must be emphasised that he does this precisely as a baptised individual, not only and not primarily as priest, bishop, as one vested with hier- archical authority in the narrower sense. For the peculiar nature of her relationship with the individual Christian is precisely determined by the fact that he is an active member of her in this sense, and that too even in cases in which she addresses herself to him in the name of Christ. Paul says at one point that God alone judges those who are without. The Church's power to judge is restricted precisely to those who are within. This is not because they must be more severely treated, but rather because they are something more than mere individuals. They are more because they have a function which is identified with that of the Church herself. When therefore the Church instructs her own members, calls them to order or sanctifies them, she is in fact safeguarding her own function as bearing witness in the world, and extending it to these as well.

In all aspects of her relationship to her own members one of the deter- mining factors is the function which the Church herself maintains and exercises precisely through these members of hers in the world in general.

Paul finds no difficulty whatever in accepting the fact that those whom he is instructing have intercourse and fellowship with non-Christians. But he forbids them to have the same intercourse and fellowship with Christians who are sinners, and he reacts far more vigorously against the smallest deviation from the gospel as preached in the Church than against errors outside the Church. Again he is sensitive with regard to the impression which a communal assembly and their liturgical celebrations make upon non-Christians, and again in the Pastoral epistles we may search in vain for any real exhortation to the clergy to exercise any external apostolate. It seems, therefore, that no provision whatever is made for any 'propaganda' to those outside the Church, and that no particular necessity for this was felt. Now behind all these phenomena, and many others which we pass over here, we can discern a single underlying conviction, namely that each individual Christian manifestly shares in the responsibility for the Church and her functions as a whole. He is made a sharer in this responsibility precisely in virtue of the fact that he is a member of this Church. This is why when he falls into sin he is treated differently from an outsider. In failing in his own individual task, the contribution which he has to make to the holiness of the Church as the visible manifestation of the victory of God's grace in the world, he compromises the Church herself and her task as well. This is why the Church withdraws herself from the sinner by means of a kind of official ban or excommunication, because otherwise she herself would betray her own task. This is why the primitive Church had no misgivings in taking it for granted that the missionary work of the Church would be carried on without anything much in the way of systematic or official organisation, because in fact each individual Christian has to bear witness in his life to the fact that by his grace God has laid hold of his life to transform it and to fill it with his grace. Baptism, therefore, in that it admits the individual Christian to a place in the Church, initiates him into the basic function of the Church herself, in that she identifies herself with the imminent advent of the kingdom of God in the victory of his grace. And even in cases in which the Church's solicitude for the salvation of mankind is directed towards the individual himself as its object the Church cannot forget that the baptised individual is an object of such solicitude on her part in a totally different sense from the unbaptised. In caring for the salvation of the baptised the Church always takes cognizance of the further fact that he can only achieve this salvation of his if, and to the extent that he exercises his active function in the Church, and in collaboration with her works for the salvation of the world by bearing witness to God's truth and God's grace.

It may be that baptism does not impart to the layman any new position in the world such as that occupied by the officials of the Church's hierarchy. In normal cases the only ones who can be official emissaries of the Church in the hierarchy of her apostolate are those who by their vocation are withdrawn from the secular position which they formerly occupied in the world in order to go forth to all peoples. But in normal cases the baptised layman, unlike these, continues in that secular sphere of life which he previously occupied in the world before he was baptised. In spite of this, however, he acquires through baptism another and a fresh task to be discharged precisely in this position in which he finds himself at the purely human level. For it is because of him that the Church is present precisely *there*. When we use the term 'Church' here this is not to be thought of simply as an externalising application of this concept to the Church as an organisation, or simply to her legal constitution, her influence as an organisation, as a 'perfect society', as visible in her own history. When we use the term 'Church' here and in *this* context what we mean by it is the grace of God, the power of God as faith, hope and charity, trust in the meaning of existence and its further projections into infinity in the deed of God. 'Church' here, therefore, is intended to signify truth, that liberating truth which alone can open up all human truth to the infinite and dazzling mystery of God. 'Church' in this context signifies the courage to commit oneself to eternity, the daring of that love in which man uncalculatingly and finally lets his entire existence fall into the incomprehensibility which we call God. When we speak of the Church then we mean by it all this precisely to the extent that this grace does not simply take effect somewhere in the deepest recesses of our conscience, so that we hardly dare to make contact with this infinite mystery of existence, but rather acquires a body, is unashamedly borne witness to (even if not in the high-flown phraseology of a Christianity that is pretentious), is joyfully lived, lovingly handed on to others, makes its impact in all dimensions of existence whether in life or in death. It is the Church in this sense, therefore, that we are speaking of here, and we shall say of the Church in this sense that through the baptised its presence must be made manifest. It must be there wherever one who is a Christian in *this* sense is there.

The mission of the baptised layman to share in the task of the Church does not begin and end with the observance of peaceful Sunday devotions. It does not consist in any primary sense in Corpus Christi processions with the notables of the parish or the political party or the good Catholics. It does not mean casting one's vote in favour of the Catholic interest, nor yet in patiently paying the Church's dues. Rather it implies an awareness, so deep and so radical that it revolutionises everything, of the fact that the baptised man is constantly confronted with the task of a Christian precisely in that environment in which he finds himself and in which his life is passed, that is to say in the wholly natural context of his calling, in his family, the circles in which he lives, his nation and state, his human and cultural milieu. And this task consists in establishing the dominion of God in truth, in selflessness and in love, and thereby making what is truly essential to the Church's nature present in the setting in which he is placed, from the position which only he can occupy, in which he cannot be replaced by any other, not even by the clergy, and where, nevertheless, the Church must be. Of course once the layman takes up his task in this position of his he will undergo a further experience: for him this Church is the Church of truth, of kindness, of selflessness, of honourable behaviour, of courage, of a tacit harmony with the dark mystery of existence, a silent attitude of readiness and sure hopefulness with regard to death, and of a practical fulfilment of duty even when no further profit is to be attained from it. And he will experience the fact that this Church has representatives and champions who never know that this community, to which they belong by being true to it in their actions in this way, is precisely *the* people of God which, according to the will of God and Christ, attains tangible form as a society and an unequivocal place in history, in other words a quasi-sacramental value as an effective sign, precisely in the Church of Jesus Christ. This is because this anonymous Christianity, present in those who only *think* that they neither are nor should be Christians, does in truth live by, and bring to its fulness, that grace of Christ which finds its historical concretisation and embodiment precisely in the Church.

Now when we speak in this way of a Church of interior grace characterised by a love and faithfulness that are effective, and an attitude of acceptance towards death (in which faith and love are always brought to their consummation), then we are not indulging in any kind of conceptual sleight of hand, so as to substitute a different concept of the Church for the usual one. No, what we have in mind here is not in any sense an 'invisible

Church', but is precisely that which manifests itself in the concrete and visible Church. And even in those cases in which the Church has less of the outward form of a visible society, the reality of which we are speaking here still belongs to the Church and is in very truth orientated towards it. Nor do we underestimate the importance of the fact that the Church as a concrete and palpable entity should have the further quality of being visible. For indeed she both is and must be the concretisation in social and historical terms of that divine reality which we call grace and spirit. Now according to the teaching of this same Church this reality both can be and is already present and powerfully at work even in those areas in which she has not yet been unequivocally manifested to the world as an historical and social fact with a concrete embodiment of its own.

What we are asserting, therefore, is that the Christian, from his position in the world, and in the power he receives from his baptism, has to render present the victory of grace, of love and of faith, of the fact that the kingdom of God has arrived. And he has the responsibility of being a sign in the world and to the world of the eternal reality of salvation. But in making this assertion we are not for one moment denying that there are other Christians too, unprofessed Christians, present in the very milieu to which the professed Christian himself belongs. It is no mere hypothesis, but a sure fact, that such unacknowledged Christians are there, and in them the same power of grace has already begun to do its work. It is on their behalf too, therefore, that the professed Christian must bear his witness. This situation may make it more difficult for the professed and acknowledged Christian to stand out from the rest so clearly in the position he occupies in the world, in his family and his calling and in the task he has to perform in the world, to the extent that these others are ultimately quite unaware of the fact that they are Christians. Yet the professed Christian has to stand apart from the rest in such a way that the Church which he represents can very clearly be distinguished from the world in the wordly milieu in which she finds embodiment. But all this does not in any way alter the task and the special responsibility of the baptised Christian to make the Church present in that context in the world which he occupies as one who has been baptised. When God of his sovereign freedom distributes talents and graces to men, and causes the Spirit to move in them through all the byways of the world, this often has the effect, if we may so express it, of creating a rival to his own Church, for in doing this he raises up men outside the visible Church who are endowed with graces belonging to his Church, men who are not yet incorporated into her visible and official structure, and who may only be so incorporated when the consummation of the ages has arrived and everything that has proved itself good and true is gathered into the Church to enjoy eternal life. But in spite of all this there is no reason for the baptised Christian to be any less conscious of his mission and his radical responsibility. Wherever he finds himself confronted by justice, right living, love, faithfulness, courage, consolation in life and strength in death in the world, there he knows that the grace of Christ is at work. Because without this grace even the natural human virtues do not in the long run endure, and therefore when they manifest themselves amid all the darkness and guilt of this world they bear witness to the grace of Christ, whether those possessing them realise it or not. And when the Christian encounters such natural human virtues in the world he cannot say 'See, even without Christianity and the Church human goodness is achieved'. Rather he must say to himself: 'There has been achieved here that for which you have been sent, commissioned and endowed with grace twice and three times over by the finger of the living God when it sealed your soul and your life with the irremovable seal of baptism. Woe to you if in your life the witness to God's goodness shines out less brightly, less convincingly, than it has shone in the primæval forest of Lambarene, or in the case of Simone Weil, or in the lives of such as Wolfram Siewers and many others of whom we may think that the sign of Christ shines upon their brows even though they themselves appear to be unconscious of it. It is a fact that the Christian who is so *ex professo* through baptism is often sent to the unacknowledged Christian who is so through an interior grace which achieves its effects within him without his knowing it. And it is precisely because of this situation that the commission to share in the Church's task which is given with baptism becomes once more a mission to perform an act of total and unconditional obedience in faith, an act in which witness is borne to God even though this witness may seem not to be successful in winning over those to whom it is addressed to the point at which the witness itself can claim any credit for his work.

One point at least is clear. Through baptism a man becomes not only subject to the Church, bound by its rules, a sharer in its blessings, but a member of the Church as well, one who has to share actively in the performance of its functions. He has to be a witness to the event in which the victory of God's eschatological grace has arrived, in which God himself

becomes the salvation of the world, and in virtue of this the baptised
Christian in the Church acquires a position which consists not primarily
or exclusively in the fact that he is a subject for the hierarchy to exercise
their authority upon, and is distinguished from the clergy simply by the
fact that he is *non*-clerical. This much is clear and unmistakable. Something
which bears upon the relationship between the various elements in the
Church should not become the first point for consideration right at the
outset. The nature of the Church cannot initially or adequately be described simply by pointing to the relationship which her individual members bear one to another, because in fact, in order rightly to determine
how two elements in a whole are related one to the other one must first
understand the nature of the whole itself. When, therefore, we set out to
establish the exact legal status, the functions and duties of those vested
with authority in the Church, and, as the outcome of this, the rest of the
duties to be performed by the other members and functionaries who have
to be subject to these established authorities, all this cannot count as a
description of the nature of the Church, however essential the functions
vested as a matter of sacred right in these officials of the hierarchy may be,
and however many blessings they may bring on the Church, and however
indispensable they may appear. But when we say that the Church is the
Body of Christ, the enduring presence in history and in the world of his
truth and grace, the effects wrought by the incarnate Word made abiding
in the flesh, and when we say that every baptised individual shares in these
because he is a member of this Body, then we have said everything, provided that we have really understood the principle which we have just
stated.

    We might, of course, go on to develop many particular aspects of what
has been said up to this point. If we were to take this course we would
have to point out that the Church's essential function as envisaged here
is far from being confined to those powers which the officials in the
Church can bring to bear, and which are of a legal and constitutional
character. We would have to point out that there is such a thing as a
charismatic factor in the Church which is no less vital as an element in its
nature than the factors of the institutional and the official. We would
have to point out that there is, and must be, an unfolding of conscious
faith in the Church, a progress in the life of faith which is unplanned
and which is the outcome of the Church's own experiences. And this is
not controlled by the human designs of the Church's officials, but rather

guided by the Holy Spirit. It is true that the official teaching authority of the Church is not juridically dependent upon these movements of faith, but it is so in fact. We would then have to point out that the Spirit is far from choosing to produce his effects always and necessarily through the officials of the Church. Thus for this charismatic element in action, in faith and in love, which operates under the direct influence of the Spirit, the 'layman', on the basis of his membership of the Church through baptism, can be, and often enough is in practice, just as much the point of entry and the medium through which the Spirit operates as the cleric, so that he too has the duty of developing the sort of sensitivity to this movement in himself which will make him adequate for his position in the Church. We could then go on to remind ourselves that according to the words of Pius XII there must be, and in fact is, something corresponding to the factor of public opinion even in the Church, and that without this the Church would suffer damage in her shepherds and her flock alike, and that the laity inevitably are and must be to a large extent the upholders of this necessary factor of public opinion in the Church. We might draw attention to the fact that there must necessarily be something like a supernatural 'existential' ethic, even though what is normally designated as 'situation' ethics is a heresy. In other words, to put it briefly, the decision which the individual Christian takes at particular points in his life must indeed be brought into line with the universal principles as proclaimed by the teaching authority of the Church, but cannot be derived in any adequate sense from these alone. At this point, therefore, every individual and every Christian stands in an immediate relationship to God, one which does not withdraw him from the visible Church, but which cannot be left to its visible authority to sustain (even though this latter still continues to have its force as a *norma negativa* against deception). Moreover it would have to be pointed out that any such decision on the part of the individual Christian, in other words on the part of the so-called individual layman too (and here it must be pointed out that the immediate relationship to God involved in this must be thought of as wholly based upon the grace of baptism), has a vital significance not only for the individual concerned in his own private life but for the Church as a whole as well.

The role of the layman in the Church as constituted by baptism is to be understood, therefore, as deriving not primarily from the position of the clergy, but from the very nature of the Church herself. Naturally in any community of men organised as a society there must be a leadership and this must be vested in specific individuals. Naturally in the Church of Christ this power of leadership is founded by Christ himself and not constituted by a democratic process from the rank and file upwards. But this is in virtue of the fact that the Church, and therefore the position, task and function of every member of the Church too, as instituted by Christ, stems from above. Thus if we take the analogy of a politically organised society, a people or nation, this does not owe its existence as such in the first instance to the fact that some political system is already available in the abstract. Rather it is the historical and human entity that is already in existence for the political constitution to be applied to it, and so to organise it into a society, in other words a people with a culture and communal organisation which has developed in the context of history. And just as the life of the people thus politically organised does not only, not originally, and not in any ultimate sense consist in the exercise of authority on the part of its officially constituted leaders, but rather these are in the position of servants contributing to the life of the people as a whole, so too it is with the Church. Even though its constitutional structure derives from above it is already in existence prior to this as the community of the redeemed, the believers, those who are impelled by the Spirit of God, those who are beloved by God, those who are called to eternal life. The life of the Church is embodied in the activities of all these. And in relation to this the members of the ecclesiastical hierarchy, precisely in their constitutional function as leaders of the Church, have to act as servants. The ultimate aim of all who work in the Church and for the Church is to ensure, as a living fact of faith, hope and love, that the grace of God shall be received as the life of God in the Church, that witness shall be born to the truth of God, to the faithfulness of God, to the hope of eternal life. In relation to this everything else in the Church, including the whole constitutional organisation into authorities and subordinates, and the provision for official leaders vested with authority, is only a means to an end. The provision for such authorities is designed for an end beyond themselves. They are there because the Church must exist, and what is in truth her primary task must be performed. But they are not in any sense an end in themselves. Their presence in the Church does not mean *ipso facto* that she has already arrived at that true flowering of her own true nature which she is intended to achieve. One might, therefore, go so far as to say in a very true and uncompromising sense that the clergy exist because the laity exist, and the term 'layman' is not in any sense derogatory, but rather is equivalent to 'member of the Church'. For the Church is composed of these laymen, and in them she achieves her own fulness as the life of Christ in the world.

We have spoken of baptism as the sacramental basis for the position of the layman in the Church. Baptism provides a sacramental basis in this sense in virtue of the fact that through it the baptised individual receives his divine calling and is established in a position, i.e. in an enduring and inalienable form of life in which he makes an active contribution to the Church in the realisation of her own nature and destiny. But all that we have said of baptism applies in a still higher degree when we come to think of the *sacrament of confirmation*. In the last analysis it is not of decisive importance when we have received this sacrament of the outpouring of the Spirit, or how we have understood it. The decisive point is rather whether as confirmed individuals we finally come to notice at any point in our lives what has been achieved in objective reality in this sacrament, and what we have subjectively to accomplish by the strength which it confers. For a dogmatic theologian it is difficult to distinguish with complete precision between the two sacraments in their meaning and their effects. It is precisely as taken both together that they constitute a single initiation into Christian existence. Sacramentally speaking these two sacraments represent two distinct aspects of our Christian calling considered as a single entity. For this reason we do not need here either to make the attempt at separating or distinguishing the two sacraments from one another in any very explicit way. All that we feel is necessary to say here is this: the sacrament of confirmation is a sacrament of witness to the faith, of charismatic fulness, of the Holy Spirit, the sacrament in which those sealed with the Spirit are sent into the world to bear witness in order that the world may be made subject to the dominion of God. It is the sacrament of strengthening in the faith against the powers and forces in this world, the powers of lying and disbelief and of the diabolical *hybris* involved in attempting to work out one's own salvation. And if this is the significance of this sacrament, then we can realise still more clearly how little the Christian as confirmed layman is a mere object for the Church's educative and directive activities as exercised through the authority and leadership of her hierarchy. We can realise how much more he is placed in the position of one who has a mission and a task, a personal responsibility for the world in virtue of his initiation into Christianity.

Of all the other sacraments too it could be shown that they have an ecclesiological aspect; that they do not merely constitute so many events in which one's own salvation as a private individual is conferred and catered for. On the contrary they are meant to contribute to the Church as a whole. So true is this, indeed, that they always have the further significance, over and above their immediate effects, of initiating the recipient into an active task in the Church. And this is the case with all the sacraments including those which every layman receives. The sacrament of *penance*, as the sacrament of reconciliation with God and the Church, is in fact the sacrament in which the fulness of what was conferred in baptism and confirmation is restored, and in which the initiation which they bring is, in a certain sense, re-activated. This is true also, therefore, with regard to being assigned a definite position in the Church. He who receives the Spirit anew receives him (as the Fathers of the Church have explicitly realised) as the Spirit of the Church and precisely in virtue of the fact of being reconciled with the Church. And therefore he receives the Spirit precisely as willing to seize upon, save and fill with the life of God himself the world which belongs to the community of the believers, these believers being themselves filled with the Spirit. It is in this guise that the Spirit bears witness to himself through the existence of the Church.

The fact that the sacrament of the *Eucharist* is a sacrament of unity with the Church achieved through being filled with the Spirit, the Church's own bread of unity in love, and that it is not, in the first instance, a sort of sacramental private audience with God in heaven – all this is in fact a recognised truth. He, therefore, who receives this Bread of life can do nothing else (provided that he knows what he is doing) than to receive from the Spirit which the Body of Christ imparts to him the power of the unity, this expression of the highest unity of eternal life, is something that *all* Christians receive in the same way; none of them, therefore, has any prior claim over the others in this, which constitutes the supreme sacramental expression of the whole essence of Christianity. Certainly this sacrament above all, as symbolising and deepening and rendering ever more effective the unity of the Church, must of its very nature give expression to the hierarchical structure of the Church in the manner in which it is celebrated. The Last Supper of the Lord, in which all share, since all are loved and redeemed in the same manner, must be celebrated in a way that has been fore-ordained, and that is in conformity with the will of Christ himself in that the bishop or priest has the presiding role. Without an officially worked out order of celebration of this kind no celebration of the Eucharist of the Lord could be conceived of as the celebration of the Church herself. But precisely as ordained in this way, the Last Supper of the Lord is designed in the intention of Christ himself, for all Christians, for the Church as a whole. Certainly it is through the officially deputed ministers of the Church that Christ extends this Bread of eternal life to us, but he extends it to all. And it is true even of the ordained minister, the member of the hierarchy, that he achieves the fulness of his personal Christian life in virtue of the fact not that he imparts, but rather that he receives this sacrament like every other Christian. It is in this way that as incorporated into the Body of the Lord he becomes filled with his Spirit and so finally achieves in this the highest act of his personal life, one which, once more, he has in common with all Christians: that he believes, hopes and loves.

The fact that *marriage* directly imparts to the Christian a social and ecclesiastical function, a position which has its basis in the world but in the Church as well, is something that hardly needs to be gone into at any great length here. It is through the sacrament of marriage that the actual common life of those who have been united by it is dedicated as the effective sign of the unity between Christ and his Church. It is through this sacrament, therefore, that the community of the married actually comes to constitute a Church. And while marriage does not impart an irremovable character to its recipients as do baptism, confirmation and orders, nevertheless it is true of marriage too that so long as it lasts as an enduring bond between two Christians in this world and in the time appropriate to it, in other words until the death of one of the two parties to the marriage, it has the force of an abiding sign of grace. It is a sign that this grace of Christ is always extended to the partners to the marriage, and always ensures that this particular state shall endure in the Church as well. For marriage has the force of inaugurating men into the closest and most intimate kind of unity that exists, and at the same time of imparting a sacramental consecration and an imperishability to this community, turning into a sort of microcosmic 'local Church'. For this community consists precisely in the 'two-in-one-flesh' relationship of two married individuals, such that the community thereby constituted represents for them a Christian grace and a Christian task to bring salvation into the world.

It must be remembered that the death of the Christian, and, together with this, the right attitude with which he endures the death-throes when these press in upon him (even in cases in which they are overcome and he is restored to health once more) is an act of dying with Christ, an acceptance of death in faith, hope and love as the ultimate reality of life which has been redeemed by Christ and accepted by him in person. It must be remembered too that the death of Christ, even though he died this death in circumstances of the most cruel loneliness that could be conceived of, was not the most private event in his life, but rather one of cosmic dimensions, in which all was redeemed and the world was cleansed of its guilt. And if this is true, then too our death as a dying with Christ must also have a significance that extends to all men. We suffer together with all, and for all in the fate in which all are ultimately made equal, and the death we die, because it is hidden in the death of Christ himself, is one that generates life. And therefore it is not suprising that even in this moment of the uttermost loneliness, the Church does not let man simply fall into this ultimate incommunicability of death, death as the most solitary of events, but actually accompanies man in this moment through the sacrament of *Extreme Unction*, the sacrament specially designed for this moment of the death throes. And she does this because the dying man, sanctified and strengthened by this prayer of faith, precisely in these moments of death achieves once more an act which affects the entire Church. When an individual 'dies in the Lord' then he has also died with the Lord on behalf of all who belong to the Lord. And in this sense the Christian never loses that position which has been conferred upon him sacramentally in the Church and for the Church until all is consummated.

At the outset of these considerations we formulated the following proposition: by sacramental consecration and the power which this confers every Christian in the Church is equipped, empowered and commissioned to take up a position of active co-operation in the Church's internal and external work. It has been impossible for us, within the brief limits of an essay such as this, to develop this statement further, or to show how it provides the most complete basis for what we have been saying, and, as an interpretation of the actual content of this essay, is the most all-comprehending that could be devised. If we could go on to develop this point the question which would now arise (though this is no longer possible within the limits we have set ourselves) would be what the significance of this is in the concrete for the individual Christian of our own times. But even as it is one point at least should have been made clear: as applied in the context of the Church the term 'layman' means the opposite of what this signifies in other contexts, when it is applied in the profane sphere, as for instance in the assertion: 'In the field of criminal law he is an utter layman.' In the secular sphere 'layman' means one who cannot take part in the discussion, who has nothing to contribute, who is excluded from a specific area of life and responsibility. But when the term 'layman' is used in the theological context it means the opposite of this. Certainly the findings of the most recent investigators may be correct when they say that the use of this term for the baptised and believing Christian in order to express the difference which exists between him and the cleric is not derived directly from the biblical concept of the 'people of God' (in other words from the concept of the λαὸς θεοῦ with which it has linguistic connections). According to these findings the manner in which this term was applied right from the beginning shows that it carried with it the further connotation of 'non-expert', 'amateur'. In practice, however, it would have the most devastating results – and to some extent these do exist in fact – if the sum total of the individual Christian's conception of his own position as a Christian was that he was not a cleric and therefore had at most a subordinate and more or less passive part to play in the Church's life. In virtue of his baptism every Christian is one who has been anointed and consecrated, a temple of God, one who has been chosen and set apart, one who has been called and summoned into the community of those who know and acknowledge that God has taken compassion upon the world, and has called her into his own life. Every Christian has a share in the active function of the Church both in her internal and external affairs. The word of God is laid upon his lips too, even though he has not the authority or the mission to preach in the officially constituted communal assembly, for in fact he has to uphold the gospel message in those areas of human life upon which the communal assembly has to make its impact if it is to have meaning and authority at all, those areas, namely, in which that life is lived which this word of God is intended to illumine and to redeem. Generally speaking the baptised Christian should convey this word by the integrity with which he conducts his life rather than by his own words, though this is not always or exclusively the case, and there may be occasions when it is legitimate for him to speak out as well. Nevertheless he is a member of the Church which possesses the word, and as such is sealed by the spirit of God. For this reason the the saying applies to him: 'Woe betide me if I have not preached, if I have not born witness.' By baptism and by all the other sacraments too, every

Christian is made responsible in his own measure for helping in the task of the Church, namely that through her the grace of God may be made present palpably and convincingly in *that* world which *has been* redeemed by the love of God and yet which still needs to be redeemed by being made to experience and to accept this fact of its own redeeemd state. This is always an act which takes place both in the Church's interior life and in the sphere of the external world as well. In the Church's interior life because all of us as Christians must constantly be re-discovering and re-living our Christian state anew. Externally because far the greatest part of the world has not yet consciously apprehended that which has, nevertheless, already been received into the depths of its *subconscious*, namely the grace and promise of being definitively possessed by God's grace which does, nevertheless, need to be explicitly and consciously grasped.

One fact remains true, and it should not be glossed over, because it is quite unnecessary to do so. There is a very real difference between the cleric and the Christian who has *not* been entrusted with specific tasks of organisation and leadership in the Church in virtue of having received the sacrament of priestly consecration or order. In this respect it is Christ's will that there should be an ascending order of rank and degree in the Church. But these differences in rank and order are so only with regard to quite specific functions in the life of the Church and her disposition and organisation as a society. They have nothing to do with the holiness of her members, or the fact that they are encompassed by the love of God. Nor do they even necessarily have anything to do with the objective significance of the function concerned for salvation. For it can be the case that a free charism in the Church, such as a layman too can be favoured with, may in practice be of greater significance for the salvation of mankind and of the world than the exercise of an institutional, official or even sacramental authority. Nor does this organisation of the Church into orders and degrees affect God's radical claim that we shall uphold and preserve the truth that the whole world in all its dimensions is that which has been brought into being by God's own creative act, and that we shall make his redemptive act effective in it too. This is a task and duty which is laid inalienably on every individual regardless of his rank or order. Now if, taking all these factors into consideration, we were asked to produce a formula which was at once concise and comprehensive enough to sum them all up in one, we might propose the following: Certainly the layman in the Church is different from the sacramentally constituted cleric because both have different tasks to perform in the Church, tasks which mutually complement and condition one another. But when that is realised and stated the best way to express the matter would be to say: the layman in the Church is not a 'layman' but – a Christian. And in either or both of these aspects of his position in the Church he is confronted by the question of whether he wills to be what in fact he is.

5

THE POSITION OF WOMAN IN THE NEW SITUATION IN WHICH THE CHURCH FINDS HERSELF

THE Church is an extremely complex and multi-dimensional structure, and this is true not merely with regard to its hierarchical structure and the diversity of tasks, rights and duties belonging to its members and which derive from the very nature of the Church herself. A further factor which we should never forget is that while the Church is *one*, this unity of hers is one in which the greatest possible diversity and multiplicity of individuals, peoples and cultures live and move. If we may so express it she includes among her members the greatest diversity of human types which it is possible to conceive of, ranging from the men of the stone age to those who, while they live in the present, really belong to the twenty-first century. All these live simultaneously side by side in the Church.

The Church's life as a society is carried on in the lives of her members through the most manifold system of interrelationships. For this reason, while it may be true that human nature as constituted by the distinction of the sexes may endure throughout as a metaphysical reality, still the actual mode in which this one nature is objectively realised in the concrete is stamped and conditioned by the special circumstances of history which correspond to this plurality of types and situations justifiably existing in the Church. The diversity to be found in the Church today, with all the different territories, nations, cultures and different types of society which she embraces, means that it is possible to speak of *the* situation of the Church only in an extremely limited sense. And in the same way there is very little that can validly be asserted of *the* woman as a single and entirely homogeneous type with a definite concrete position in the Church capable of being investigated. On these grounds alone this is a subject which can be treated of only with the strictest reservations. Of course in raising this question of the position of woman we are thinking of her position in our society and in the Church as we know it, and not, for instance of the position of an Indian woman in the Church as it exists in the primaeval forests of Brazil. But even so the reservation expressed above still applies. For even the Church as it exists among us and woman as she exists in our society are still abstract concepts, and the realities corresponding to them in the life of the Church and of women today are extremely diverse in character.

It is true that in answer to our question it might be possible to adopt an approach of prudent conjecture, and so to sketch in the basic outlines in a portrait of woman, her potentialities and tasks such as would gradually become more typical as our *'big city' culture* developed its rational, technical and cosmic potentialities. But in all this there is one point upon which we must be clear, namely that this process of predicting a future type or category is uncertain in the extreme, so that the sort of conclusions we can draw and the sort of estimates that we can make of what will be required on the basis of such a portrayal can only be conditional in so far as they can be applied at all in any effective or universal sense to woman today and her position in the Church. Any of our contemporaries who is really serious in accepting history for what it is and who recognises it as the will of God must take the representatives of the past just as seriously, and allow them to have just as much value as those who feel themselves to be the spokesmen for the future of mankind. For the past is just as much with us as a reality present and divinely willed as is the future, and for this reason even what is out of date still has its significance. And the power to render present everything of the past which should be preserved as well as everything which is to come and must come in the future is nowhere summed up in any one individual person. It is true of the woman of the past and the woman of the future alike that we can only rightly understand the Christian position and the Christian task of each of these types in so far as we recognise that each has a value for the other, and that their full value is only appreciated when they are brought together in the unity of an understanding love.

To this first point a second must now be added: every present conceals within itself, combined in an unity in which they cannot ultimately or totally be distinguished one from another, the following factors: the nature of man himself which endures through all change, the fact that he is called upon to enter into an immediate relationship with God, the guilt of the past and the present, the legitimate impulse to advance towards the future, the failure to understand what this impulse signifies whether this failure be blameworthy or not, and finally the assent of God to man which creates salvation for him and again and again rises superior to all his sins. And because of this the attitude of the Church in response to the demands of the times and to man's will to advance towards some future still unrealised can in all cases only be one which is both critical and positive at the same time. The Church cannot simply join in the general chorus of those who demand a new age and with this a transformation of the Church herself and of her life as well. For in all this an element of shortsightedness is inevitably involved as well, as the heritage of the past and as the guilt of the present, a guilt which belongs to us all since we are, and continue to be, sinners.

Unlike the world, therefore, the Church cannot simply issue watchwords to set the spirits alight of those who belong to her. Conscious of the duty which her past lays upon her, she will always adopt a critical attitude even, once more, to those estimates which are made of the future of the world and of the Church herself. But it is no less true that she cannot simply wage a defensive battle on behalf of the concrete realities which survive from the past of the world and of her own life. For this past is itself subject to the same law which we have mentioned above, namely that a whole series of factors are united in the present: the enduring nature of man himself, the process of becoming in history to which he is subject, the providence of God in its salvific effects upon him and his own guilt. And for this reason the past can never simply provide the ideal pattern according to which the future should be constructed. This realism, in which the Church identifies herself neither with the past as it has been in concrete fact nor with the future as it is postulated, is inevitably felt by the members of the Church to be tiresome. And it must be borne with patience and hope. It is in this realism that the hope and faith of the individual Christian is made effective, for in it two essential factors are brought together, namely the incalculable and uncontrollable complexities of the world on the one hand, and the abstract rigidity of man's own conception of the future on the other. These are viewed as under the control of the Lord of history himself, whose designs, for all our planning and proposing, always remain ultimately hidden from us.

A final point which must be added is this: By reason of the unbridgeable *gulf which exists between the universal and the concrete particular* all those rules of action which can be deduced from the natural law and the gospel, and which can be laid down for the future, remain at the abstract level. They never admit of being reduced to directly concrete terms or into imperatives which are binding absolutely and in all cases, and which can be laid clearly and unequivocally upon all Christians as an absolute duty. For this reason even within the Church and within the unity of her faith and her love there are inevitably differences of opinion as to what should be done in the here and now, and this divergence of opinion must be borne with in patience and love, and can only be resolved in the concrete through our own free decisions as exercised in history itself. And this history can neither be controlled by any authority nor catered for by any theory in any adequate sense.

All this must be borne in mind if we are to make any attempt at stating what the position of woman should be in the new situation in which the Church finds herself. If we do attempt anything of this kind then we must begin with certain theories which remain at the abstract level, and which, while they may in themselves be binding upon all, are necessarily applied in the concrete in terms of an outlook which is historically conditioned. And this outlook does not have the same degree of binding force as the theories themselves. A further factor, apart from these theories, which we have to take into account is the arbitrary demands for a particular kind of future which are made, and which, basically speaking, cannot be regarded as binding upon any Christian in virtue of the nature of Christianity itself. Now when we attempt to define what the position of woman in the new situation of the Church should be then inevitably these two factors are blended into an unity which can no longer be analysed or resolved into its constituent elements in any adequate sense. This fusion of abstract theory and concrete demand, therefore, always manifests itself in the concrete form of that which is historically conditioned, in other words in a form which Christians do not necessarily have to agree with each other about.

I. THE UNITY OF THE WORLD AND THE CONSEQUENCES OF THIS FOR THE CHURCH

When we say that the Church now stands in a new situation we mean that this situation is new in a deeper and more far-reaching sense than could have been said of any given age in the past as it followed upon the preceding one in the general process of history. Without prejudice to the supernatural dynamism of the Church, which is the work of the Spirit within her, it seems that we should ascribe this new situation to the new situation which prevails in the world in its purely secular aspects. This in turn is a situation which has been brought into being by the fact that the 'new age' is coming to an end, and a future one has already begun. It is this, then, that we should look to if we are ever really to come to some definite conclusions about this new situation which prevails in the Church, to some extent to arrive at some definite theory with regard to its significance, and to anticipate how it will develop, instead of merely enduring it without comprehending it.

The new epoch in world history is one in which that history has achieved a real and concrete unity such that all the particular histories of peoples and of continents which have hitherto remained separate one from another have been brought into communication. The result of this is that the fate of each individual member of the human race and of each individual, country and nation, constitutes a factor in the historical, situation of all the other individuals and all the other nations too. We might put it this way: in the scriptural narrative of the Tower of Babel we are given an insight, in terms of the theology of history, into what the consequences are of this episode. God is represented as intervening providentially, and ultimately for the sake of saving mankind, in order to prevent men from adopting an united stand against him. This is viewed as the beginning of the process by which the individual peoples and nations departed one from another on their separate ways of salvation. Today this process has been reversed by an act which is just as providential and at the same time just as dangerous too. Mankind has once more been drawn into a unity, and in this *a real possibility has arisen of a collective and cosmic atheism, but also of a world Church really coming into being to afford universal access to God to all history and to all men.*

This cosmic unity, by which history becomes one, has its origins in the West. And from here it is possible for the saving history of Christianity to be extended to all the world. As viewed in its ultimate and deepest sense this unity is itself the outcome of a Christian interpretation of man's meaning and mission. This cosmic unity, comprised by the saving history which proceeds from the Christianised West, is the unity of a world that has been divested of the numinous, a world what is dominated by human reason and human technical achievements. It is a world which man no longer accepts simply as the natural order, directly controlled by God, but which he himself constructs according to his own plans by his reason and technical mastery, and in this sense it is a 'humanised' world. This world is one in which man takes over personal responsibility for his own moral decisions, shapes his life and works out or fails to work out his own salvation. But over and above this it is also the world in which man can use his technical mastery in an ever-increasing measure to manipulate himself and his nature. He can actively transform and reconstruct his own real selfhood, which hitherto he had simply to take more or less as given. This world is a world in which mankind is increasing and multiplying at an immense speed, and therefore necessarily requires far more developed and precise patterns of social living than has been the case hitherto. At the same time, without denying the tendency of this world towards this cosmic unity and these more intense forms of social living, it is still a *complex* world with many different elements in its make-up. And this is precisely due to the fact that because man has been freed from the dominion of nature and has been able to rationalise his environment to a far greater extent the objective impact of the human intellect in the arts and sciences has increased rather than decreased, while the differences which exist between nations and the complexities inherent in the one history of mankind, so far from disappearing have actually intensified.

It is this world, then, that exercises so decisive an influence upon the situation of the Church. She has become a world Church not only by definition but in real fact as well. For this reason she is no longer materially to be identified with the culture of the West, but embraces a whole range of national histories and cultures. Formerly she could have been accused of an almost naïve *symbiosis*, of identifying herself with a particular form of civilization which in practice she herself more or less controlled, but now she is to an ever-increasing extent emancipated from this, and is developing into a Church in a secularised world, a world that is made up of numerous and complex elements, and is the outcome of rational planning. The inner dynamism proper to this world does indeed remain encompassed by the creative and salvific will of God. But to a large extent it can no longer be directly shaped by the Church's official authority or integrated into her life by being presented with her concrete imperatives. The Church is the Church, and, as instituted by God, she offers salvation to all men and is aware that she is basically and fundamentally the Church of all men. But on any realistic assessment of the future she cannot count on being able to include all men among her members as those who actually and explicitly confess her faith and receive her sacraments. With regard to the generality of mankind and its development she will, upon all human calculations, continue to be, and that to a still greater extent than hitherto, the 'little flock', and this in spite of all missionary endeavours on her part. Indeed, relatively speaking, she will become a still smaller flock despite all the efforts which are rightly made to ensure that she shall remain a Church of the ordinary people. To a still greater extent than in former times she will become the Church of those who believe as a matter of individual and personal responsibility. Hence she will recognise her role still more clearly as the leaven in the lump that is the unified history of the world, as the 'arch-sacrament', i.e. as the sign of salvation which God has set up in the dimension of history for the salvation of those, too, who are not numbered among her members as a visible society.

II. CONCRETE REQUIREMENTS FOR THE EQUAL STATUS OF WOMAN TO BE MADE EFFECTIVE IN THE CHURCH

What is the significance for this new situation of the Church in a new world? We cannot, of course, undertake here to provide a systematic or comprehensive answer to this question, nor even to indicate the lines along which such an answer might be developed. All that is possible here is to provide a few partial answers chosen more or less at random, and these can only be given with the proviso that other points are not being dealt with here, even though they may be more important.

1. First certain consequences must be mentioned of what has been said above, which apply to the Church herself in the exercise of her authority, and which bear upon her attitude towards women. *In her own personal life too the Church must recognise without reserve the fact that women have equal value and equal rights with men.* Contemporary theology has had much to say in general terms about the position and function of the layman as based upon the baptism and confirmation which he has received. And all this applies directly, and in an equal degree, to women as well as to men: the right attitude for the authorities of the Church to adopt towards them, the universal priesthood of all believers, the fact that whole areas of human knowledge are relatively autonomous and independent of the Church, the fact that the world has legitimately become secularised, and the task of the layman in the world, which is to bring redemption and

sanctification into it. No-one, of course, would contest this as a general principle. But the actual practice of the Church falls away in many respects from this principle, manifest though it may be.

When the doors of the Second Vatican Council were opened to laymen as well as to clerics it was taken for granted that this applied initially to men only. But in reality the correctness of this assumption is far from self-evident. Of course, there is a point at which limits do seem to be imposed to the equality of rights which women in the Church should enjoy: the impossibility of women receiving the sacrament of order in its various degrees or being consecrated as priests, and thereby becoming members of the official heirarchy. Whatever the position may be with regard to the theological arguments which are put forward in support of this doctrine (and undoubtedly in many instances at least those who put forward these arguments are unconsciously and without realizing it working from positions deriving from an age which is no longer with us and with which we no longer need to identify ourselves), there can be no real point or prospect of achieving anything by pursuing this question at this particular point in the history of the Church's understanding of her own faith and of her practice outside the specialist circles of those engaged in scientific theology. Nor is it of any avail to point to the developments in theology and in actual practice with regard to this question which have taken place among Evangelical Christians. For these do not in fact recognise any official priesthood based on sacramental consecration such as provides the basis for the fundamental distinction between clergy and people. For the present, therefore, it is legitimate to pass over this question in a spirit of patience, whatever conclusions one may arrive at with regard to the binding force of that theological principle which excludes women from the official priesthood. For even without this we still have much to achieve before we can say that we have effectively put into practice the principle that women should have equal rights with men in the Church.

The more the world changes in terms of culture and social living, the more fresh tasks and fresh patterns of living emerge in the lives of individuals and of society, the more man and woman emerge amid these changes in the human environment as equal in capabilities and equal in rights to exploit these new potentialities and to ensure that they are actualised, the more the life of the Church too changes in proportion to these other changes in her human situation. For the life of the Church must be projected and extended into all these new and different spheres of life in the world, and for this reason there is a proliferation in the Church of those tasks and opportunities which can be entrusted unreservedly to women just as much as to men, and which in fact must be entrusted to them.

It would take us too far afield to describe these new opportunities in detail at this point. But they are there, and the Church, just as much as contemporary society, which in practice has become so emancipated from her, must gradually learn to rid herself of the prejudice that the ones to exploit these opportunities and perform these tasks should properly and in the first instance be exclusively of the male sex. The fact that society in the world and in the Church has become so multi-dimensional, and that the work to be done has been broken down into so many subdivisions means that we have perforce to recognise the whole new complex range of tasks which can be performed equally well by either sex, and to which the differences between the sexes are wholly irrelevant. At the same time, however, in the concrete manner in which these tasks are performed, men and women will each bring their special qualities to bear, and this cannot be otherwise than beneficial in ensuring that in the execution of these tasks, to which the sex of the actual performer makes no difference, every aspect of them shall in fact be catered for. When the Church speaks of the position and the task of the layman in the Church and in the world she must apply equal standards to men and women in real fact and not simply by paying lip-service to the principle of equality between them.

2. *In her preaching and in her cure of souls the Church must take into account the unmarried, independent and professional woman no less than the mother and the housewife.* If we abstract for a moment from the ideal of Christian virginity as undertaken for sake of the Lord we may hold as an absolute principle that the fulfilment of woman's vocation as human and Christian is to be found first and foremost, and in normal cases, in partnership with her husband and in the exercise of married love and motherhood But there is a further point which the representatives of the Church must be resolved unreservedly and realistically to take into account in the present and the future of the Church, and which the first point does not for one moment invalidate. This is that both in the preaching and the practice of the Chuch justice must be done to the number of unmarried independent and professional women, including those who do not belong to religious orders or secular institutes. What has just been said about the

rights and duties of the Church, namely that she must respect the principle that women have equal rights with men in the life of the Church as well, and must turn this to good account for the Church's mission, naturally applies in a special degree to women in this unmarried and independent state. Such women should tell the Church what new forms of specialised pastoral activity, what new types of vocational groups within the Christian community, and what new kinds of active mutual 'pastoral' help between women in this state are appropriate to them in their situation and to the times in which we live.

3. Apart from the personal position of these single women a further factor which does have a bearing on the situation, even if it is not an essential reason for introducing changes, is the dearth of priests. This is one reason why the Church of today has been forced actively to call upon women to a greater extent than formerly to help in fulfilling those tasks in her apostolic mission which belong originally and primarily to the members of her hierarchy. In other words she has had to give women *a share in the apostolate of the hierarchy itself*. In discharging tasks of this kind women act as social workers, catechists, parish helpers, etc., and this must not be confused with that mission and task, that apostolate, which every woman is equipped and commissioned to perform in virtue of the fact that she has been baptised and confirmed and on the basis of the royal priesthood which belongs to her, and which she has to exercise from her own position in the world. Nor should this function which belongs specifically and *ex officio to the Christian woman in the world* be thought of as a lesser and more restricted way of 'participating' in the apostolate of the Church's hierarchy. On the contrary it is to be understood as the function of the laity *ab initio* and in its own right. Certainly this participation on the part of the layman in the apostolate of the Church's hierarchy is understood by him as having a further significance beyond this, and as having the force of a permanent vocation. In this sense it has a meaning, an indispensability and a value of its own. But precisely because of this it is a necessary condition that those who have an official position of this kind must not be regarded by the clergy as subordinate helpers and auxiliaries to be exploited for their own advantage.

Opinions may vary as to how precisely we should interpret the ancient Christian institution of deaconess and its relationship to the institution of deacon. But whatever conclusions we may arrive at on this point any theology of the diaconate does show that the deacon too is not merely an insignificant and subordinate auxiliary designed for the help of the priests, but is directly under the authority of the bishop, and that he has a task to perform in the Church which belongs to him personally *ab initio* and in his own right. The same could also be said of those functions which are performed *ex officio* by women, and which likewise belong fully and properly to the apostolate of the hierarchy. Those members of the Church who *ex officio* have such tasks entrusted to them must, therefore, be accorded the dignity, independence and responsibility due to them and necessary for them to discharge their functions properly. This dignity and personal responsibility should not be regarded as deriving from a concession granted to them by the condescension of the clergy. Rather, while always remaining under the control and authority of the bishop, it must gradually, yet at the same time boldly, establish itself as properly belonging to a legally authorised institution in order that there may no longer be even an impression that it needs to be left to the short-sighted caprice of the individual parish priest or chaplain whether there shall be such participation in the apostolate of the Church's hierarchy.

4. From many points of view the Church will have to develop new and better kinds of relationship between the clergy and women, such as are more appropriate to the times. In this respect much may already have been achieved, but nevertheless much still remains to be done. Relics of patriarchal attitudes in the relationship between priests and women still survive, which belong to past ages and do not derive essentially or necessarily from the spiritual authority of the priest as pastor and confessor in relation to the individual Christian.

5. *The Church must be bold and far-sighted in demanding that the religious communities of women shall be shaped in accordance with the needs of the time.* This applies to the secular institutes which have recently emerged, in which the women have to exercise their own creative powers in finding a form of life which corresponds to the evangelical counsels in the midst of the world, and in which they are not simply the objects of apostolic zeal on the part of the founders of orders of priests. But the same principle also applies to the communities of the women's orders which were founded in former times. In recent times the popes have called for the life in women's orders to be adapted and remodelled in conformity with the needs of the age, and in a manner which corresponds to the outlook on life of women of today, and the tasks they have to perform within the unity of their orders. But sometimes one has the impression that these

appeals have met with too much caution and respect for secondary traditions, and too little boldness or readiness to undertake genuine experiments. Obviously the evangelical counsels and the act of embracing the Cross of Christ must uncompromisingly be preserved. But this does not exclude courage and boldness in undertaking a genuine and radical reshaping of many of the day-to-day customs practised in the religious orders. There must be a place for contemporary woman too in the religious communities if she is to be able to make fruitful her efforts to become a disciple of Christ uncompromisingly and without reserve, and if she is to be given an opportunity to fulfil her role in the Church in a manner which is genuinely and effectively human and Christian at the same time. If in this respect the women's orders may be said to show too little courage and trust in the Spirit, who is present with us even today, then there can be no doubt that it is for the authorities in the Church to strengthen this courage and to open up the way for this resolve to take effect in the concrete. The prescriptions of the Second Vatican Council relating to life in the religious orders today clearly point in this direction at least in principle.

III. THE INDISPENSIBILITY OF WOMEN FOR THE NEW TASKS THAT ARE THEIRS

Certain further consequences arising from the new situation in which the Church finds herself must be mentioned here, since they have a bearing on the actual position of women. In view of the undeniable complexity of human, social and cultural factors in the midst of which the life of women in the Church and the world is lived, and necessarily has to be lived today, they are such as can be spoken of only with the greatest reserve. This is true both with regard to their application to the individual woman, and because of the fact that these consequences have been selected somewhat at random.

1. In the new situation in history of the world and of society woman is presented with fresh problems to solve for the world. These are such as can be solved by woman herself and in her own way, and not, in any direct or adequate sense, by directives issued by the authorities of the Church and in their preaching. Probably no single or absolute solution can be found to the question of what form should be imparted to those aspects of human living at the earthly level which are of special concern to

women. And yet what is being treated of here is, in the strictest sense, a Christian task.

The task of woman in the purely secular sphere and in society, with which she is presented as a secular and *at the same time too, as a Christian task*, is of such a nature that the problems which it involves must necessarily be left for the most part to woman herself as she exists today to find solutions to both in theory and practice. Obviously in her official preaching the Church both can and must proclaim the immutable principles of the natural law and of the gospel message as these affect the lives of women, just as she has done in former ages. She must stand firm in defence of these principles and this message, and constantly bring them home to woman anew in a manner appropriate to the particular epoch. But it would be a mistake not only in practice but in theory too, if we were to believe that these basic principles were sufficient of themselves to enable woman to recognise in the concrete what the concrete situation of these present times demands that woman herself shall accept as the task of her womanly life and in the role she assumes in contemporary society. The more complex and intricate the present has become – a present in which it is precisely man's own manipulation of himself and the construction of a humanised world that has made the situation of human life so complex and incalculable – the wider the gulf becomes between the abstract norms, the abiding validity of which is upheld by the Church's authority, and their realization in the concrete; the gulf between the principles and the imperatives, between an abstract statement of what is the case and the concrete constructive plan to be followed. It is quite impossible for it to be otherwise. It is something that is inherent in the nature of the case and in the contemporary situation which makes the ontological difference between the universal and the concrete particular into a gulf which is experienced as such in our everyday lives more clearly than ever before.

It would be foolish and un-Christian to make this a reproach against the Church, and in particular against her preaching, carried on as it is by human intermediaries, or to condemn her on the grounds that today she is unable to produce any living models, any convincing pattern for the life of contemporary woman such as has an immediately formative influence upon life itself, and such as in fact can and must be produced in this age. It is true that in the official preaching of the norms which govern the conduct of the life of woman today it generally seems as though the Church can no longer rise above a confusing ambiguity full of phrases such as 'On the one hand . . . on the other', 'Not only . . . but also', 'Yes, but we must not exaggerate'. But this is entirely right to the extent that the official authorities of the Church recognise their own limitations, with which they must come to terms, and beyond which they cannot go without special charismatic powers. But this observation must not be interpreted as a denial of the Church. Over and above this official and abstract kind of preaching she has another and totally different task to perform, namely to provide the concrete model, the constructive pattern of life which is necessary for woman in the present age.

At the same time, however, the Church which both can and must perform this task is not, in any direct sense, the Church of officialdom as such, but rather the Church of women themselves. Supported by the message of the gospel and the power of the Spirit they can both discover and present this concrete pattern of life for women today as something over and above the basic norms and principles of Christianity with their permanent and unchanging validity. This task belongs inalienably and exclusively to woman. It cannot be taken away from her by the official authorities. Certainly the manner in which it is performed must always be subject to control and criticism on the part of the Church's authorities, and must be in compliance with their demands. But it is, and continues to be, a task for woman herself, and not, in any direct sense, for these officially constituted authorities of the Church.

In earlier times it was, in a certain measure, possible to translate the universal norms and principles of the Church directly into practical imperatives because the process of translation did not involve any intermediary stages between the two such as could be consciously and explicitly pointed to. The result was that one always knew what actually had to be done, and the only question was whether one was willing in actual fact really to carry out this duty which one had recognised clearly and concretely as such. Today, however, the way which leads from the norms and principles of the gospel to the point of putting them into practice in the concrete has grown longer. The gulf between the teaching of the gospel and the concrete realities of life needs to be bridged by means of a concrete model or plan. But in this context to construct such a plan is the task of women themselves. The question is how in the concrete a woman can uncompromisingly and fully be human and a woman of this age, and precisely as such a Christian who bears witness in faith, hope and love in her professional and social life, in marriage, in the worlds of fashion, politics, science and art. And the answer to this question in all its convincing clarity must be discovered and presented by woman herself. Therefore a quite specific task is laid upon her, one that is greater than in former ages, in which the official Church could tell her more or less directly how she should act as human and as Christian.

Now to this problem which has to be left to woman herself to solve, it is presumably quite impossible to find any one single solution universally valid in all cases at all times and for all individuals. Indeed it is not even desirable to aim at producing such a solution. *There must be a whole range of constructive patterns and models for the life of contemporary woman in the world, and these must be of various kinds.* The situation is similar to that which in earlier times applied to the individual religious orders. A whole range of quite realistic and nevertheless very different forms were found for these, and were put forward and developed as permanent constitutions. And in these forms one and the same Spirit of grace and one and the same Christian ideal were presented in a way in which they could really take effect and generate new life. And in the same way we have boldly to take into account the fact that there must be a whole range of such productive patterns and models in the Church devised and presented by women under the impulse of the Spirit.

This process of discovering and presenting the concrete forms which the life of the Christian woman should assume in the dimension of the worldly and profane is a truly Christian – *indeed actually a theological task of the Church herself inasmuch as the women who are her members are representative of her.* Admittedly it is necessary to draw a very clear and realistic distinction between the sphere of the worldly and the profane with its relative autonomy on the one hand and the specifically religious and ecclesiastical sphere on the other. But at the same time it would be false to regard this wholly profane sphere as being of no concern to Christians as such. The worldly can indeed be distinguished from the Christian in the sense of that which pertains to the official Church. But the worldly itself as such constitutes a truly Christian task. For in it salvation is worked out and the grace of God with its power to save and to liberate is lived and attempted. Thus the question arises of how women should live in those states of life which seem to be purely worldly in character in all their dimensions. But it is for Christian woman herself to decide this question as her primary, proper and inalienable task. If she fulfils this apparently worldly task, if she shows in the concrete how the life of woman today in the world both can and must be lived in faith and in the Spirit, so that this life itself constitutes salvation and is a part of Christian life as a whole, then she has fulfilled the task of the Church as such – fulfilled it in the Church and for the Church.

All this may sound extremely abstract and theoretical. But if it is correct, and if it is understood, then what follows from it is precisely the truth that it cannot be the task of the priests or of the male sex themselves to develop and to present this concrete pattern for the life of the Christian woman in the world.

2. To discover and to exemplify in her way of life this concrete, constructive and inviting pattern of what the life of contemporary woman should be, and to discover this from the age itself – this, therefore, is the inalienable task of the Christian woman. But precisely because this creative task belongs exclusively to her, and because it is a new task, it can only be performed by her when her life as a mature Christian derives its strength from the centre and source of the Christian reality. Indeed this task consists in a discerning of spirits, as well as in the loving acceptance of whatever the Lord of history wills to make real precisely in this age of ours. It also involves a use of the critical faculties to set on one side all elements of error and sinfulness in this reality, with which woman is presented in history. Woman, therefore, in that she is made inalienably responsible for the performance of this task has to adopt a complex attitude in which she both gives herself to, and withholds herself from the historical reality with which she is confronted. But she can only achieve this if she really lives by the grace of God and the truth of the gospel.

The present age, however, does not hesitate to impose upon life patterns which are, in the most intense degree, the outcome of conscious thought and deliberation, and for this reason a task such as we have outlined above demands the highest thought and deliberation likewise. Moreover this is a fresh task, and is laid upon woman herself. And for these reasons the manner in which the task is performed must be consciously religious and spiritual today to an extent which did not need to be demanded in earlier ages. To this end a certain theological knowledge is required, though today the situation is different from those former ages in which only those of the male sex who had official positions in the Church could have such knowledge at their command. That capacity for illuminating and critical speculation which is needful for the solution of the problems confronting women must be present, therefore, in woman herself as the person responsible for carrying out the task. In spite of the fact that the official Church continues undismayed to preach the principles of Christianity, there are today a thousand moral questions and problems which can only be solved by the individual Christian himself in the concrete realities of his own life, and which, moreover, must be solved in that context even when this Christian has accepted the norms and principles declared by the official Church as the true expression of the Spirit which moves him personally in a clear attitude of obedient faith. But for this purpose it is necessary that there shall be in the layman, and therefore in woman too, *a far deeper theological awareness*, a far more direct and more living contact with scripture, a far more autonomous exercise of moral decision than in former ages. It is vitally important, indeed indispensable, that women shall mutually impart one to another a deepened awareness of the Christian faith of this kind, and over and above this a certain mystical insight into the original Christian experience. For what is in question here is precisely not merely the imparting of some theoretical or abstract knowledge of the norms of faith and morals, but rather the imparting of a kind of religious knowledge that can already be characterised as existential and is directly assimilable, one which, therefore, so far as woman is concerned, must already bear precisely a feminine stamp. In saying this we have no intention of conjuring up a vision of learned women theologians well-versed in science. The catechists, teachers of religious knowledge, mothers with children to instruct and women leaders of bible-reading circles, etc., are just as indispensable.

3. The contemporary age of the Church will demand from woman as a member of the Church that she shall devise a kind of religious life which is clear enough to understand and powerful enough in practice really to be lived effectively. Of course the requirement as stated here applies just as much to men as to women, because the basic forms of life in the present, and the forms of religious life corresponding to these, are the same for men and women alike. Nevertheless particular mention must be made of this requirement in this context because the special characteristics of the feminine nature, or what many women or many members of the clergy too, regard as typically feminine qualities might seem incompatible in some respect or other with a form of devotion and of religious life which has been made conformable to the present age in the manner described. Not only the men but the women of the present

D

age too, must learn to live in a situation of religious diaspora. They must learn that faith as it exists today is under attack. That it must be a faith that is constantly striven for anew, and that this is not incompatible with its true nature or its firmness and constancy. Both for her own sake and on behalf of those entrusted to her care woman must learn that faith is not a kind of folklore, not in any sense like the sort of heritage of local customs that are handed down from one generation to the next, and which woman's temperament and her readiness to find security in what she can take for granted make her particularly prone to opt for. But woman must learn that so far from this faith is in fact the exercise of the most elemental, radical and irreversible kind of decision.

Religion as practised by women, if it is to convince the world as being genuine, must be discreet and restrained. It must not make any false claims as being immediately obvious. It must establish its credentials in the sober realities of everyday life. There must be no attempt to suppress the specifically feminine qualities which legitimately belong to this approach to religion in favour of a kind of religion that is masculine in character. It must clearly be rooted in the sources of scripture and the classic spiritual teaching of the Church. It must accept that which is of decisive importance and which must have a decisive influence for what it is and let that which is secondary and immaterial be secondary and immaterial. Even though this faith may rightly involve great solicitude and great fear for the salvation of the woman's husband and children, and perhaps for relatives too, when these have fallen into unbelief, still it must be the faith of a bold and trustful hope that God's grace can still be effective in saving men even in those cases in which we can no longer perceive it at work. Woman's faith and the expression of her religious life must be joyful. It must not seem to be a false substitute for what life has denied to her in purely human terms. It must not appear to be the means by which she maintains a false kind of self-assertion and self-justification as though she had been denied the opportunity of a real task in life. In her religion she must discover the source within herself, the grace which from the very outset her human heart has received into its innermost depths as life and love, and she will experience it there as a supernatural vocation to share in the life of God himself, though this is not incompatible with the fact that she will also experience and endure her habitual down-to-earth everyday life as well. *Religion must not appear as a kind of ideological superstructure,* such that, if it were removed, the life that still continued without it would be the same as the lives of those who do not believe or suppose that they do not believe.

I realise that I have not said much, and this may be due to my own limitations. But I also believe that we must and should have patience with an age of uncertainty, in which fresh quests have constantly to be embarked upon. It is at once the task and the grace of the Christian to hold out, in this way, without falling into any attitude of embittered cynicism in which he allows everything to take its course. It is his task and his grace in a world which will always remain characterised by darkness and guilt. Today there is much of which we have a clearer and more penetrating knowledge than in earlier times. But our lot in the present is not really harder than that of earlier generations, in which all too often the only attitude possible for man was one of a dumb and silent acceptance of his lot. Then there was much in his life which he simply had to accept without question. Above all he was unable even to raise the question as to whether and how he could do something to alter the life to which he was subjected.

Not the least important of the factors contributing to the new situation in which the Church finds herself is the altered structures of contemporary life in the purely profane sphere. It is a situation which provides fresh opportunities for woman to question her own lot. What woman is or should be is a matter for woman herself to decide, and it is better to wait in patience than to provide over-hasty or ill-considered answers. When we do what we can to understand ourselves, and in doing this do not forget that God is greater than our own heart and our own deeds, then in truth, even though we may not always yet know how the future will turn out, still we should trust in the fact that the future in the ultimate and definitive sense holds nothing else for us than the protection and the love of God.

6

ON THE SITUATION OF THE CATHOLIC INTELLECTUAL

THE aim which we have set ourselves in the modest essay which follows is to make certain observations about the position of the Catholic 'intellectual' in the world of ideas, and also about the tasks which he has to perform. It is no part of our intention here to look into the problems of the 'intellectuals' in the realms of sociology or political theory. The area which we have set ourselves to investigate is narrower and less complex than this. What we mean by the term 'intellectual' in this context is simply the 'professor' and the 'scientist' in the broadest sense. For this reason all the three designations which we have used are used in the same sense. Theory and science are factors which affect the lives of all men of the present age, but here we are envisaging the kind of Catholic for whom theory and science have an even greater significance. He is one who has dedicated himself to the pursuit of science in one or other of its departments and made it his central interest and the object of his life's work. We are presupposing that the sort of scientist we have in mind is a Christian and a believing Catholic. The subject into which we are enquiring, therefore, is not the relationship which exists between the unbelieving scientist on the one hand and Christianity and the Church on the other, a relationship, therefore, which has certainly undergone a number of changes from the Church's side as a result of the Second Vatican Council. We are enquiring into the situation of a scientist who is at the same time a convinced Christian and into the sort of tasks which confront such an one, and this to the extent that the scientific life of an intellectual is also of significance for his life as a Christian, while conversely the fact that he is a Christian also has its significance for his life in the world of science. If both spheres of his life were completely separated one from the other and simply existed side by side without either of them having any significance for the other then this question would simply not arise at all. Likewise a question of this kind could not be posed if both departments in the life of the Christian intellectual were simply identical one with the other. It is therefore to be taken as axiomatic for our whole approach to the problem that there is both difference and mutual interconnection between both these objective factors in the life of the intellectual. We shall not be making this axiom an object of investigation in its own right here, even though in the course of our considerations it is inevitable that we shall constantly be touching upon it.

I

The first point that must be stated with regard to the situation of the intellectual in the Church and in relation to the Church is the principle that as a result of the Second Vatican Council a wider sphere of intellectual freedom now lies open to him than was formerly the case. We are not, of course, thinking here of an explicit formal declaration to the effect that this sphere of freedom open to the intellectual in the Church has been expanded in this way, but rather of a broadening which has in fact taken place in the concrete, or, to put it another way, of the fact that the Church and her official representatives have been willing boldly to allow that freedom in thought and research which has always been permitted in principle, but which is now a concrete and practical reality as well.

In order correctly to evaluate the real though limited significance of the fact to which we are referring we must first of all recognise that there has been scope for thought and research to be carried on freely in this way. The First Vatican Council itself explicitly taught that the methods of arriving at human knowledge proceeded from a multiplicity of sources, and rejected the idea that revelation was the sole and unique source of the sort of knowledge that was significant for human living. The Church herself (in this opposing in part the findings of Protestant theology) has never presented saving history, revelation and faith in such a way that these realities could from the outset have no points of contact with the secular sciences, or, conversely, that there could be no cases in which secular science could have any contribution to make by being brought into the discussion of the Christian faith. When we ask, therefore, what the relationship is between secular knowledge (including knowledge of God from natural causes) and faith (theology) we must say that each is fundamentally and right from the outset different from the other and possessing its own autonomy, but at the same time that there is a mutual interconnection between them. But we must also recognise that the situation between them is one in which sincere dialogue is possible, and that concrete and positive results may accrue from this. It is also one of conflict, though of a conflict which, while it may not be possible to solve it straightway, is not in principle impossible to solve. All this means that in view of the fact of the relative autonomy of faith, theology and the Church on the one hand, and of profane science on the other, the former must accord to the latter a sphere of freedom for its own thought and action, and that too not merely in questions which are from the outset of no concern to faith and theology, but also in respect of the problems and conclusions of the secular sciences, natural sciences and human sciences which certainly do have a relevance, and perhaps a very vital one, for faith and theology, and therefore for the Church as well. As has been said, in principle the Church and her theologians have always conceded to the secular sciences this scope for freedom. In principle the Church has always allowed questions and challenges to be addressed to her by the exponents of the secular sciences, has been willing to enter into dialogue with science, and has regarded this dialogue as important for her own faith, her life, and the tasks confronting her.

But this attitude has remained at the level of principle alone. It has never been put into practice in the Church's concrete life. Even though this basic principle has never been radically opposed, in the manner in which it is applied in practice it is possible to grant a greater or a lesser degree of freedom, and Christians can bring a greater or lesser degree of courage to bear in coming to grips with the problems, whether real or supposed, raised by the conclusions of the sciences. It can be that in particular instances a dialogue of this kind is broken off too precipitately or that Christians are over-hasty in believing that they have a ready-made answer to some question, some problem raised by the sciences and put to believers to solve. To that extent it can probably be said with some confidence that as a result of the Second Vatican Council courage and readiness to enter into dialogue with the secular sciences has increased in the official Church even with regard to questions which are 'ideologically' important. She is readier now to face up to the questions and conclusions of the modern sciences in all their branches, and not to be too hasty in giving a theological answer to such questions, to give due value to the position of the Christian scientist which in some circumstances can be so full of difficulty and strain, and finally not to underestimate or evade the real problems with which she is confronted. This is already apparent from the Pastoral Constitution, 'On the Church in the World Today', where the Church takes cognizance in a far clearer and more explicit manner than formerly of the existence, extent and significance of the sciences for the modern world, which is also the situation in which the Church herself is placed (cf. Nos. 7, 53f.). She recognises ' . . . the enormous growth of natural, human and social sciences' (No. 54). She recognises that 'The so-called exact sciences sharpen critical judgment to a very fine edge. Recent psychological research explains human activity more profoundly. Historical studies make a signal contribution to bringing men to see things in their changeable and evolutionary aspects' (No. 54). She clearly acknowledges the autonomy of these sciences, which today are no longer at the level of mere theory, but actually provide the means and incentive for a transformation of the human sphere of existence planned and carried through by man himself, and indeed for man to manipulate and re-shape *himself* according to his own preconceived plan (No. 56 f.). The Church recognises the ethos proper to the scientist: to be scrupulously careful to preserve truth in his scientific investigations, the need for teamwork, which today has become indispensable, the spirit of international solidarity, an awareness of the responsibility of specialists which is becoming ever clearer (No. 57). The Church realises the importance of the secular sciences for theology and of the necessity for theology to enter into dialogue with them (no. 62). 'For recent studies and findings of science, history, and philosophy raise new questions which influence life and demand new theological investigations . . . In pastoral care too appropriate use must be made not only of theological principles, but also of the findings of the secular sciences, especially of psychology and sociology . . . Let them (the faithful) blend modern science and its theories and the understanding of the most recent discoveries with Christian morality and doctrine. Thus their religious practice and morality can keep pace with their scientific knowledge and with an ever-advancing technology. Thus too, they (the faithful) will be able to test and interpret all things in a truly Christian spirit. . . . In order that such persons (Christian scientists) may fulfil their proper function let it be recognised that all the faithful, clerical and lay, possess a lawful freedom of enquiry and of thought, and the freedom to express their minds humbly and courageously about those matters in which they enjoy competence' (No. 62).

It is the will of the Church, then, to pay due attention to the secular sciences of today in their whole range. She recognizes the swiftness of their development and their significance for the whole of human life and therefore for Christian living as well, a significance which is still continually increasing. Thus she wishes to grant these sciences genuine scope and freedom for research, for speculation and for the expression of opinion. But this attitude of hers has found expression in the Second Vatican Council not merely in declarations of principle of the kind which we have quoted, but also in the conrete approach adopted by the members of the Council. Thus, for instance, in the preparatory documents made ready before the Council commenced a particular attitude was adopted upon the question of so-called monogenism, the question namely of whether there was a single human couple at the beginning of the history of mankind or whether humanity originated in many human couples appearing independently of one another. But in the actual Council itself a quite different approach to this question was adopted. Previous explanations were abandoned and the Council fathers deliberately avoided pronouncing upon this question, and so left it open so far as the Council itself was concerned. Again on the question of marital ethics the experts have come to be extremely cautious in their approach to the question of what degree of moral responsibility modern man has to bear in this area in view of the modern population explosion and the social situation as a whole into which mankind is moving as it becomes increasingly bound together in a real and effective unity. In the Dogmatic Constitution 'On Divine Revelation' the members of the Council have been prudent indeed, but still far bolder than formerly, in taking cognizance of the findings and methods evolved by the contemporary sciences of history and philosophy as well as by modern exegetes and biblical scholars, and in applying these to the sacred books of Christendom. There is a new desire that in the specialised departments of systematic theology too, the history of dogma shall be explored and the questions of the historical origin and development of the teaching of the faith shall be approached more boldly and clearer conclusions shall be arrived at than has formerly been the case. There is a new and genuine desire to enter effectively into dialogue with the theologians of the non-Catholic Christian bodies in order to establish the conditions necessary for a genuine and unprejudiced study of Orthodox and Evangelical theology. In Catholic theology too, it is explicitly acknowledged that there can be differing schools and differing approaches – indeed that there should be such; that Christian theology should not merely be the product of Western culture, but should have to enter into dialogue with the philosophy and wisdom of non-European cultures as well. In respect both of its theological approach and of the questions it raises the Council has avoided identifying itself simply with the idiom and approach of neo-Scholastic theology as this has been practised almost universally in the Church for the past fifteen hundred years. With regard to the theology of Thomas Aquinas in particular, in spite of the fact that his works have been quoted from time to time in the Council documents and that at one point there is a very brief and cautious recommendation to follow his teaching, he has been given a far less significant place in the theological curriculum than was accorded to him by Roman theologians before the Council. However highly we may prize the teaching of Aquinas, we still have to be realistic enough to face this as a sheer matter of fact. In a word, in practice as well as in theory the Council has subscribed to the principles of autonomy and freedom for the secular sciences, and has thereby shown its readiness to enter into genuine and candid dialogue with them. This would become still clearer if we could examine in detail the Pastoral Constitution 'On the Church in the World Today', especially the second part of this Constitution. Here we find a discussion of such questions as marriage and the family, the just demand for advances in civilisation and culture, human life in its economic and social aspects, the political systems by which communal life is regulated, peace and unity between peoples. The manner in which all these questions are handled is such that it entails a dialogue with those sciences to which these questions are of particular concern as a matter of worldly experience. This becomes all the clearer when it is remembered that the Constitution shows itself aware of the fact that it is quite impossible to find a concrete solution to all these questions on the basis of revelation alone. The only way of arriving at such a conclusion is to provide in all cases a synthesis appropriate to the needs of the particular epoch between an ultimately Christian orientation on the one hand, and that concrete 'this-worldly' experience on the other, which is, today in particular, so largely subject to control by secular science.

It would, however, be both un-Christian and untheological as well as unfair if one were willing to abandon everything for the sake of this increase in the real scope and freedom for thought and research made available to the Christian scientist, and for the sake of friendly dialogue between the Church and the representatives of secular science. If we are to be both Catholic and honest we must add to all that has been said hitherto that the Catholic Church even now never ceases to regard herself as an 'absolute system', and that in a sense every bit as decisive as formerly, although the term 'absolute system' which we have chosen is intentionally a somewhat provocative one, and needs to be taken in the right sense. We may even adopt the jargon of Marxism and say that the Church is not some kind of debating society in which one can say anything, call anything in question and continually introduce radical alterations of every kind. The Church is aware of her role as the absolute and definitive self-bestowal of God in Jesus Christ made present in the here and now, as she who receives the saving deed of God for mankind in faith and proclaims it as a deed so final that the only thing still to come is its own definitive consummation. This will take the form of a direct and immediate confrontation with God in the kingdom of God himself which is without end, and which no longer belongs to the changing course of the history of this world. To this extent the Church will continue to claim the allegiance of her members in just as absolute a sense in the future as she has in the past when she asserts that she is vested with absolute authority as their teacher. But what of those who, in obedience to the dictates of their own consciences with regard to truth, have to refuse this claim of the Church to be the bearer of absolute and binding truth in this sense? For such as these the Church's claim is not in the concrete absolute or binding in duty upon their individual consciences at all. But then they cannot really be Catholic Christians at all either. Basically speaking they have no really compelling reason for wishing to associate themselves with the Church as members of her flock. Conversely, the intellectual, the scientist who is really following the dictates of his own conscience in deciding to be a Catholic Christian cannot set himself up in opposition to the declared teaching of the Church, or to the Church's teaching authority, as though he were nothing more than one party in a dialogue such as might lead to any and every kind of conclusion or to no conclusion at all. This is a kind of dialogue in which one of the partners can, in certain circumstances, draw conclusions that are authoritative and binding in conscience upon the other. The ultimate authority of the Church herself can only be real and effective in its application to a given individual and a Christian if, independently of this authority, he recognises that it is his religious and moral duty to acknowledge the Church herself. But once he has accepted this authority he can no longer refuse the pronouncements of the Church upon specific questions upon the pretext that the grounds adduced by the Church for making this pronouncement are insufficiently cogent so far as he is concerned. In fact in the last analysis it is not for the individual, not even for the individual scientist, to discover what can be believed and thought in the Church. Rather it is for the Church herself, constituted as a society by the Pope and bishops who are her representatives and who embody her teaching authority to discover this. But she does this through them, with the assistance of the Holy Spirit promised to her, by consciously explicitating the content of her own faith and so deciding what is or is not reconcilable with that content in the findings of secular science. Nevertheless the believing Catholic who is a scientist is not afraid on that account that by acknowledging the binding force of the Church's teaching authority he must necessarily arrive at a radical and absolutely irreconcilable conflict. On the one hand, it is true, he has in principle acknowledged the teaching authority of the Church, and the effect of this is that he also gives his interior assent to the concrete decisions of that teaching authority in individual cases, while on the other hand he has to maintain the integrity of his conscience as a scientist with regard to truth, and this obliges him as an intellectual to accept and publicly to uphold any assured scientific conclusions which he has arrived at, and also to conduct his researches without prejudice. But these two factors in his life do not necessarily create an irreconcilable conflict within him. For the Catholic Christian proceeds from the justifiable presupposition (which is necessary in other contexts too), that two recognised and assured truths cannot contradict one another even though they may have been arrived at by quite different processes of reasoning. There is a further principle which the Catholic Christian rightly takes as axiomatic, and which, moreover, is not controverted by history. This is that the Spirit of the Church prevents her from teaching in an absolute or definitive manner, such as requires the assent of faith from the Catholic Christian as a matter of duty, anything which is proved by the subsequent findings of science to be in reality false, and which therefore has to be abandoned. Admittedly in this connection the Catholic Christian recognises that the teaching authority of the Church is justified in sparing no efforts to preserve divine revelation in its fulness and purity, and is, indeed, bound to do this, and he finds no embarrassment in reckoning with the possibility that to this end the Church can produce provisional and non-definitive decisions which are subsequently proved to be either false or exaggerated in their formulation or else too one-sided, measured by the genuine findings of science, which they only seem to deny. There is a further factor which the Catholic Christian, no less than the genuine scientist, can and must take into account. This is that those findings of his science which seem to be assured remain, in the last analysis, always open to future revision when different methods are applied and in the light of new experiences and conclusions. Moreover this revision may be extremely radical in its effects, and may even necessitate that the original formulation of the scientific findings concerned actually has to be abandoned altogether.

It is not possible at this point to develop the 'case history' involved in this problem in detail, to provide a fully developed answer to the question of what the attitude of a Catholic scientist should be in order to be both Catholic and at the same time a scientist in the true sense. This becomes a problem in cases in which there seems to be a contradiction between a decision on the part of the teaching authorities of the Church on the one hand, and a scientific conclusion which he has arrived at on the other. The decision of the Church may, indeed, only be provisional. It may be capable of 'revision' by the Church herself. But nevertheless at the time it is, in a true sense, binding in conscience upon him. Again the scientific conclusion may either seem to be assured or be so in real fact. But in any case the effect is that he is faced with a conflict which, though ultimately and basically capable of solution, seems at the time to be irreconcilable. What attitude is he to adopt in such a case? Only a few scattered observations bearing on this problem can be offered here. But we are in a position to confine ourselves to these few observations because, as a matter of concrete fact, it seems that at this particular point in history there is a total absence of any such cases of conflict, at any rate in the realm of the natural sciences (admittedly it is easier to conceive of a concrete instance of conflict even today in the area of the historical sciences. But then again, in view of the fact that historical conclusions remain problematical and always open to further revision, a conflict in this area is less intolerable). But to commence: It is often taken as axiomatic by secular science as well as by the exponents of a kind of Christian apologetics which is too brash and self-assured in its approach, that in every case where a conflict seems to arise between secular science and the teaching of the Church, it must always be possible to find a clear and obvious solution straight away. But this is not so. It is perfectly possible that both the theologian and the scientist (who is, *ex hypothesi,* a Catholic in this case, are convinced that the seeming conflict is ultimately capable of solution, even though so far they have not been able to discover where the solution lies. In such a case it is necessary for them to have respect for, and patience with one another. In fact similar cases do arise, in which the conclusions of one particular science seem to be in conflict with those of another. Such a situation as is envisaged here, therefore, should not occasion surprise, and does not justify the scientist in every case in bitterly protesting against an allegedly reactionary attitude on the part of the theologian. It is also understandable that the tempo at which the content of the Church's faith becomes consciously explicitated is different from that which is possible in the secular sciences of today. And again even the modern scientist, if he intends to conduct his intellectual life as a Catholic, must today have a certain knowledge and a certain understanding of the 'theological qualifications' as they are called in theological parlance. As in other spheres of human life so too in the theology of the Church the Church herself is aware that it is not always, or necessarily the case that a given statement is either absolutely and certainly true, or else that it has no binding force whatever and can be left to the caprice of the individual to accept or not as he wishes. There are statements which cannot of themselves claim to have an absolute binding force in the realm of theology, and which, nevertheless, have to be respected both in theory and also in the practice of one's life. There are many statements in Catholic teaching which, while they do not in any sense amount to an absolute dogma such as has to be responded to with a totally unconditional assent of faith, still do, on the other hand, have a definite degree of binding force for the Catholic believer. For the intellectual this means that he cannot simply abolish such statements from his mind as matters of indifference which are, from the outset, irrelevant to him and to his work, even though he may find it difficult to reconcile them in any clear sense with his scientific views. Situations may even arise in which it is not altogether clear whether a given statement really is a dogma or merely a doctrine which, though it has a certain degree of binding force, is, nevertheless, capable of revision. On these grounds alone it can be realised how necessary it is for theologians and scientists of all branches to enter into dialogue with each other. This is the only way in which problems still open to discussion can profitably be viewed, in which the real meaning of the Church's teaching can be shielded from misunderstandings (and these can also arise on the side of the theologians), in which the precise degree of binding force which a given theological doctrine may have becomes clearer, and so on.

II

What we have said up to this point does not, of course, cover every aspect of the situation of the Catholic intellectual in the period following the Second Vatican Council. But we are compelled to break off our attempts to describe this situation at this point because we still have something further to say about the task of the Catholic scientist. To begin with we must enunciate a principle which may seem to be self-evident but is not so in reality, namely that the Catholic intellectual can and must accept the fact that he, just as much as other intellectuals, is a scientist who belongs to the present world. His life, no less than theirs, has this significance. We have said that this seems to be self-evident, and certainly there are many Catholic scientists who do not experience any problem in this. They accept unquestioningly their status as scientists dedicated to their field of enquiry. Side by side with this they have a further status of being sincere Christians and men of religion, in the same sense as they obviously have, in addition to their status as scientists, the further status of being husbands and wives, fathers, men with musical interests, citizens, perhaps sportsmen, etc. But this 'interior pluralism' in the individual in itself entails a problem, especially when it is a question of a pluralism of status involving the individual's religious commitment and task on the one hand, and his worldly calling on the other. It is precisely the sincerely religious man who, faced with this pluralism, can ask himself 'How do all these different aspects of my life fit together? Ought I not, right from the outset, to be directing all my activities and efforts in the world, together with the goals I set myself and the results I achieve in these, to a single supreme goal with which my religion presents me? Ought not all these activities to be permeated and inspired by a religious motivation, to be done for the "honour of God" and the "salvation of my neighbour"? Ought not my whole life to be stamped explicitly and directly with my Christianity?' To these questions it must be replied: A Christian scientist must indeed have present in his heart an ultimate awareness that his life is *ultimately* orientated to God, and that God himself has made him responsible for the way in which he conducts his life as a whole. But if he really understands his own Christianity in a wholly Christian sense it must be no less clear to him that in his scientific work he not only may, but actually must also live a life that is genuinely 'worldly'. Even the scientist who is a convinced Christian does not need constantly to be asking himself in his scientific work: 'What direct contribution are my researches making to the salvation either of my own soul or of the souls of others?' He needs to be sustained in his work by a spirit of enquiry in the purely worldly sense, a desire for new knowledge. And he should give himself unreservedly to this, even though it has no direct relevance to his beliefs at the ideological level. In other words, even in his science he must help to construct a world that is 'worldly'. It might seem to be Christian and pious to wish to let religion enter directly and explicitly into everything always and everywhere, and to be 'religious' even in one's approach to the material realities with which one has to cope in the achievement of one's aims. But in reality this is a measure of the degree to which the finite creature refuses to entrust the ultimate unity of its own life to the mystery of God, choosing instead to retain control of this for itself. Perhaps, therefore, we may be permitted to formulate the matter as follows: The scientist does not need to submit his science to interrogation by the Church as to what contribution it makes in the fields of apologetics and ecclesiastical politics. In the last analysis he has already done enough in this regard if he is a really sound scientist and a convinced Christian at the same time.

For the Christian scientist of today it is, furthermore, of great importance that he really knows what it is which he believes and lives as a Christian. It is important that he does not continually labour under the impression that his science, both in its individual tenets in the concrete and still more in the general attitude of criticism appropriate to a scientist, exists in a situation more or less of conflict with his Christian faith. And precisely for this reason it is necessary that the idea which he has of his own Christianity is one which does not from the outset come into conflict with the contemporary outlook, characterised as it is by a spirit of scientific investigation. To ensure this it is necessary that the scientist in particular sees clearly that the Christian faith is at basis not a huge amalgam of complicated doctrines and propositions which are in constant and imminent danger of coming into conflict with the questions and findings of the various sciences. Certainly in our introductory remarks we laid emphasis upon the fact that in one's understanding of Catholicism one cannot simply relegate the content of the Christian faith to an 'other-worldly' sphere in such a way that right from the first it has no point of contact whatever, and so no possibility of coming into conflict with that reality with which the sciences are concerned. Nevertheless Christianity, rightly understood, is something very simple. The Second Vatican Council has actually formulated it as follows: Man has to recognise that he who has been withdrawn from a state of sinfulness, encounters the mystery of the love of God imparted to him in Jesus Christ. We can also express the matter by saying: Man is aware of himself as a free and respon-sible being, as one who can fall into sin. He knows that no science, how-ever sublime and however worth striving for it may be in its results, can ever comprehend or define in any adequate sense what man is as a whole, as he brings himself to his fulness as a whole and single entity in his life. Man knows that the sources of his conscious being are based on an absolute mystery which encompasses him, and that he dwells in this mys-tery whom we call God. The message of Christianity to this man is that the eternal mystery of his being, which is called God, not only encompasses his existence as the horizon, eternally distant, of all that he can think of or control in his life, but actually gives itself to this spiritual existence of his in the form of grace and eternal life to impart to this existence a value that is eternal, to blot out his sins and to make itself his own. Christianity asserts further that this self-bestowal of God in the Spirit of God has been made manifest in history and has been made firm and irrevocable in Jesus Christ, the man whom we recognise as him in whom God has definitively made himself present in our history. This is the real substance of Chris-tianity, the basis on which the whole complex hierarchy of truths pertain-ing to the Christian faith rests, that hierarchy of which the Second Vatican Council speaks. All these truths are credible and able to be accepted by the spirit only to the extent that they maintain a constant and living con-nection with this true kernel of Christianity. Once we have realised this we can then go on to realise that this faith in the self-bestowal of God in the grace which achieves its definitive manifestation in history in the person of Jesus Christ constitutes a community of those who believe which can legitimately claim to trace its origins back through history to Jesus Christ himself, and which assembles itself about him. We can further perceive that this community expresses its faith in the form of credal confession and cult, and that it has a form of leadership which corresponds to the eschatological and indestructible nature of this community of believers considered as the enduring presence of Christ himself. All this becomes, in fact, in a true sense self-evident, once we realise what constitutes the heart and essence of Christianity, and provided we do not misunderstand the nature of man himself by taking it in a sense that is over-individualist and so utterly out of date by contemporary standards. Moreover for a mature and realistic man it no longer occasions any surprise that this community of faith, made up as it is of men, even though it is gathered together about the God-man himself and in his Spirit, nevertheless has to bear the burden of history, of factors which are all too human, and the difficulty of constantly having to adjust the relationship between the individual and the social factors in this community anew. If we take Christianity in this sense, and view it from what is its true heart and essence, and if in so doing we make allowances for human nature in all its dimensions, then there is certainly nothing in the nature of Christianity which could be said to be irreconcilable with the mentality of contemporary man when this is realistic, rational and, in the best sense, critical. All that Christianity demands of modern man is that he shall not restrict himself in his reasoning exclusively to the data of science and to that which can be technically manipulated. It demands of him that he shall recognise that at the centre of his own existence a Mystery lies concealed, and one which ought to be responded to with adoration and love, that he shall have the courage to believe in the self-bestowal of this Mystery made immediately present and close to him, and to direct his life in hope towards a future that is absolute.

We have said at an earlier stage that the Christian precisely as such can and must be bold enough to be thoroughly and unreservedly 'worldly' in his approach to his science, and not to seek to give it a directly religious orientation. But this is not to deny that science as such can and must also be a *praeparatio evangelii*, a way into what is specifically Christian. An anthropology that is Christian rightly contests the view that human life in its entirety can be regarded as sacralised, and teaches that the explicitly religious and ecclesiastical factors in human life represent one section of it, and not the whole. But precisely this same Christian anthropology does teach that there is a concealed consecration of the whole of human life, in other words that the effect of grace upon human life in all its dimensions causes it to be open to the immediate influence of God, and to have an interior impulse which pushes it towards God's immediate presence, the only proviso here being that the individual concerned has accepted, if only in a quite subconscious and unexplicitated manner, the ultimate Mystery of his existence in a spirit of obedience, hope and love, and has thereby been 'justified'. But for human life in all its dimensions to be open in this way to 'consecration' from above it is not necessary that it shall invariably and in all cases be interpreted in an explicitly religious sense. All dimensions of human life are, from the outset, subsumed, even though, it may be, only in the subconscious, in the unity and ultimate orientation imparted by the radical decision which man himself takes in response to the self-bestowal of God which is offered to him. This of itself is enough. Over and above this there is a basic ethos for the true scientist which has an intrinsic connection with the ultimate attitude of the Christian, and which causes him to exercise this basic attitude again and again in the concrete way in which he conducts his life. The will to truth, the determination to be self-critical, the basic realism which causes him to distinguish between what really is known and what is not, the attitude of reverence towards that which is not, and of its nature cannot be, explored, the attitude of objectivity and of a sense of responsibility, the resolve to serve truth rather than one's own prejudices — these and similar attitudes are indeed not gifts which belong to any and every individual who calls himself a scientist, and who may, perhaps, achieve very noteworthy successes in his special field. But they are attitudes which are certainly demanded by science as such, if one still understands science in a sense that is genuinely human, and they are attitudes which can be practised in the process of 'proving oneself daily in hard service' in the field of science. But such attitudes are not only human but Christian too. In virtue of the grace of God which constantly precedes all human activities such attitudes are always and of themselves open to the ineffable Mystery of God as he imparts himself to us. If then the scientist approaches his science in this way as a genuinely human activity, then the scientific work which he actually accomplishes and the goal which he sets himself to achieve, while remaining fully and uncompromisingly 'this-worldly' in character, are, nevertheless, Christian too, in their significance, even though this may be only implicit and at the subconscious level. And the explicit Christianity of such a scientist is properly speaking nothing else than the true self-realisation of his own humanity, already subconsciously divinised by the grace of God, which he achieves and develops in his actual scientific work.

Over and above this the position of the scientist must be one of genuine dialogue with the Church, and even of active collaboration with her. It may be that references to the 'apostolate of the laity' in the Church and with the Church have connotations which are displeasing to modern man, and most of all to a scientist. They do sound – even though this may be against the genuine basic meaning of such references – as though the mission of God to man may all too easily be interpreted in terms of a brash propaganda, an egoistic self-assertion on the Church's part in the struggle for power in society, of striving for prestige, of intruding upon the privacy of others in the sphere of religion. Of course, such attitudes are most of all repugnant to a scientist. But what the Church really means by the 'apostolate of the laity', and so of the scientist too, can be expressed even without references of this kind. What is really meant by this can, of course, not be developed in its total extent and all its aspects at this point. Here we must confine ourselves to mentioning a few specific points which have a special urgency for today. The scientist should not shrink from a dialogue with the officially established Church. He should put his know-ledge and his experience at the Church's disposal. Admittedly more opportunities must be provided for this in the concrete than was formerly the case, even to the point of setting up permanent institutions for the purpose. The established representatives of the Church's authority should be borne up by the conviction that today it is no longer possible for the leadership of the Church to be conducted in a paternalist manner, and solely on the basis of their own abilities and experience of life. At this time, rather, in which human life has achieved an extreme degree of complexity, there is a need to supplement this by systematically planned experiment and research such as can only be achieved by methods which have been scientifically proved. But scientists in every field must be ready to place themselves at the disposal of the established authorities in the Church. They must themselves take the initiative in making the sort of contacts which are necessary for the Church's authorities to be equipped with information of this kind. The situation is not in fact such that every science and every scientific finding has in the concrete the same degree of ideological or ecclesiastical significance, or that the Christian scientist has to evaluate the importance of his own particular science according to the degree of its importance for the Church. Nor should he use such a criterion in determining what lines of investigation to follow in his science, what aims to set himself, etc. But when we survey the chief and basic branches of the natural, social and human sciences, then we are forced to recognise that all of them have a real significance for the Church too, for her official policy and for her preaching of the gospel inasmuch as this is adapted to the special needs of the age. Earlier the Church could help herself in this regard by ensuring that she always had a sufficient number of specialists in the various branches of science, even among the ranks of the clergy. Today, however, there are various factors which render this ever more impossible of attainment. Today the dialogue between Church and science must be a dialogue between her established authorities on the one hand and scientists who are laymen on the other. Indeed it will soon be the case that in many questions there will not be enough Catholic scientists even in the ranks of the laity, and the Church will be forced to seek her information without embarrassment even from those who are not Christians at all. This is not the place to adduce examples showing what the implications of this can be in the concrete. One such example is sufficient to show that the Church is genuinely in earnest in entering into dialogue with science. It is that of the commission summoned by the Pope to prepare an official declaration of the Church on the problems entailed by the increase in population and family problems, including that of legitimate methods of regulating births. Here not only theologians but also physicians, sociologists, psychologists, etc., were brought together to constitute a *single* commission which often met for weeks at a time. Moreover there was full freedom of discussion, and the findings of these specialists were genuinely not already laid down *a priori*.

Of course, for the scientist to make a constructive and critical contribution of this kind to the discharge of the Church's task in the contemporary world it is not always necessary to set up an official and institutionalised structure of this kind. Certainly there are many other and simpler forms which such collaboration can take. To a large extent, in fact, the educated man and so the scientist exercises a decisive influence upon public opinion in the Church, errors in which, as Pius XII has actually said, would be damaging to the Church in the highest degree. The scientist should be aware of his own significance and so of his responsibility in shaping public opinion of this kind in the Church, and should take this responsibility seriously. To a large extent the mission and task of the Christian scientist in the present age covers the same ground as the mission and task which every intelligent man of responsibility and good will ascribes to the scientist in general in the sphere of human, social and political life.

It can be stated with confidence: If the Catholic scientist of today is true to his duty and task in its human aspects in his science then he has already to a large extent fulfilled his Christian task as a scientist. It can be understood that the officially constituted Church cannot lay down any very concrete directives or rules for the Christian scientist as to how he should fulfil this task of his in its human aspects. This is something which must to a large extent be left to his own specialised knowledge and his personal conscience alone to decide. But the fulfilment of this task, which has to be discharged by the mature Christian as his own personal one, can in the case of the Catholic scientist be inspired by his faith and supported by a specifically Christian attitude on his part. In his case it is not only demanded by merely humanistic considerations but by his responsibility before God and by his awareness that all science must, in the last analysis, serve the interests of humanity, for man has a validity in God's eyes that is eternal, and to serve him represents an absolute value which does not disappear when the finite history of the individual or of mankind comes to an end. In the case of the Christian he is upheld in the fulfilment of the task by the religious conviction that every service of love on man's part is an actualisation of his love for the eternal God. And when he performs a service for his neighbour as part of the service which it is always the duty of all science to perform, it has for him as a Christian this significance of also being an act of love for God.

It has not been possible here, and probably it would not have been desirable either, to provide a detailed presentation of what the Second Vatican Council has to say about the scientist, his value and his task in the Pastoral Constitution 'On the Church in the World Today', or to comment on the individual points in this Constitution. In conclusion let us refer once more to the actual Constitution itself. It may be that the scientist, when he reads the relevant passages in this Constitution, might have the impression that all that it contains is self-evident propositions (here as also elsewhere). But the genuine scientist understands that it is good when he is not overloaded with detailed prescriptions as to how he should live his life, and he knows that that which is most obvious of all in theory with regard to the reverence due to truth and to his fellow men, and with regard to love and service, is in practice the most difficult of all tasks. Yet it is precisely this which is laid upon the scientist no less than upon others.

7

THE TASK OF THE WRITER IN RELATION TO CHRISTIAN LIVING

THE essay which follows is concerned with the role of the creative writer or author. It is permissible to include a discussion of this subject in the present volume only to the extent that we are treating of it strictly from the standpoint of the *theologian as such*, for certainly, apart from a specialised knowledge of theology, we have no other qualifications to make judgments in this field. If therefore the theologian is asked for his special views on the subject of creative writers and authors then what he has to say will naturally fall under the heading '"Authorship" and Christian Living'.

I

The basic thesis which we have initially to state and to develop here is expressed in the following simple proposition: the author as such stands under the summons of Christ in grace, and his Christianity must be conditioned by this fact. Authorship as a human activity has a special Christian relevance of its own.

Such a proposition may seem abrupt and enigmatic in the extreme, and for this reason certain introductory remarks may be permitted, though admittedly these are incapable of solving all the problems raised in this thesis.[1] Thus we are in a position to set out our thesis in this manner because and to the extent that every man is in a true and decisive sense (even though it may be not in a full and adequate one) 'Christian'. In

---

[1] The concept of 'anonymous Christianity' is one that is very often used in contemporary theological parlance (and also in the actual conclusions arrived at in contemporary theology) in a manner in which the present author would not wish it to be taken. For a right understanding of this concept we may refer to the essay 'Anonymous Christians' in *Theological Investigations* VI, pp. 390–398.

other words he has been summoned by Christ and has already taken up a permanent attitude in response to this summons. Of course, there must be differences in the way a statement of this sort is applied to particular cases. But the statement that every author is 'Christian' and is so precisely *as such* is not necessarily or immediately proved false by the assertion that many men are not Christians at all in any sense, and could not therefore become so merely by the fact of being authors. What is being asserted here is not that every man intends to be a Christian, or that every man knows explicitly or in a way that could be formulated propositionally that he is such, still less that every man is a member of the visible Church. But it has to be recognised that human existence as such is inevitably and inescapably subject to certain transcendent conditions or 'existentials', such that, while they may indeed be denied, they do not thereby cease to be so, but simply remain in force even though they are denied and rejected, and continue to be in force whether we recognise them consciously or not, whether we accept them or protest against them. And once this is realised then Christianity itself will, in a radical sense be numbered among these 'existentials', and will not be assigned to the category of those ordinary conditions of life (as for instance one's calling as a citizen, the fact that one is or is not staying at some particular place, etc.) which can be accepted or refused according as the individual concerned wishes.

When, therefore, we have to draw a general distinction between the chance circumstances which affect human living on the one hand and the enduring existentials which condition it on the other, then the state of being summoned by the grace of Christ belongs to the enduring existentials which apply absolutely to every man. He can, in fact, be baptised or unbaptised. He can belong in a visible and sociological sense to the Catholic Church or not. Only in this sense and to this extent does Christianity also belong to the chance circumstances of human life, and these factors in Christian existence, freely ordained by God and either accepted or effectively denied by man, must not be underestimated as though they were insignificant or inessential (though at this point we are in no position to treat of their significance for salvation). But all this makes no difference to one essential fact: no man can prevent the fact that he is loved by God with the absolute and unreserved self-offering of the innermost depths of God's own triune life. No man can prevent the fact that he is redeemed, that God has willed the incarnation of the eternal Logos to take effect in his existence. No man can escape the fact – even when his whole life is one great protest against and denial of it – that the grace of God is applied to him permanently and enduringly, and that thereby his existence in all its dimensions is constantly open to the infinite. He cannot escape from the fact that grace is present to him at least as something that appeals to, empowers and invites him, and that, in virtue of this, everything in his life is included in a self-transcendence in which his own free decision is already foreseen and provided for. He cannot escape from the fact that the whole of human existence rests upon a single unique basis, namely the immeasurable depths of that mystery which is absolute love.

This reality may be received into man's conscious awareness, may be believed in and loved, or it may not. It remains a reality, and its purpose is, even when it is denied, to support the life of man from within. It wells up from the depths of man's heart in a thousand secret ways, penetrating into all spheres of his life. It makes him restless; makes him doubt whether existence is really finite and restricted to this present world, fills him with a sense of the immeasurability of that claim which can only be fulfilled by the infinity of God. It renders all the experiences which he makes of himself lead on to a further dimension beyond themselves. It reveals further and deeper levels of significance in them and makes them open to the ineffable and the incomprehensible. Man cannot rest. He can no longer be content to take his own finitude as something that is obvious. In the very moment that he becomes conscious of it the movement which carries him on to the incomprehensible, the fall into the infinite depths, is already taking place. Man may protest against this, may seek to suppress it, may employ the most subtle devices in order to hush it up. Even then he is still involved with it, even then it is still there. It (considered as that which he experiences in the very act of fleeing from it) is the ineffable mystery of which we Christians say without embarrassment and almost facilely, as of something that is obvious, that it is not something that repels us but something that is near, protecting, forgiving, 'giving' of itself and forgiving of us.

In one word: no man can escape the fact that he is 'Christian' in this all important sense of being summoned by God, and in the sense that however secret his acceptance of the claims made upon his existence may be, in accepting them he accepts *this* claim, which permeates his whole existence: the claim that in accepting them he is, in a true sense, a Christian – an anonymous Christian, perhaps, a Christian who denies his own Christianity, a Christian who has not the least suspicion of the significance of what has been achieved in him, a Christian who is constantly running away from himself, one who betrays the fact that he is a Christian in spite of himself, but still precisely a Christian. And even in cases in which an individual becomes a Christian in the usual sense of the term all that is achieved in this (though admittedly this in itself is a miracle of blessing) is that someone accepts in faith what and who he in any case is, and that this loving acceptance is 'manifested' at the historical and social level in the sacramental sign and in the fact that he belongs to the community of those who can say in a definitive sense what they both are and will to be, and what all others too are, even though they may outwardly deny it.

It is in the light of this, then, that we say that the author as such is called by Christ, and has to be a Christian. First it must be recognised that this proposition is not simply a self-evident one. There are indeed realities pertaining to the life of man, without which he cannot exist at all, yet which as such have nothing specifically Christian in them, not even in that sense which we have already adverted to of a Christianity that is still concealed and anonymous. The laws of physics and biology, for instance, of their very nature point to such realities, which in themselves are still at the pre-Christian level and 'neutral'.

But the first thing to be recognised is that every human act of writing, just as every human act of speaking, is a free act on man's part, and as such has a moral relevance which is prior to, and independent of the actual content of what is being said. For in such an act, man is exercising control over *himself*, his spirit, his freedom, and directing himself towards a specific object; he addresses his fellow man indisputably as human even in those cases – indeed precisely in those cases – in which he requires the other to concentrate his attention exclusively upon a limited and no longer fully human subject-matter. But in the very act of saying or writing something, or alternatively of listening to or reading something, our specifically human qualities are engaged at least in virtue of the *formal* quality of the process, and so the process in itself acquires a moral relevance.

There are several different levels in the responsibility which a speaker assumes for the content of what he says. He is responsible for ensuring that what he says agrees with his own convictions as the speaker (truthfulness). He is responsible for making sincere efforts to ensure that his actual statement corresponds to the reality which it is intended to designate (truth). He is responsible for the effect which he foresees that his statement will make upon those who hear it, those to whom it is addressed.

He is responsible for ensuring that his statement is conveyed in the appropriate manner and measure having regard to the general intellectual environment of speaker and hearer alike. He is responsible for doing his utmost to make sure that what he says can be understood and assimilated (this is a duty of love which he owes to the individual, and of respect which he owes to the community in its intellectual and social aspects). He is responsible as a matter of duty for saying what needs to be said because it is urgently relevant and should be said in the here and now. This responsiblity is laid upon those who put themselves forward to speak in public life, and who therefore must speak (each according to his particular opportunities and abilities and according to the position he occupies) in order to make their contribution to the general debate considered as a whole, and in the manner appropriate to this kind of situation (even though in this context it is clearly quite impossible to calculate or to foresee what the effect of the word will be, and so the free exercise of the mind leads ultimately to an outcome over which there is no control and the deed returns at last upon the doer's head as that which he has to endure).

The mere fact that his statements have this kind of moral relevance of itself means that the author as such is already drawn into the sphere of the Christian, and there are two basic reasons for this. First it must be remembered that every act, even one which is in the first instance made to conform merely to the norms of natural morality and the natural law, and which is judged by Christendom to be so conformed, is preserved and protected in its essential 'rightness' (its conformity to natural norms), and this in itself gives it a salvific import (at least in a negative sense). It means that the doing of it has an effect upon human existence as a whole, and in this context of the totality of human existence it can only be done aright with the help of God. This help in turn can safely be regarded as a grace bestowed by Christ. The second basic reason is that in the order of salvation as it actually exists in practice and in the concrete every human act which is morally relevant possesses (for reasons which cannot be gone into in greater detail here), a certain intrinsic salvific power within itself such that through it the doer either becomes one with God and filled with his grace, or else guilty in his sight. In other words every such act constitutes a response, either affirmative or negative, to Christianity as such, even though the Christianity involved here may be of the unacknowledged and unexplicit kind with which every human being is inescapably confronted.

The moment the author makes *man* the subject of his assertions he *ipso facto* passes beyond the limits of the purely natural sciences and the conclusions which they are capable of yielding, and becomes a philosopher, a poet, a visionary, a sage, a committed believer or a prophet. When he takes *man* as his subject and formulates propositions about him, makes him the theme of his argument as a whole, produces definitions of him or preliminary statements about him, then the very content of what he is asserting as an author necessarily means that he is answering either 'yes' or 'no' to Christianity itself. For a factor which must always be borne in mind is that human nature is realised in a complex multitude of created individuals, and it belongs precisely and by definition to the Catholic attitude towards humanity as a whole that it maintains unreservedly, and accords full value to this complexity and multiplicity in mankind. And it is precisely this multiplicity that makes it possible in speaking about man to assert something which applies only to a part of humanity and not to the whole.* In themselves, therefore, statements of this kind are still neutral in content, and, from the ideological aspect, it makes no difference whether they are accepted or denied. But if a part of a given reality really is a part, and if there is indeed a unity in human existence whether actual or, in a true sense, potential, such that this unity constitutes either a fact to be recognised or a goal to be striven for, and if this single all-embracing unity is truly a Christian unity, then it follows that the part of the reality as such (i.e. as a single 'subdivision' of it, for this is an essential specification of what it means to be a part, even if it is not one which is necessarily adverted to) has an objective bearing upon the Christianity inherent in the whole. For this reason such a statement about a part of reality is constantly open to further supplementation when the vision of the whole is arrived at. In that sense the partial statement is already Christian at least in an 'adventist' sense, in the sense namely that it is capable of bringing the one who makes it to the Christianity of the whole. Alternatively, a rejection of this openness is a denial of that Christianity which is already present at least in an implicit and anonymous sense in the whole, and is already making its impact through the partial statement about humanity.

This inescapably Christian dimension in the statements which a human author makes, only really achieves its full force when he forms the intention of isolating and throwing into relief the essential totality of human existence by pointing to the causes which constitute it as one and whole.

It can be the case that in pursuing this aim he never arrives at this essential wholeness of humanity at all, and that through no fault of his own, but where and to the extent that he intends to make or actually makes the all-embracing statement about existence, he speaks as a Christian, and either appeals to or denies the Christian message. The Christianity in his statement can be an anonymous Christianity, but it is Christian for all that. He may not understand the full significance of what he is saying. He may be saying more than he intended (as, for instance, if his message is one of love of neighbour and so of fulfilment of the law. This message may be Christian in an Old Testament sense, an expression of adoration for the unknown God. He may perhaps in some dumb and inarticulate way be proclaiming that anguished atheism which is, in reality, a sharing in the desolation of the Cross). But what is quite impossible is that this message should be of a kind that is really irrelevant to Christ. This would only be possible if he were not real. Even in cases in which Christianity is explicitly or implicitly denied, or seems to be so in the course of pursuing this aim to express existence as a totality, caution is required in coming to a judgment on this. A statement such as this, which sounds like a denial and perhaps actually is one, can nevertheless be the expression of a new situation for the Christian and for Christendom as a whole which is unfamiliar and which has not yet been brought under control. Such a statement can be the false or inadequate explanation and interpretation of a quest for the fulness of life which is, nevertheless, under God's blessing, which is Christian. It can be the statement of a man who only supposes that he does not believe in God, but does in fact accept with a sort of ultimate inarticulate obedience that absolute mystery which is called God, and that mystery of his own life which is Christ.

Indeed we can go further than this and add the following: in a human statement of this kind it is not mere words that are uttered, but the human reality itself which is expressed and put forward (put forward as something that is representative of the totality of being to which it belongs). For this reason it is necessarily ambiguous, since it is, in the nature of things, impossible to achieve absolute clarity or to eliminate all ambiguity in any objectifying statement of what human freedom means. Otherwise the abiding mystery of how man can exercise a free decision would finally and totally be unveiled, and this is not possible. But there are two sides to this truth. If in explaining what is meant we must still confine our attention more or less to what is actually stated in the writing, then we shall be compelled to say: this writing contains an explicit denial of Christianity, which as such is explicitly false, and constitutes a temptation and a danger.

There is no need to discuss any further at this point the practical norms that should be deduced from this with regard to how far such writings and such creative work should be tolerated, disseminated or read. In this connection the following factors have to be borne in mind: It is a general principle that everything capable of producing false and evil effects depends for its survival on the existence of good. It would not be Christian at all, but rather Manichaean, to forget this in its concrete application to the conduct and attitude of Christians (though this does in fact happen all too often). For this reason, it is true to say, those theories in which Christianity is attacked, and which represent a real danger to it, depend for their very existence upon the fact that there are certain genuine questions which the Christians themselves have not yet sufficiently coped with, and that existential rejection of Christianity which represents a real danger to it can only derive its strength from a genuine love for a genuine reality which the Christians have not yet made their own as warmly and uncompromisingly as they should.

From this it is clear and obvious that in the concrete anyone can be a 'fine fellow' and, in the social sense, a good Christian, while still being a wretchedly bad writer. And yet there is an intrinsic connection between a really great Christianity and really great writing. Certainly they are not to be identified one with another. Great writing is achieved only in those cases in which man achieves a radical self-confrontation, in which he realises what he himself is. But even when he does this he can indeed become ensnared in guilt, perversity, self-hatred and even demonic pride. He can confront himself as a sinner, and identify himself with this, yet even in this case he would still stand to a greater degree in that blessed peril which consists in encountering God than the narrow-minded and superficial bourgeois, who right from the first anxiously evades the imponderable factors in existence, fleeing from them into that attitude of superficiality in which there is admittedly no encounter with doubt, but no encounter with God either. Therefore for those who are still only approaching maturity the question of what sort of reading matter is suitable for their education can be a serious problem in itself. But the mature Christian must be fully and unreservedly free to explore all writings that are truly great, bringing to them an attitude of reverence and sympathetic love, even when this may entail pain for him. He will do this because such writings contain a message about man either as redeemed or else in need of redemption and capable of receiving it. And in any case such writing will give us a deeper insight into the truth than if we simply adopt that attitude of superficiality which has only too often and for too long been regarded as appropriate for so-called good Christians, an attitude namely in which man is regarded as the two-legged animal which has become somewhat craftier than the other animals and therefore less predictable than they.

The further man is led by the message of great writing into the immeasurable depths upon which his existence is founded, the more he is compelled by such writing to face up to the hidden depths which a man can find within himself, depths which are dark and obscure, and which are buried in that twilight of ambiguity in which man can no longer say with any ultimate certainty whether he is in a state of grace or one of radical desolation. It is no accident, but rather inherent in the nature of the case, that the great creative writings of mankind are obscure, and for the most part leave us with the unanswered question of whether it is the mystery of grace or that of perdition which takes place and which is described in their pages. How indeed could it be otherwise? Creative or imaginative writing must be concerned with the concrete, and not try to manipulate abstract principles like puppets in a dance. But that which is individual and concrete is a mystery which will only be unveiled by that unique judgment which belongs to God alone, yet which the creative writer makes present in his writing as a mystery. It is not in the least necessary, therefore, that his writing should have that simplicity and clarity of structure which many bad teachers would so much like it to have in their anxiety to protect the minds of their pupils from any harm.

If we are not Manichees then as Christians we recognise that a sin that is truly great is terrible indeed because it is a sin and because it is so great, but that the only possible way in which it can come to be so great is that in it much of the greatness of humanity itself is realised and revealed. For evil as such is nothing. Moreover we know that God allows sin to exist in this world, and to be great and powerful, and yet that for this very reason it is not so easy to confine ourselves to the saints when we seek to find examples in the concrete of the greatness of humanity. Moreover we recall Paul's instruction that we Christians must not withdraw ourselves from the world, but actually can and must, in a certain sense, have fellowship (though admittedly a different kind of fellowship from that which we have with our brethren in the faith) with unbelievers and the unchaste (1 Cor 5:9–13). And in view of all this we Christians are not only not forbidden, but positively commanded to take seriously into consideration and to familiarise ourselves with that creative writing which genuinely is such, even if it is not in conformity with the moral standards of Christianity, though admittedly here we have to distinguish this genuine creative writing from that which conveys a message of sheer unbelief and immorality under the pretence of being creative writing. And in all this we must not judge those who do not share our Christian belief.

There is such a thing as a Christianity that is anonymous. There are men who merely think that they are not Christians when in reality they are so in God's sight and under his grace. Thus it is possible for the individual to be raised to a level of human living which is already imbued with grace even though he does not realise it, and even though he supposes that he is still at the purely human level. We Christians are in a better position to understand this than one who is actually in the state to which we refer. We lay down as part of the teaching of our faith that even human morality at the 'this-worldly' level has need of the grace of God in order to be able to maintain itself in its fulness or for any length of time. It is our belief, therefore, precisely as Christians that to achieve this supreme level of human living, wherever it manifests itself in its genuine form, and even when it is found outside the limits of professed and acknowledged Christianity, is a gift of God's grace and a fruit of the redemption itself even though the individual who has attained to this level is not himself yet aware of it. Why should we not love this exalted level of human living when we find it in such an individual? For we would actually be despising the grace of God itself if we were to remain indifferent to it.

II

The *second* thesis, which I would present as the development and application of the first, may be stated as follows: an author can justifiably be Christian in various ways. In order to explain this thesis and to establish it I would like to attempt to enumerate the most important of these ways. In doing this I shall be using a nomenclature that is unfamiliar, and for this I apologise. Despite every effort to the contrary, I have not succeeded in avoiding this use of strange and unfamiliar designations.

1. An author can be Christian in that he is and remains one who *frankly restricts himself to a limited field*. By way of preliminary it should be noticed that every author is free to choose what he wishes to speak and write about. Of course this choice is, in itself, subject to moral, and therefore to Christian considerations too (since we have to render account for every idle word if it really is such). But even allowing for this, it is justifiable to write about anything which is a subject for human discussion, about the weather, therefore, the advantages of the Volkswagen, the absurdities of everyday life – everything, in short, which is an object of investigation for one or other of the particular sciences. Now when a writer takes this course his work can be genuinely human and – precisely because of this – genuinely Christian too, precisely in the modesty of its aims, in that it is restricted in this way to that which is in the immediate foreground, that which has no directly ideological relevance. The reason for this is that this very modesty implies a tacit acknowledgment of the pluralism of creaturehood, and of the fact that the ultimate unity of it remains hidden in ineffable and impenetrable mystery in God and is reserved to him alone to comprehend.

It is here that a truer and more Christian 'positivism' than that which is now in vogue might be in place. The 'positive' element in such a positivism would have to be evaluated from this standpoint. For a positivism of this sort, which restricts itself to the apprehensible in human life, does not thereby erect itself into an absolute ideology (this would in fact be anti-positivist) by claiming to be either in theory or in the concrete existing situation the only possible right and rational attitude to adopt. And provided it does not make any such claim then it is something for which the modern Christian can have full understanding. For he will understand the attitude of silence, reserve and modesty, of being slow and cautious with regard to all 'ideological' assertions as a sign that the statements reflecting these attitudes are genuine and of real value. He too does not like to hear God spoken of as though the speaker imagined that he had actually resolved the mystery of the divine. A Christian of this sort, therefore, does not for one moment expect that the honest positivist, the one who, in all honesty, restricts his field of discourse in this way, will always attain to God in everything that he says. Such a Christian recognises that there really is a pluralism of beings, and that these are precisely not identical with God. Taken in their formal aspect as so many particular things they have no direct reference to God at all. The most genuinely Christian way of speaking of such things, therefore, is the one in which the speaker simply and honestly remains within the limited field of discourse he has set himself, and shows himself fully and sincerely aware that it is restricted, even though he does not explicitly refer to that fact in what he says.

2. *The man who is overwhelmed by questions*, whose statement of his experiences takes the form of an *open* question. At this point attention must be drawn once more to certain factors which we have already mentioned. Wherever creative writers seek to present word-pictures of man as he is there will always be some whose presentation of him is based upon his radical insufficiency and utter insecurity, who represent man as a question to which there is no answer. A writer of this kind will do this without giving the positive answer to this question which Christianity supplies. For him man constitutes a problem which is insoluble. He will say that it has not been given to him to achieve anything more, that as a creative writer he can put into words only what he experiences, and that he is no preacher or theologian. Can an author write in this vein? Can he take this approach and actually in doing so be a Christian? For our present purpose we are abstracting from the special question (which must, however, be taken seriously) of how far statements of this kind can be out of place for specific circles of readers for whom they might be regarded as morally perverted and therefore unChristian. This might be argued on the grounds that these particular readers will predictably be drawn into the false opinion that the particular problem which this author has left unsolved in the here and now is insoluble in itself, that there is no solution to it which the reader could in his own right supply in response to the question put to him. Here we are rather considering the question that has been raised in itself, in the absolute.

If the creative writer or thinker who raises this question and leaves it unanswered believes, or intends to assert, that there is no answer, that man constitutes the absurdity of a question launched into the void of nothingness, then he is in error, and an answer of this kind (whether taken in this sense by him or by others) is false or unChristian. Admittedly there is a further question which may be raised in such a case, that namely of whether the very fact of posing the question and of calling man himself in question in this radical sense cannot have a salutary effect upon the

E

complacent and the superficial (a type which is extremely common even among 'believing' Christians) by shaking them out of their complacency in such a way that they can no longer be soothed and quietened by the specious solutions offered by well-meaning 'average' Christians. And then in such a case we could go on to ask a second question, namely whether what is ostensibly a denial that there is any solution to the problem of man, a denial which is more or less expressed as a theory, does not in fact proceed from a deeper, although unexpressed acceptance of the solution constituted by the mystery of the forgiving God, a solution which would be present in the creative writer himself and in his basic attitude – the more so since, in cases of genuine creative inspiration, this basic attitude and impulse often go far beyond the writer's own conscious intuitions.

At all events it is often the case that the Christian reader can take the question, with all the radical despair which it involves, in a way that conduces to his own salvation. He can take it as a summons to him to call up the ultimate resources of faith within him, which he would otherwise never have brought to bear. But there are cases in which the question is genuinely left open, and then it should not be rejected on the grounds that such questions should never be asked unless the answer to them is supplied. Every piece of creative writing and every philosophical position is in fact only *one element* in a continuous and incessant discussion carried on among men. And it is impossible for the whole discussion to stand revealed in any one such element taken in isolation. What is true of human life as a whole applies in this instance too: the experience of each particular moment must remain open to the greater breadth and fulness of life as a whole. No one moment can be the measure of its own value, nor have we any right to expect of it that it should contain the whole of life within itself. It is a necessary fact of creaturely existence, and one which Christians have to accept, that the moment of fear is *not* the moment of love, that of desolation is not *ipso facto* that of consolation, that of death is not also and in itself that of resurrection. He who, whether in life or in creative writing, is unwilling to endure this fact and to bear with it constantly experiences a 'watering down' of life's due fulness. For such a one seizes life before it is ready for him, so that for him it is always flat and insipid. Nothing in it has come to the full ripeness and maturity of its being. This is true alike of the questions which life puts to him and of the answers which it can supply. But where he is humble enough and obedient enough to bear with the question and to allow it to be completely open the answer is already present even though only in a hidden manner, even though it is still buried in silence, just as even before Easter, while Christ was still on the Cross or in the grave on Good Friday, the victory of life had already been won. There is a real need for writers of the type which we are considering here, who are overwhelmed by the magnitude of the questions life puts to them; writers who state what they experience in the form of an open question. There should be such, and even as such they are Christian.

3. *The writer who is a full, though anonymous Christian.* We have already said that according to Catholic teaching there is a type of man who has been wholly justified in faith, hope and love, and endowed with the grace of the triune life of God, even though, so far as those ideas are concerned which well up from the innermost dynamism of his being to become the expressions of his real self, he is not a Christian and a Catholic in any explicit sense, or as incorporated into the visible society of the Church and governed by her laws. This situation is not only something that was possible in former ages, or is possible in pagan lands. It is also possible among us and in our own time. And in view of the doctrine of God's will to save all men and of the victory of Christ over sin we have every right to assume that the case envisaged is of frequent occurrence among us. But if this is true then it is also perfectly possible to imagine that a man who has received and been touched by the ultimate reality of redemption and been endowed with the Spirit of faith and love in this way may go on to use his powers as an author to express this and to embody it in his words. And let it not be imagined that in cases in which a man does intend to express a reality of this kind about himself he is inescapably confronted by the following dilemma: either to profess himself as a fully committed member of the official Church, and to do this in some sense by a formula already prescribed by the Church as a society, or else to refrain from defining his position in any way at all. No such dilemma need necessarily apply to a man who finds himself in this situation.

Of course the ideal case, both from the personal and social point of view, for such a declaration would be one in which an individual who was explicitly and consciously a Catholic and member of the Church expressed his belief in such a way that it was not merely theologically correct but living, actual, able to be understood and proceeding from his own personal experience and from the innermost grace with which he was endowed. But while this is true, it does not render the other case impossible, namely that precisely this Christian reality can be expressed in ways in which the individual making the statement about himself is totally unconscious in any explicit sense of the Christian significance of what he is saying. And yet in the case supposed a professed Christian can recognise in this statement the same Christianity which he himself professes, and, it may be, expressed in a more cogent and more comprehensible form than it is in merely traditional formulae which, while they may be dogmatically correct, are not really understood or able to make their full impact in the concrete existential situation. Of course statements of an anonymous Christianity of this kind can meet with indifference on our part. We can fail to recognise them as Christian at all (though in fact they are so). We can be deaf to them. Nevertheless we are in contact with authors who are Christian in this sense, and we should train our ears to be ready for statements of this kind from them. For all other considerations apart we could take over the modes of expression and style present in such statements and develop them further so as to make them express a more explicit kind of Christianity for our own salvation and that of many others. And this would fulfil an urgent need.

4. *The professedly non-Catholic writer who fails to realise that his position is in fact a Catholic one.* What kind of author this description is intended to designate can be deduced from what has just been said. Just as there are authors who profess themselves to be non-Christians but only suppose themselves to be such, so too there are non-Catholic authors who only suppose that their actual position is not a Catholic one. The outcome of four hundred years of division in the Christendom of the West is that we have drawn so far apart in our modes of thought and expression, in the tenour of our ideas and in our attitude and outlook that in addition to the real differences in doctrine and life which do exist between us there is also much else which we believe to be opposed to the teaching of our Church, but which in reality either does belong fully and unreservedly to Catholicism in all its breadth and fulness, or else which ought to be introduced into it. Several factors have to be borne in mind here. First let us take the case of the non-Catholic Christian whom I believe to be in good faith and justified by God's grace. With regard to the basic tenets of the Christian faith he holds these in common with me. But what of the points in which he deviates from Catholic teaching? To the extent that he is in fact in good faith he is actually *quite incapable* of maintaining these with the faith that comes from the Holy Spirit, or with the absolute

and basic decision of faith which he personally has made in his concrete existential situation. With regard to those tenets which we both have in common he does indeed do this in real fact, but with regard to the points which are in dispute between us he only *seems* to do so. Moreover this difference, which cannot be otherwise than real and objective, is one to which we ourselves must pay due heed. A further point for consideration is that often there is not even a real disagreement as to the actual object of belief, but rather differences in mode of expression, of perspective or outlook, or at least the difference is about something which has not been perceived, but which if it were perceived would not be denied. The implications of this cannot be developed any further at this point. But at any rate this type of Catholic author too, does exist.

5. *The author who is a professed Catholic.* It might seem that there is not much to be said about this type. There is, however, a great deal that might be pointed out and yet that is very difficult to express. First we should consider the explicitly Catholic author who does not pretend to be stating the revealed fulness of the divine and human reality in the name of the Church in the manner of a teacher laying down what is her official doctrine or for her members at large. He is not in any sense preaching the Church's official message, or seeking to bring it home to men. Rather he speaks as a 'private' individual, as a layman. As such he is the creative writer, and at the same time always the professed believer too, who expresses the Christian reality as he himself experiences it and lives it, the gospel message as brought home and made actual in his life. The first point to be made is that there both can and must be authors who are Catholics in this explicit and professed sense too. Why indeed should there not be? Should the creative writer and author be ashamed of the gospel merely on the grounds that he does not feel himself called to preach, and because he seeks to express concrete reality and not merely abstract theory? Or is there no such thing as a Christianity that is made actual in the concrete? Or does this process of actualisation take place only in a hidden manner and at so deep a level that even the most exalted of creative writing or poetry could not conjure it up or give it expression? And if this were the case how could it continue to be preached at all? How could it be that God-given reality which is intended to permeate all dimensions of human life with forgiveness and new creation?

Certainly every creative writer must say only what he really has touched upon and understood. But it must be remembered that we have been redeemed. God, and not the devil, has had the last word. And in view of this no-one should be the sort of creative writer who regards only the interior hell within man as a suitable subject for the genuine poet or author. Or do we, in the last analysis, still have to rely on the message of that current of creative writing that comes from the East to teach us that a man can still be a creative writer even when he is bold enough to aim at 'edifying' (using this term in the best biblical sense)? If we are considering statements about the specific achievements of Christianity, about forgiveness and redemption, grace and consolation, eternity and the living God, who is in no sense a figment of man's mind, then of course these have a quality of their own that is unique. The very nature of the subject matter of such statements sets them apart from all others. For this subject matter is present only in that faith which comes as a pure grace of God. And this faith ever-present within us is hidden in the ineffable mystery of God. To this extent, therefore, every explicitly Christian statement shares in the same absolute and unique quality, as also in the same obscurity, indirectness, difficulty and sense of mystery that constantly challenges us anew, for this is unmistakably a quality of the word of faith.

It is in no sense to be regretted, therefore, but rather something that is inherent in the very nature of the case, that a message of faith of this kind should come from the lips or from the pen only with the greatest hesitation and reserve, and that it should be expressed in few and modest words. In this connection one might almost say: if the theologians were more cautious and more careful in formulating their theories, and if the laity were bolder in their faith, more open and more trustful in letting the light of the creed they profess shine out, then the message explicitly pertaining to Christianity, that which emanates from God and his Church, and from the event of salvation and new life as actually achieved − that message would be more comprehensible, more penetrating and more convincing.

The point which we have now reached in our considerations would be the appropriate place to speak of the author who is explicitly Christian and Catholic and is so more or less *ex professo*. In other words his writings are directly theological or religious in character. This, however, would constitute a new and quite distinct subject, and in order to deal with it we would have to return to the fundamentals and begin all over again. Instead of taking this course, let us put forward a *third* thesis, though one which, admittedly, we cannot spend any further time in establishing here. It is this: the author is wholly — and even, in the last analysis, always — susceptible of being judged and criticised by Christian standards. Such standards are not extrinsic to the special character of the author and his work, but are inherently present in them from the first. If we were explicitly to point out the implications which follow from this statement, then it would be made apparent what we meant by the assertion with which this study opened: the author as such stands under the grace of Christ and has to be a Christian in this sense.

8

PRAYER FOR CREATIVE THINKERS

ETERNAL God, Creator of all men and of all things, invisible and visible alike, God of all history, you who are the Lord and the goal, the power and the light of all the activities of the human spirit, today we bring before you our prayer of intercession for all those who have a creative contribution to make in this field.

Lord, who else offers prayers on their behalf? And yet we know that the goal they set themselves, their creative power, their work and their achievements are willed by you. For your will is extended unreservedly to those men who are engaged in constantly producing new expressions of their own nature and spirit, men who are the architects of themselves. You love the sort of man who realises his own being in what he achieves and produces, who discovers and expresses that nature which is an image and likeness of your own glory. That which your will intends them to be, that they can only become with the help of your grace, O Father of poets, eternal source of all light, Spirit of all true inspiration!

It is for this, then, that we entreat you and invoke your Holy Spirit upon them. Raise up among us men endowed with creative powers, thinkers, poets, artists. We have need of them! Remember that saying that man cannot live by the bread of the body alone, that unless the word that proceeds from your mouth becomes his nourishment he will go hungry. That saying applies to them too. Give to these young men the courage to respond to their inner call, to bear the burden and the pain which such a call involves, not to be led into betraying their task in the quest for money and the cheap applause of the superficial, who wish merely to be diverted. In words and in images, in their whole attitude and presentation they express what is in man because they proclaim what they themselves experience. And in expressing this let them express *everything*! Grant them the experience that man is not merely the frustrated hell of his own nothingness, but also the fair and blessed land over which stretches the heaven of your own infinitude and freedom. They do not need to be constantly bringing you into everything they say. They must make mention of you by name only when they are filled with the spirit of the purest happiness or the deepest pain. For the rest let them honour you with their silence. For the rest let them praise the earth and humanity. But in doing this they must always bear you silently in their hearts, for it is here that their creative work has its source. Then even the slightest song becomes an echo of the rejoicing that takes place in your heaven, and even when they have to tell of the most sombre depths to which man can sink, still their record of this is encompassed by your compassion and permeated by a longing for light, virtue and the eternal love. Then even an attempt to entertain is still a reflection of the gentleness and patience with which you love us in our daily lives. Give them the courage to attain to the light and to the joy in the darkness of this age and in all the hunger and poverty of our hearts. Such courage is a grace that comes from you. But give it to them, for we have need of such high courage. Give them the courage to distinguish and to decide. They do not need to be so very subtle, but their work must manifest the fact that an undivided heart has wrought them, one which, while it is open to everything, still in everything seeks you and seeks everything in you, recognising no craven compromise of peace between the good and the evil, the light and the darkness. Give them the courage constantly to begin anew, because only so do they find their source in that which is true from all eternity. Let them say what *your* Spirit has given into their hearts, rather than that which would make pleasant hearing to those who represent the forces of all that is average. When they make experience of the fact that all their work is in vain, of the frustration of their creativity and the insensitivity of their age, let them believe even then that in your sight what seems to be so futile is not futile, that *you* have regarded their work with delight, and have gently taken their heart when it was breaking into your own.

Your eternal Word, the effulgence of your nature and the image of your glory has himself come in our flesh. He has taken upon himself all that is human as *his own* reality. With a power that is greater and more ultimate, and a love that is deeper than that of any other creative worker for the work of his own hands he has set his own heart in the very centre of the image his hands have wrought. He has done this in order that man himself may be the expression and the image of your glory. And therefore, whether we realise it or not, every creative activity of the human spirit has become an element in the personal history of your Word, because everything has come to belong to his own world, the world into which he came in order to share with it in its living experiences, to suffer with it and to glorify it with himself. It is the world from which this Word of yours will never more be separated for all eternity. Let those for whom we pray understand this truth. What they create is inevitably either a part of the Cross to which they nail your Son in guilt, and therefore a condemnation of themselves, or else a factor contributing to the coming of the eternal kingdom of this same Son, and therefore a grace for them. For this kingdom does not only come from without as the end and the final judgment of this present world. It emerges as the hidden grace which has been present in the midst of this earthly reality ever since your own Word descended into his own creation and became the heart of all things. Therefore everything which they create can and must be a promise that your eternal kingdom is already on the way, the kingdom of truth and of love, the kingdom of the glorification of man in his undivided nature, in body and soul, earth and heaven. Therefore grant to them too, that they may be proclaimers and promoters of this kingdom. For everything which man himself has fashioned as sharer in your creative power will be redeemed and taken into this kingdom for all eternity, transferred and glorified. May the Spirit of your Son come upon them in order that your name may be praised now in this time and throughout all eternity, Amen.

9

ON THE EVANGELICAL COUNSELS

I. STATEMENT OF THE PROBLEM

IT is a recognised fact that the Dogmatic Constitution 'On the Church' includes, among other things, one section on life in the religious orders. It is also recognised – and this is equally true of the discussions which have arisen of the decree concerning the orders – that a notable difference of opinion arose in the debate preceding the promulgation of these enactments as to the precise formulations in which they should be expressed.

One point on which there was indeed general agreement was *the actual fact* that some mention of life in the religious orders (in the broadest sense, i.e. including the secular institutes as well) should be included in this scheme. Now this is not simply a self-evident proposition. The schema on the Church which was prepared for the First Vatican Council (and in substance drawn up by theologians belonging to the religious orders) contained no specific statements with regard to life in the orders. To the authors of the preliminary draft it seemed manifestly unnecessary to include this in so brief a dogmatic exposition of the theology of the Church, which must necessarily confine itself to what is essential. Thus it is not so immediately obvious as in some strange way seems to be generally accepted that today everyone should expect a section dealing with life in the orders to be included in the Constitution on the Church or should accept a subsection dealing with this topic without discussion. In this the desire evinces itself for a realistic presentation of the Church, one which does not merely describe its abstract juridical structure and composition conceived of as the characteristic forms of a 'perfect society'. This is what might have been produced by those who are hostile to reform. What we seek for today is something more than this: a treatment which also takes into account the inward mystery of grace in the Church, her role as the people of God and as the Church of sinners and pilgrims. But yet a further point of interest which manifests itself here is that there is a desire to perceive, in addition to the institutional and juridical structures in the Church, the 'charismatic structure' as well; to see her as a Church of fresh 'breakthrough', a Church which is in constant process of reformation, a Church in which the Spirit operates freely and unrestrainedly. For it is precisely in all this that those committed to the religious life have, or should have, an essential part to play.

In contrast to this disagreements arose in the conciliar debates as to whether a whole section (a chapter) should be set aside to be devoted exclusively to the religious life (as was provided for in a pre-conciliar schema) or whether it should find its proper place in the wider context of a chapter on the holiness of the Church, the calling of all her members to develop to the full that participation in the holiness of Christ and God implanted in the roots of their being in baptism, and to put into practice the spirit of the Sermon on the Mount and the evangelical counsels as constituting the gift and at the same time the task of the Church as a whole (this is, in fact, what the schema actually laid before the Council does). Moreover if we were to listen closely and seriously to the arguments in favour of each of these two different solutions we would find it impossible to deny that both the parties upholding them were influenced by certain secondary considerations. *Some* of the factors (though certainly not the only ones) by which the defenders of the first solution were motivated were a certain *esprit de corps* on the part of the orders, a desire to be accorded their due value, a certain anxiety lest their role in the Church should be underestimated, and a preoccupation with the need to recruit sufficient fresh blood. These and similar considerations, though in themselves secondary, did exercise a real influence. Again it would become apparent that the champions of the second solution were not always wholly free from a tendency to *undervalue*, in theological and practical terms alike, the significance of life in the religious orders both in itself and for the Church of today. The point that they emphasise is that *all* Christians of all classes and in all situations in life are called to bring Christian living to its full maturity. They also emphasise the ideal of the priesthood, and of the secular priesthood in particular, as a perfect state, and in all this their outlook is coloured here and there with a certain resentment (in view of past history this is understandable) against the members of orders and the importance attached to them in the Church.[1]

But all this is so much 'atmospherics' or the deceptive façade behind which lies a genuine problem, for it is this that really lies concealed behind this strange conflict concerning the manner in which the ecclesiastical schema should be drawn up. And in reality, however much this problem may impinge upon our attention, in the last analysis both sides have been unanimous in arriving at one and the same solution to it. For both sides are in complete agreement on the point that every Christian has a radical vocation to develop to the full, and to prove his being a Christian, which has been given to him by God's own act in baptism. He is called to that maturity of Christian living which is called 'perfection' or 'holiness'. For however much distrust these words may arouse in us today they are, in the last analysis, the words of the bible itself.

In accordance with this the Council itself has acted as a reconciler in arriving at a solution to these problems to the extent that it treats of the two points in two successive chapters of the ecclesiastical schema, the first dealing with the universal call of all Christians in the Church to holiness (Chapter V, Nos. 39–42), and the second dealing with the religious orders (Chapter VI, Nos. 43–47).[2]

Of course it might be said that in terms of biblical theology and so of dogmatic theology too, the proposition we have just referred to is self-evident. It might be said that no real or radical opposition has ever been offered to the actual principle which it embodies. It might be pointed out that in the actual practice of the Church as well this principle has always been upheld, for she has repeatedly canonised Christians who belonged neither to the clergy nor to the religious orders. And yet this unanimity which has arisen in the Church, and which, viewed as a whole,

[1] Of course one might take the view that a special chapter devoted to the holiness of the Church and to the fact that all are called to holiness would better meet the case. This could not be argued on the grounds that so important a topic as this must not appear to serve simply as an introduction to a statement about the religious life. But provided that both points – first that all are called universally to Christian perfection and second that one of the ways of attaining to this is that of the evangelical counsels – are clearly stated, and both the difficulties and the common ground between them are brought out, then it is certain that all can approve of the division into two chapters.

[2] For a more detailed explanation of chapters V and VI cf. recently F. Wulf, *Das zweite Vatikanische Konzil. Konstitutionen, Dekrete und Erklärungen. Kommentare*, Vol I (Freiburg 1966), pp. 284–313 (with bibliography).

is entirely spontaneous in its demand for a conciliar statement (this too, has to be taken into account), is an astonishing event. For so far as the spontaneous attitude and outlook of the Church throughout almost two centuries is concerned the truth embodied in this proposition has precisely *not* been self-evident. Of course *in point of fact* there always are Christians in all situations and walks of life who have been and are holy. But over and above this it has not been so immediately obvious that on God's side there is also a *positive vocation* and mission to marriage and to a worldly calling, to earthly tasks precisely as the manner positively ordained by God for the individual concerned, in which precisely he is to attain to the fulness of his Christian existence, the maturity of the baptismal grace bestowed upon him and in which he is to bring to their fulness the fruits of the Spirit. Has not (Catholic) Christendom always been confronted, in a manner which is quite simple and which already seems to leave no questions unanswered, with a saying of Jesus which has the force of a summons to *all* in heart and spirit: 'If you will be perfect sell all you have . . . and follow me?' Have not the Fathers of the Church stated uncompromisingly (and without drawing any further distinctions) that it is the virgins who bring forth the fruit one hundred- or sixty-fold from the field of the gospel, whereas married people only bring forth fruit thirty-fold?[3] Has it not been defined by the Council of Trent (without drawing any further distinctions) in the words of scripture itself that it is 'better and more blessed' to renounce marriage 'for the kingdom of heaven's sake'. Is it not the unassailable teaching of Catholic theology (even if, with Thomas Aquinas, it draws a prudent distinction between the essence of holiness and the means of attaining holiness) that it is precisely the fulfilment of the evangelical counsels in concrete practice (and not merely the 'spirit' of them) that is the *better* means of attaining to Christian perfection? And even if the phrase 'at least in itself' is added, even if this statement is tempered by the concession that the situation may '*per accidens*' be otherwise, even then do we not really mean (even though

---

[3] cf. M. Viller, K. Rahner, *Aszese und Mystik in der Väterzeit* (Freiburg 1939), pp. 45 f. Thus in Augustine (Serm. 354 Ad Continentes, 9, P. L. 39, 1568) we read: 'Because she is married a mother will be granted a lesser place in the kingdom of heaven than her daughter who is a virgin. But both will be there like a brighter and a darker star which, nevertheless, are both in the heavens.' Distortions of the truth of this kind are not rectified by the fact that Augustine then goes on to warn the virgin against falling into pride, which can still corrupt everything for her.

we may not say so in so many words) that for the *majority* of men (how otherwise could the complementary *'per se'* retain its validity?) these counsels constitute the better means – in other words that if they do not follow these counsels they *de facto* radically renounce the quest for perfection or at least in the majority of cases do not attain to it in the degree that God's grace had intended for them? In the Middle Ages and later too, has not the distinction often been drawn between two distinct 'perfections', the perfection of the commandments and that of the counsels, and does not this imply a distinction in the goal itself and not merely in the 'means' of attaining to it? In other words does not this imply, precisely with regard to the ultimate and deepest call itself, that Christians are divided into two different classes, and that, so far as holiness is concerned, the religious orders constitute an élite? Is it not significant that in referring to married women who are saints, the liturgy only knows of the designation 'non virgines'? Has not so classic a moralist as Lehmkuhl explained that the summons to follow Christ by practising the evangelical counsels is addressed to all men, and to that extent it is for the individual to show cause why he should not respond to this summons, and not simply to take it for granted that he has a right not to do so? In other words it is the calling to the secular state, and not that to the religious life that needs to be justified. Is not the religious life spoken of even today without reservation or further distinction as a way of following Christ that is closer and more totally committed than life in the world? Is it not held that members of religious orders have made a total oblation, of their lives to God and Christ without any reserve (implying, therefore, that Christians in the world have in principle failed to do this?). Has there so far been any clear explicit or comprehensible statement on the part of the exponents of the theology of the religious life to the effect that there is also such a thing as a God-given vocation (which also represents a gift of grace) to marriage (1 Cor 7:7) and to worldly callings, and that this too, constitutes a factor which contributes positively to the sanctification of man? Or is it rather the case that up till the present the only really intelligible thing that these theologians have said is that when someone marries or devotes himself to a worldly calling he can be sanctified by God's grace *in* that state (though not, properly speaking, *through* it)? When we consider all this is not the explanation offered by the ecclesiastical Constitution (an explanation which has been accepted almost without celebration or acclamation of any kind) to the effect that every Christian who is in the married state and in a (morally justified) worldly calling is called to Christian perfection – is not this, I say, an event of immense significance in the history of the Church and in the process by which Christianity comes to realise itself? Is it not one that has gone unnoticed only because no-one contradicts it, or (better) because in the practice of their daily lives Christians have already come spontaneously to anticipate this official explanation?

But this very fact means that the question of the nature and the function of the religious life in the Church of today has been set on a new footing. For it is certainly shown precisely in this Constitution that the Church intends neither to contest nor to obscure the fact that the religious life has this part to play in the Church. The very nature of a conciliar schema is such that it can only provide a cautious indication, or else refrain from taking up any position at all on the question of *how*, in more precise terms, these two doctrines are to be reconciled: on the one hand the doctrine that *all* Christians are called universally to bring their Christian living to its fulness, and on the other the doctrine that a life governed by the evangelical counsels has a special value and a special function. Here we encounter the same situation as with many other elements in Christian teaching. In the process of consciously explicitating the content of our faith, two propositions are put forward side by side which do not seem to be altogether reconcilable one with the other.[4] Yet for all this the Church does uphold both doctrines with unshakeable firmness in the explicit awareness of her faith, and leaves the task – immensely important though this admittedly is – of reconciling the two to be worked out by her theologians. In the process of doing this they have also to acquire a more precise understanding of the finer shades of meaning involved in each of the two statements. Theology, then, has the task of synthesising these two truths by a process of dialectical confrontation, and in performing this task it may actually be the case that a deepened understanding of each of the two statements is arrived at, one that has been clarified by criticism and purged of the unconscious errors which it has carried along with it. Of course, this degree of precision in an individual's understanding

---

[4] e.g. 'Sacred scripture, as inspired, has God for its author. But it is also a genuinely human document produced by a human author.' Or 'The plenitude of official power in the Church belongs to the Pope alone. But it is also vested in the college of bishops together with the Pope as the head of this college'. Again, 'Jesus is a true and perfect man, yet not a human person'.

of a statement of this kind (as well as the amount of understanding required to arrive at such precision) can only be expected of one who is capable of taking seriously and effectively into consideration, in theological and human terms alike, that other statement which is dialectically opposed to the first.[5]

II. SOME THESES

The questions with which we are concerned then turn upon the relationship between the calling of all Christians to perfection and the special calling of some to the life of the evangelical counsels. These questions have been resolved in the new theological situation in which the Church stands, but certain observations concerning them must be offered at this point. These are primarily concerned with the nature of the religious state itself, insofar as this is constituted by the evangelical counsels. It is of decisive significance for members of religious orders and the life they lead that they expose both themselves and their life, unreservedly and in the searching light of reality, to the questions which the contemporary 'age' puts to them both from the point of view of the world and from that of the Church. They must do this even if they are not yet ready with an answer which is sufficient to satisfy all sides. Their life in the Church provides them with an *a priori* guarantee that such an answer is to be found, but does not dispense them from searching for it, and they will only find these answers, which are of literally vital importance for them, if they really submit themselves to the questions. Today it is easier for a man to lose face by acting as though he always had an answer for everything pat and ready to hand than by calmly conceding that he is at a loss. This simple point does not seem to be realised everywhere throughout all classes of religious. We too shall have answers to supply in the considerations which follow, but these are only meant as statements which, since they are probably far from being universally accepted, cannot constitute anything more than a stimulus to further enquiry. If anyone

[5] For instance how many theologians there may still be even today who either gloss over or minimise the fact that the concept of sin is used in a merely *analogous* sense in the doctrine of original sin! They do this because they have never attained to a really theological and existential understanding of the free subjectivity of the person. They have never understood that a man can never become a sinner through the deed of Adam 'in the same sense' as he becomes a sinner by his own free decision.

feels that such statements do in fact constitute a satisfying answer, so much the better.

An attempt must be made to develop, almost in thesis form, an account of what is essential to this subject, i.e. the nature of the evangelical counsels. This must be done in such a way as to include from the outset the treatment of the problems touched upon in the introduction.

1. The Fact that All Are Called to Perfection

Every Christian is called to 'perfection'. The summons of grace, to which man has a moral duty to respond, calls him to love God and his neighbour with his *whole* heart and with all his strength. Now *this* love is the perfection and goal of Christian living. One question which, though difficult, needs to be taken seriously, and is rich in implications, is that of whether it is conceivable for a man to have renounced precisely that fulness of perfection intended for him by God, and that too, definitively and in death itself (and not merely during specific phases in his life), and still, in spite of this, to attain to salvation. Or is this quite impossible? In that case even though the second view seems to entail an optmiism that is all too bold, it nevertheless does include the full rigour of the doctrine that he who has decided to confine himself merely to avoiding mortal sin, and does not trouble himself or make any effort to strive for a *greater* love, by that very fact has already imperilled his own salvation.[6] This is the question, then, which must be developed here. It is apparent that God has

---

[6] Nevertheless it does seem certain that he who *in principle* excludes the will to the greater love (on the pretext that it is enough for him simply to keep the commandments of God whenever *in concreto* these are binding upon him under pain of grave sin) does sin gravely because he is refusing to submit to the 'commandment' which contains all others within itself, the commandment namely of the love which must ever be greater, the commandment which stems from the inexhaustible dynamism of the Spirit of God. According to Thomas perfection consists essentially in that love which in its *entire fulness* is '*de praecepto*' (S.T. II-II, q. 184, 3). On this basis it is already clear that for a correct Catholic understanding the works of 'supererogation' do not signify a 'supplementary achievement' added onto the 'works of precept' of love as something over and above them. Beyond the fulness of love which is the subject of the gospel commandment there is nothing more. The works of '*super*erogation' fall under that love as the means of attaining it. The element of freedom in these works is present only because the duty that is laid upon us is of a love that tolerates no limits, and it is only in virtue of this fact that it is truly free. On this basis it also becomes immediately clear that the spirit of the Sermon on the Mount (and therefore of the evangelical counsels as well) is necessary for every Christian life, and for salvation as such.

offered to each individual the possibility, and at the same time laid upon him the duty, of loving God and his neighbour with his *whole* heart. Everyone therefore has the possibility and the duty to attain to perfection in *this* sense, and apart from this there is no other perfection. The particular circumstances of the individual and of the age, and of the paths by which he is led in the concrete by the grace of God, can cause variations in the manner in which this *one* perfection is realised in the concrete. But there is no holiness and no perfection apart from it, and every further factor which could be conceived of as belonging to perfection 'in addition to' love as such is, in the last analysis, only intelligible and 'pertaining to perfection' because it is an element in *that* love[7] (an integral part of it and freely posited by it) to the fulness of which every individual is called. While it is true that not every individual is called to *that particular* concretisation of the love concerned in which it is brought to its fulness in the life of *some other* man, still it cannot be concluded from this that the individual is not himself called to achieve the fulness of love in his own life. For this love has in fact to come to its fulness and perfection by being concretised in other works distinct from itself (virtues, trials, etc.), yet is not on that account to be identified with such works. It is not merely the sum total of them all. For this reason it can be the same love even though it is exercised in all these diverse works. Every individual is offered the grace to attain to this consummation of Christian living. But the manner in which he does so varies in each individual case, being unique just as every free human being is himself unique. It may be felt desirable to throw light upon this diversity in personal and individual modes of existence by means of a 'quantitative' concept, by saying that God himself so arranges things that one is called to a greater or lesser degree of perfection, and that too prior to any question of a greater or lesser degree of co-operation with his grace.[8] But the decisive factor in this question of a perfection that varies from individual to individual is that each one is called by God himself, and that this is prior to any position which he freely adopts on his side with regard to *his own* perfection. It follows that this perfection is not the same with each individual, yet that

---

[7] cf. K. Rahner, *Theological Investigations* V, pp. 439–459.

[8] This may be true even though the perfection in question is always *his* (the individual's) perfection, i.e. the perfection that makes actual the possibilities offered to *him* as an individual, so that as an individual when he reaches heaven he will not have to be saddened by being brought face to face with what he could and would have been.

it still remains unquestionably a fact that *all without exception* are called to holiness.[9]

2. *Man's Concrete Stations in Life Considered as a Calling to Perfection*

The perfection to which all are called can be attained in all walks and situations of life which are not morally objectionable. These can constitute not merely the sphere and the 'situation' *within which* Christian living can be brought to its maturity and its fulness, but are also the means *through* which and the basis *upon* which the individual concerned grows towards this fulness of his perfection. And they constitute an *intrinsic* element in this fulness itself.[10] Hence it is that the actual concrete circumstances of a man's life and calling can themselves be, precisely as such, a factor in his vocation to holiness. The individual is called not merely 'in' a given state of life of this kind *to* holiness, but actually 'to' a specific *state of life*. He has to sanctify the state of life itself and himself in it, and this because man is called to holiness and to holiness in the particular form appropriate to him as an individual. In accordance with this, marriage for those who are called to it is not merely 'permitted', but is actually a vocation, a positive contributing factor in that holiness which God has made

---

[9] It must again be reiterated at this point that the true and effective theological concept of perfection has nothing, or at any rate very little, to do with the concept of quantitative increase. For this perfection is of one and the same nature wherever it is realised. In other words it consists in a boundless love between God and man in Christ. In essence, therefore, it does not admit of any quantitative concept. The possibility of growing in such perfection is primarily a question of how far the individual concerned realises the possibilities offered to him in particular. No comparison is possible in any primary sense between his case and that of another man to whom different possibilities are open, and who realises these in different ways.

[10] This does not, of course, mean in their temporal and physical being, for this passes away. But the concrete situations in life (calling, age, marriage, the spirit of the times, etc.) also constitute something more than the external circumstances 'by reason of' which the appropriate virtue is practised. There is no need to interpret the concrete circumstances of human life, as Hofmannstahl does in his concept of 'everyman', as some kind of arbitrary 'role', by assuming which man proves his ability to play a part regardless of what the part itself is intended to represent. Again these concrete circumstances and occupations should not be thought of as analogous to the rush baskets which the Fathers of the desert used to make, weaving them in the morning only to take them to pieces again in the evening, simply for the sake of occupying their time in a virtuous manner.

it possible for them to attain to, and a factor intended by God himself. From this we can and must go on to say that marriage (and, by implication, any kind of 'worldly' state of life) actually constitutes for the vast majority of Christians the *better* means positively offered to them by God himself to attain to that perfection which God himself intends for them. This assertion, therefore, is not intended to be taken in so obvious a sense as it might sound. Behind it lies the whole group of problems concerning the relationship between the order of creation and that of redemption, between nature and grace, one's earthly state and one's calling to the life beyond. And this statement will have to be evaluated as the outcome of an historical experience which has only gradually emerged, and which in turn shows that a statement of this kind is precisely *not* self-evident. If Christians had to think of themselves simply as *nothing more than* the few who have been called out of a world which is in a radically corrupt state, in which everything earthly falls under the curse of sin, in which all 'natural' potentialities invariably lead to *hybris* and a collapse into sin as soon as they are 'developed', and in which evil with its principalities and powers reigns supreme, then they would not be far from arriving at a position in which they regarded the unmarried state as the 'normal' one for these few Christians. It may well be, they would say, that many fall short of this position (without thereby having *ipso facto* to be consigned to the great mass of the damned), but still this unmarried state does constitute the true goal and the calling which is intended for all these Christians. And this was, in fact, to a large extent, if not actually the worked out *theory* of the early and mediaeval Christians (they were preserved from this by scripture and also by the realities of everyday life), still a certain basic attitude on their part which should not be condemned as Platonist, Manichaean, etc., too quickly or before one has one's self been subjected to the tragedy in man's experience of life on this earth and in his activities in this world. (For that matter what else could have been the origin of all Platonism and Manichaeism, the conclusions of which are certainly not foolish or wicked?), or finally before one has really opened one's self to the inalienable 'other-worldliness' of Christianity. But without going into the reasons for this in greater detail at this point the following statement is, nevertheless correct, and the outcome of the historical experience of the Church from which the Church is no longer in a position to withdraw herself: marriage is a positive vocation for the majority of men, addressed to them by the God of creation *and* of redemption, and not merely an element in the old order tragically perverted by sin, which is tolerated even in the case of the redeemed reason of their weakness and hardness of heart.

Of course marriage as conceived of here has itself in turn a specific history of its own in each individual case. As the married man grows older it can initiate him into an interior disposition and frame of mind which is no longer very different from that which the unmarried have taken upon themselves for the sake of the kingdom of heaven. But even then this outlook is an element in, and a fruit of the marriage as such, and therefore part of the actual summons of grace which constitutes his vocation to marriage. And therefore this attitude of mind precisely does not signify that he who is called to marriage might have been able to attain to the 'more direct' way even without having entered into marriage. What we have still to consider is in what sense the evangelical counsels, and virginity as included in these, constitute the means which are 'in themselves better' for attaining to Christian perfection. But already at this stage it can be stated that the meaning of this theological statement concerning virginity cannot be that for the majority of individuals in the concrete it would have been better if they had chosen virginity. If they did this they would be choosing that 'means' (or better that 'situation', those concrete circumstances in which their Christian life is achieved) which was less fitting for them. Certainly it is quite possible, and even probable, that among those who *de facto* have entered into marriage a number of men (precisely how many it is impossible to determine) are to be found who have refused to follow the evangelical counsels even though these were offered to them as the means better fitted to their particular cases. But in view of the nature of man in the concrete and the task of humanity as a whole it certainly cannot be maintained that God's creative and redemptive will was such that this applies to the majority of married men. On the contrary they are positively called by God to marriage as that means of attaining to Christian perfection which is better *for them*. The very fact that scripture regards *all* as called to perfection, and presents the unmarried state as the exception offered by God to the few – this fact alone is enough to establish that marriage can be and is a positive vocation in this sense. That for the majority marriage is the better means is not controverted by the everyday experience (to the extent that this does prove anything at all) that the great majority of sinful men do not make a very good use of this better means for them, or even make a positively bad use of it. For on this showing it might equally be argued that the shortcomings of the majority of members of religious orders prove that the evangelical counsels are not the better means for them (or indeed for anyone).

3. *The Character of Every Christian Vocation to Perfection as Pertaining to Saving History*

In the present order of salvation and the contemporary situation in saving history (i.e. in the post-Christian 'eschatological' age) this perfection of love for God and man, to which every man is called in the particular situation in life proper to him and according to his own particular 'gifts', has in *all* cases (not merely for members of religious orders) a significance as part of saving history, i.e. a specifically *soteriological, ecclesiological* and *eschatological* character. It is a sharing in the destiny of the Cross and the death of Christ himself for the salvation of all. It is a love of that God who in freedom has irrevocably summoned the world in the person and in the fate of Christ to a sharing in his own life, which extends beyond all the possibilities of life in this world, and who has already victoriously made this call, which is his own 'kingdom', effective in Christ and in the Church, even if its full effects are still hidden in faith. That is why all are bound to the 'spirit' of the evangelical counsels and to the basic attitude embodied in the Sermon on the Mount. The message sought to be conveyed here is as follows: In every Christian life we must put into practice, as the characteristic within us of our love for God, that attitude which can be called 'faith' to the extent that in it God is conceived of as the one who cannot simply be attained by the actualisation of the possibilities of human experience in this world, since he intends to bestow himself directly as he is in himself, that is in his absoluteness and unattainability. We shall have more to say on this subject when we come to the question of the nature (and practice) of the evangelical counsels. For this reason this 'definition' of the spirit of the Sermon on the Mount and of the evangelical counsels may suffice for the present. When we speak of 'spirit' and 'attitude' we do not of course refer to a mere abstract theoretical 'feeling' of a merely 'interior' kind. An attitude, if it is to be genuine, must be actualised in real life. It must find expression and concretisation in space and time, in physical and palpable reality. In referring to what is demanded here as 'spirit' and 'attitude' we intend merely to give expression to the fact that this concretisation does not, and need not have that temporal 'permanence', that 'degree of organisation', that state of being conceived of as a class apart, that emphasis, that predominance over all else which is characteristic of the 'life of the practice' of the evangelical counsels as lived in the religious orders.

4 . The Duty to Strive for that Perfection which is made possible for us by God

Every Christian has his 'own gift'. However true it may be that man has been accorded a sphere of freedom by God within which he can dispose of his own life and be, to a limited extent, the creator of his own subjective state, still this sphere itself, together with the limited and finite number of possibilities which it entails, is precisely given to him beforehand by God, and is not under his control. And even the true decision of freedom in its uniqueness and autonomy is of its nature and in the very mode in which it is exercised a gift of God which cannot be otherwise. From this it follows that where the 'better means'[11] is offered in the concrete, and really recognised as such as possible in the here and now,[12] this entails not merely a moral possibility but a moral *demand* for the individual concerned, a demand which is not merely posited but at the same time made possible of achievement, even though the alternative course may in itself have a positive moral value of its own. To refuse the better means offered in the concrete would be an explicit denial of the will to a greater increase in the love of God, and therefore culpable and a sin.

5. The Evangelical Counsels as a Means of Personal Perfection

There is such a thing as a divine vocation to the evangelical counsels which entails the renunciation of marriage 'for the sake of the kingdom of

[11] This is not to exclude the fact that the basic moral attitude can be realised in the concrete in ways which are materially different, yet which, considered as actualisations of religious and moral potentialities, are of equal value, or at any rate for all practical purposes not distinguishable.

[12] In this it is clear *a priori* that it is quite impossible to arrive at any *absolute theory* that provides an all-comprehending clarification of the moral significance in the concrete of a given concrete decision. No attempt at such a theory should be undertaken. For this reason it is a Christian virtue in itself not to try to solve *all* the questions involved in every decision, a virtue which is the opposite of the erroneous attitude of scrupulosity.

heaven'; and conversely for a life lived by the evangelical counsels a special vocation is required. The 'universal' vocation of all Christians as presented in the gospels has in the first instance simply the force of an explanation that the life of the evangelical counsels constitutes a genuine possibility for Christians in general, and means that a Christian must ask himself in all seriousness whether *he* may perhaps be called to live that life in the concrete. This light which scripture throws on the question, however, does not simply constitute a direct demand to all, as though the only question remaining was whether one actually 'willed' to respond to it, and if one did not so 'will' one would have refused something that had actually been offered to one *in concreto*. To take the phrase 'If you will be perfect' (Mt 19:21) in this sense is purely arbitrary, and is an interpretation which overlooks the fact that Jesus utters this phrase to one specific individual, one who 'was able to take it'. Nevertheless when we say that there is a 'universal' call to all Christians this should not be taken in the sense that this call is *only* transformed into an effective and personally binding call *in the exceptional case* in the concrete. This would be to contradict what has been stated above in the second subsection. For those who are called in this sense to the evangelical counsels, to whom it 'has been given', this call signifies the 'better means' of attaining that Christian perfection to which they are bound in virtue of the commandment to strive for an ever greater love.

In this connection and at this point there are several questions which we shall not be entering into: the question of what in more precise terms the actual content of the evangelical counsels is, the question of whether they must be conceived of as necessarily interconnected (though, of course, this is not in fact the case), the question of how such a calling can be recognised. Here it is presupposed that answers have already been found to all these questions. But if there is a calling to such a mode of life, then the evangelical counsels are, *for those that are called*, the 'better means', and in that case what has been said in subsection 3 applies to them. When, therefore, we speak of the evangelical counsels as the 'better means' for the attainment of the maturity of the love of God and man, then our statements upon this subject are *in the first instance*[13] to be taken in a *relative* sense. In other words they are better *in relation to* those to whom it has been *given* to be able to act in this way in freedom. Nor can this

[13] At a later stage we shall be treating of another sense in which these means are to be regarded as 'better', and one that is 'absolute'.

'relative' interpretation of the traditional statements concerning the evangelical counsels be refuted on the grounds that by taking them in this way we shall be reducing these traditional statements to mere self-evident propositions. For this is far from being the case. Certainly upon this interpretation the statement: 'There is such a thing as a vocation to the evangelical counsels' is the fundamental statement, and the further assertion that these counsels are – precisely for those called to them – the better means is a straightforward consequence following from this basic proposition. But precisely this basic proposition is in itself far from being self-evident. For to say that the renunciation of marriage above all can be due not merely to the compulsion of exterior circumstances (like the renunciation of many other things which are positively beneficial to the human individual and his life), but can actually be positively striven for and willed (if only as a means of attaining to and a mode of exercising the love of God and neighbour) – all this is anything but self-evident. It represents a possibility in human existence which is only seriously entertainable as such in the eschatological situation which Christ has inaugurated, a point to which we shall have to give further consideration at a later stage. This statement is not self-evident because when it is viewed in its full and basic significance[14] it is not so easy to say why the renuncia-

_____

[14] For with regard to the possibility of renouncing marriage for the sake of Christ and the kingdom of heaven this basic outlook must not, in the nature of the case, reduce this to the banal consideration that within the restricted possibilities available in human existence it can *de facto* often be the case that one is compelled to renounce one moral and personal aim in order to attain to another. Of course this situation does often arise. A daughter renounces marriage in order to look after her sick mother. A scholar remains single because he is too intensely absorbed in his researches and because these constitute a danger to his life. A man remains single because he fails to find a wife really suited to him. Such cases really are *per accidens*. Anyone who assigns this as the basic and ultimate reason for the gospel teaching on the unmarried state, or who misunderstands the relevant teaching of Paul in this sense (for Paul only *seems* to assign reasons of this kind for remaining unmarried) is being excessively superficial, or is, by implication, maintaining something which is radically false, namely that the two loves, the love for God and Christ on the one hand, and the human love which finds its fulfilment in marriage on the other, are opposed one to another as rivals, so that as one increases the other diminishes. Now this is simply untrue. Yet the idea involved does lie at the roots of many arguments which are offered in defence of the evangelical counsel of virginity. God is regarded from the outset as one particular being amongst others such that within the finite sphere of human living these others represent further values and goals *besides* him, or even in competition with him. On this conception, therefore, he had to 'share' this finite sphere of human existence with other beings constituting rival goals and values for

tion of a human love can be a 'means' of attaining to a greater love of God. When, therefore the tradition of the Church on the basis of scripture explains that the evangelical counsels are the better means of attaining to the fulness of love of God and of man, and when we take this statement – at any rate at first – in a relative sense, namely as applying to those who are called to this state, then in very truth this does not imply that we are in any sense reducing this statement to a mere self-evident proposition. Indeed even when taken in this sense it is precisely a scandal for many. For many imagine that the evangelical counsels cannot be the better means for *anyone* (except *'per accidens'*, i.e. in circumstances which in themselves are unfortunate and which one could have wished otherwise, circumstances relating to the social status, the psychology, or the personal history of the individual. Clearly when these circumstances prevail the individual can indeed embrace the religious life precisely in order to make the best of what is possible for him).

---

the human subject. Now from the standpoint not only of metaphysics but of Christianity too this view is false. It is precisely the 'world' (as that which God has created) that increases or decreases in proportion as God takes a greater or a lesser place in our lives. In all genuine human immanence there is a factor of transcendence, and *e converso*. Love of God and love of man grow in the same proportion to one another. And it is radically untrue to suggest that married love, as a particular instance of love of neighbour, constitutes an exception to this principle. The true way of raising one's self up to God is to participate actively in the process of the Incarnation by which God came down and entered into the world. True 'spiritualisation' so far as *man* is concerned (for it is never demanded of man that he should be an angel) is the progressive personalisation of the material element, culminating in the resurrection of the body. All this must be borne in mind and accorded its full weight by anyone who undertakes to give a correct explanation of how Christian virginity is justified. He must not present his case in such a way as to suggest that the renunciation of married love *ipso facto* and *in itself* offers a better chance of attaining to love of God, as though one could love God more if one loved one's neighbour less. The defender of Christian virginity must show that in the concrete existing situation with regard to salvation the renunciation of *one* genuine possibility of loving or learning to love one's neighbour (that namely of marriage) itself provides a genuine possibility of learning to love God. But at the same time he must show that these two loves are not for one moment two rival entities which grow in inverse proportion one to another. He must show that when a man foregoes marriage 'for the kingdom of heaven's sake' he does not thereby renounce the possibility of learning to love God by loving his fellow men, for according to the gospel itself there is no other way whatever of loving God. The only possible way of learning to love God is to divide one's heart between love of God and love of neighbour.

6. Renunciation Considered as the Realisation and the Confirmation of Faith

The essence of the evangelical counsels consists in the fact that they constitute the *concrete* and comprehensible realisation of belief (reinforced by love and hope) in the grace of God that overcomes the world and is our salvation.

It is not possible at this point to examine each of the individual evangelical counsels in turn in order to arrive at the distinctive characteristics of each of them. Certainly the evangelical counsels are distinguished from one another by such characteristics, and the distinction between them is great enough and important enough for one to be able to ask whether they really can be brought under a common heading at all. The history of the way in which they have been practised in the Church likewise points to this difference between them. Major variations appear in the way in which they have been practised and in the estimation in which they have been held. So far as the New Testament is concerned the only one of them which can immediately be understood as a general counsel is the counsel of virginity. Poverty[15] is included in the New Testament primarily in the concrete manner of life followed by those who accompanied Jesus. Obedience goes unmentioned. Such major differences appear in the later practices of the religious orders with regard to poverty and obedience that it is not easy to bring everything included in this under a single common denominator such that the concept thus arrived at still retains some real content. For this reason it would be of the utmost importance to perform the necessary task of examining these characteristics and differences in the evangelical counsels taken one by one. But it is not possible to undertake this in the present context. The reason that we take these three counsels as falling under a single concept is that we regard them as exercises in Christian living which, in the last analysis, are of one and the same theological nature. As such they are renunciations[16]

[15] It is in fact interesting that outside the gospels there is no mention of 'poverty' in the New Testament. The holding of property in common as witnessed in Acts has a different basis.

[16] It is not possible here to analyse the deeper or existential meaning latent in an act of renunciation as such, though this might enable us to unveil the special properties and difficulties inherent in such an act, and so to recognise its true nature and origins. At this point we must confine ourselves to noticing that there is material here for a special epistemological investigation. An act of renunciation in which he had a

of supreme benefits in human life. This renunciation or self-denial can only be achieved in its true and genuine nature provided that the 'value' of what is renounced is not falsely underestimated, provided that there is no reaction against it whether already present or artificially cultivated. Rather it must be viewed and valued as it really is. Only one who loves the richness of life, one for whom domestic blessings constitute an opportunity and a means for self-expression, only one who possesses the courage of self-responsibility, only one who is capable of genuine personal love, can have a real understanding of what is involved in the renunciation

---

total and absolute understanding of all the factors involved, and had completely thought them out, would no longer be such at all. The negative aspects of it would have been resolved. This must be borne in mind if the considerations offered here are to be accorded their correct value. In their *a priori* approach, therefore, they are neither capable of rendering, nor intended to render, superfluous the demand in the gospels that we shall follow Christ by means of such renunciations. They are intended merely to throw light upon that limited measure of insight (it is far from being total comprehension) which must be possessed even by one who listens to the gospel and submits himself in a spirit of unconditional obedience – i.e. by surrendering his own insights – to following Christ crucified. A further factor which must be borne in mind in the considerations which follow is this: There is no possibility whatever of developing the point we wish to make without simultaneously arriving at and bringing to light that factor in the phenomenon of renunciation, flight from the world, etc., which must necessarily be present in the practice of every Christian life. Indeed the evangelical counsels cannot be intended to be anything else than realisations in the concrete (for *many* Christians) of that spirit of the gospel which is demanded of *all* Christians, and which must be put into practice by all in one form or another. And finally what we are seeking to achieve in this consideration is not to establish an intrinsic connection either between renunciation and faith as reinforced by hope or between it and love. The reason why we are working out the connection which exists between renunciation and faith at this point is that by these means the specifically Christian element in a renunciation of this kind can more easily be made clear. This does not entail any opposition to that approach to the problem in which the evangelical counsels are taken primarily as actualisations and realizations of the specifically Christian *love* for God (as we have done in *Theological Investigations* III, pp. 47–57). For we only understand the essentially Christian character of this love when we see it as love for that God who, in supernaturally bestowing himself in grace and revelation, encounters us in faith, and as a love which is still advancing in hope on the way which will lead to God in his inconceivability and his inaccessible light. In the nature of the case, therefore, the question which we shall be seeking to answer throughout is that of how the Christian attitude of renunciation is related to the complex of faith, hope and love considered as a single entity in which the first two elements of their own intrinsic natures demand to be raised to the level of love, and in which the love of the Christian still journeying towards God necessarily contains faith and hope as intrinsic constitutive elements within it.

prescribed by the evangelical counsels. If these are not present they become a means for the weak and cowardly to flee from life's realities. The renunciation is only possible for the sake of a higher good.[17] Otherwise it is perverse. But this 'for the sake of' must imply an *objective* connection between the surrender of the one good and the attainment of the other which is of higher value. This objective connection, however, need not always and in every case be of such a kind that the renunciation is the sole and indispensable means of attaining that which is of higher value. It is sufficient that it is a possible and reasonable means.[18] Now an act of renunciation can only be a means in the sense intended here if the surrender of the good in question actually constitutes the concrete realisation of the subject's will to attain to a higher good. This becomes possible and reasonable in cases in which the *will*[19] to attain to the higher good either cannot attain to its goal at all without this surrender of the lesser good, or else if it can only attain it with difficulty or with a lack of certainty as to whether it has in fact attained it unless this surrender is made.[20]

[17] This does not exclude, but rather '*in*cludes' the truth that the higher good must be loved for its own sake, and not simply as 'valuable for the individual himself'. This is possible if, and to the extent that this value is attached to the person of the other who is loved. This 'ecstatic' love (a love which draws the individual away from himself and towards the other, regarding that other and not the lover himself) does not, therefore once more, imply the ultimate paradox of a love that is self-annihilating, for the nature of man as capable of free personal love finds its fulfilment precisely in exercising a love that is selfless. For man finds 'himself', his true nature, only in the act of loving, and not, therefore, in the act of self-seeking.

[18] It is precisely as such that it makes possible those acts of obedience and self-commitment to the unknown which are essential for the renunciation of which we are speaking here.

[19] Notice that the words used are not 'If the higher good . . . ' but '*If the will to attain to* the higher good . . .'.

[20] There are cases in which the will to attain to a higher good can be fulfilled and actually achieve this higher good directly, and in which the sincerity of the resolve to attain to it is immediately evident in the very fact that the possibility of attaining to it has been successfully actualised. In such cases the surrender of the one good *can only* be a means of attaining to the other when it is, in the nature of the case, impossible to possess both goods at the same time. But *precisely in the case which we are here envisaging* this is not so. To attain to God in love and to entertain a love for one's personal fulfilment in the world are in themselves wholly compatible – indeed the one may actually postulate the other. In the particular case we are envisaging here, therefore, everything turns upon the fact that the higher good is available in such a way that the renunciation of some other benefit can be understood as a possible (if not actually necessary) means of attaining to it, and as an expression of the will to attain to it.

In the case we are envisaging here, therefore, the higher good is such that (a) it constitutes a free and unmerited act of grace on God's part, one which transcends all the opportunities and potentialities of this world, which is his own personal self-bestowal, and as such can only be received, and cannot be attained to by the subject's own autonomous powers; (b) it stands in contradiction to the *sinful* corruption of the world, a corruption which, once more, the mind of pilgrim man is incapable of separating off in any sure or adequate sense from the pure state of creaturely reality.[21] Thus man's refusal of the sinful corruption, and his assent to the creaturely reality are mutually interdependent in such a way that within the historical process, still unfolding, by which the two elements are disentangled one from another, man's refusal of the sinful corruption of the world (considered as an assent to God himself) must have a certain pre-eminence over his assent to the goods of the creaturely world (cf. Mt 16:26); (c) the higher good has been bestowed upon us as a future good, i.e. as an object of faith and hope, and therefore the will to attain to it and by which it must be accepted is itself precisely what we call faith and hope. In other words, therefore, it cannot depend for its certainty directly upon the object itself, but must depend on something else apart from the object to prove that it is real and radical. In relation to a good *of this kind* the renunciation of a supreme 'this-worldly' good is a reasonable and logical outcome of the will to attain to the higher good which takes the form of faith and hope, these in turn being the factors which sustain and specify a truly Christian love for God on the part of the pilgrim Christian.

[21] The fulness of personal existence can never be attained to in the concrete in any adequate sense solely by a process of reflexion, or the formulation of theories capable of 'distinguishing' between the 'order of creation' (whether in the natural or supernatural dimension) in itself, and the sinful corruption of the world (its state of 'lying helpless in evil'). For in considering the goods which the world has to offer from the Christian standpoint as the objects of a conscious motivation we can never abstract from the fact that the world that is presented to us to choose from, and which represents the sole object which is really available to us to shape and control, is already radically conditioned by sin. Confronted with a world so conditioned, therefore, we can never give our sheer, unconditional and unreserved assent to any one of the goods which it has to offer. To formulate the matter in terms of the categories of moral theology this point might be stated as follows: Viewed in its radical theological significance any object of human choice is *invariably* presented to man 'cum duplici effectu'. For this reason in every Christian choice, even when it is directed towards (finite) goods, a basic reserve must be maintained and actually practised with regard to the consequences arising from the fact that *de facto* every good in the world has been conditioned by sin in this way (cf. 1 Cor 7:29–31).

This faith that is inspired by hope,[22] considered as a reaching out for the future of God who bestows himself without being able to be 'taken by force', can only really achieve its fulness and an assurance that it is truly present in a surrender of 'this-worldly' values. It is not as though these were directly opposed to faith, hope and love, and could not even positively be integrated into the full exercise of these virtues. But how otherwise could this faith and hope be anything more than a mere appendage, a mere supplementary ideology superimposed upon an attitude to the world which as such would be and would remain exactly the same even without this faith and hope? How otherwise could this faith permeate the whole of existence as its determinative form? How could it achieve any assurance of its own reality (at any rate in some of its aspects), and of the fact that it is sincere in the dimension in which a reflexive process of this kind is possible and therefore commanded too? Of course the obedient acceptance of 'passion' as an inevitable factor in human existence does constitute such an actualisation of this faith, permeating and dominating the whole of human life. Indeed it is the only possible absolute,[23] for only in the *prolixitas mortis* which dominates the whole of life can man be he who surrenders the whole of himself, since in 'passion' he becomes wholly drawn out of himself. And it is in this process that there takes place that exercise of faith and love in which man gives himself *wholly*

[22] Of course faith too has its elements of 'renunciation' precisely to the extent that it is a cognitive process; the surrender of the cognitive faculty to the mystery, the obedience of one who acknowledges precisely as acknowledging, a renunciation of the demand that that which is accepted by faith should have any intrinsic credentials of its own, a readiness to allow the basic acknowledgment of faith to grow and develop, and to endure the darkness of faith, etc. All these are factors which cannot be treated of in any further detail at this point. But the faith that is precisely *saving* is always something more than a mere acknowledgment (as the acceptance of knowledge), and the acknowledgment of faith as such is always brought to its fulness in an act which goes beyond that of merely accepting some proposition to be acknowledged, engaging the subject in a movement which at least impels him towards love and can only finally be brought to rest when it achieves its fulness in love. (In spite of the distinction which exists between the three theological virtues it is in fact unthinkable that at death man, as a lost sinner, should still possess the 'infused virtue' of faith and yet should finally have lost that of infused love.) It follows that for faith to be real faith it must, in the real, concrete and existential mode of its realization, contain in itself elements of renunciation which apparently belong to a quite different category than that of knowledge.

[23] cf. K. Rahner, 'The Passion and Asceticism', *Theological Investigations* III, pp. 58–85; *On the Theology of Death*, 'Quaestiones Disputatae' 2nd ed.

over to that which is no longer his own and no longer under his control. But precisely this passion can, nevertheless, only be the highest and ultimate act and so the act of faith and hope in which man gives himself over to God over whom he has no control if man freely goes to meet this event of 'passion' in the absolute by renouncing a positive 'this-worldly' good, one that he can experience, possess and enjoy.[24] Otherwise this faith remains at the level of mere 'theory' formulated in a state of withdrawal from the world, or of ideological consolation which is only entertained when the world is no longer able to console. The 'bird in the bush' is only believed in when one in deed and in truth lets the 'bird in the hand' fly away, and that too before it is taken away from one and before the 'bird in the bush' has yet been laid hold of. If we were only to avoid the evil as such which stands revealed as devoid of value, no act would be posited, so far as the self-realisation of our personal existence is concerned, which need necessarily be more (unless it is to be absurd) than an assent to those 'this-worldly' values with which human existence can and must seek to satisfy itself even when it is not understood as the gift of God's own self-bestowal as an act of free grace. From what has been said it follows (a) that in *every* Christian life there must be asceticism (taken in this theological sense)[25] because every Christian life is one of faith; (b) that it has *not* been asserted that the nature of the Christian decision of faith is simply *identical* with its 'ascetical' aspect and the element of ascetism inherent in its nature;[26] (c) that it is further asserted that while

[24] Footnote 22 above is also relevant at this point.

[25] In other words precisely *not* as a 'training' in ethical self-control over one's personal impulses when we have not yet gained the mastery over them, and *not* as training in mystical experience on the part of a subject who has been spiritually purified.

[26] In fact it belongs to *every* Christian life (and therefore to those governed by the evangelical counsels and to the most radical forms of the discipleship of Christ crucified as well) to make actual, and to live out in one's own particular concrete circumstances the conviction that it is the grace of God in Christ which comes from beyond the world that establishes the world itself, redeems it and glorifies it. An *absolute* renunciation, therefore, is in real terms neither possible nor Christian. It would, perhaps, be in conformity with the Buddhist philosophy, and would involve, amongst other things, the heretical conviction that the renunciation *is*, of its own intrinsic nature, identical with the onset of God's presence in man, or else that of its nature it compels this. From this aspect, too, great caution is required in accepting statements to the effect that members of religious orders renounce 'everything', follow Christ 'totally', or present a 'whole offering' of themselves. The man who becomes a *total* sacrifice in the obedience of faith is the one who believes to the point where he

F

there necessarily must be in every Christian life a certain dialectical opposition between 'flight from the world' and 'assent to the world', both factors being present in their due measure, this measure can vary in the concrete from one case to another according to the particular calling of the individual concerned.[27] This faith which, in the concrete circumstances of the individual, is made real in the sacrifice of 'this worldly' values, now acquires a specific form in the taking over of the evangelical counsels. In these that element in the exercise of faith which consists in *renunciation*, as distinct from that element in faith which consists in *laying hold of* the sanctification of the 'this worldly' realities and values which are available to human experience, acquires a certain predominance. The renunciation entailed in the evangelical counsels as such is not simply identical with faith as lived out in hope and love. But it is a possible way of concretely exercising that faith, a way in which that faith is made manifest and (to a certain degree) assured. Indeed it entails a renunciation of benefits to renounce which in positive and direct terms is only rational and justified in the act of opening one's self to, and contenting one's self with that grace which comes from above, which is unmerited, and which transcends all the powers proper to man. Only so does this renunciation constitute a concrete form of living one's faith to the full. But this precisely does *not* mean that this is the sole way in which such a fulness can be achieved. The act of accepting the world as that which can be saved

---

submits to being totally taken up by death itself; now this is something which will be demanded of everyone, and which is made possible by grace for every Christian. In comparison with this all the evangelical counsels can only be mere timid and cautious attempts to practise in preparation for this ultimate kind of obedience and ultimate kind of poverty.

[27] Here we cannot embark upon an investigation of the fact that presumably this dialectical unity, which nevertheless admits of variation between the two factors mentioned, has undergone an historical process of development in the Church as well as in the lives of individuals. In Protestant Christendom a premium has constantly been set upon worldly callings as opposed to 'monkishness', while in the Catholic Church of the late Middle Ages the rise of the active orders, the development of lay spirituality, etc., undoubtedly took place under the influence of this Protestant revaluation. These factors alone attest the reality of the historical process in the Church, to which we have referred. Again when we consider the protest which arose in non-Catholic circles against the religious life as lived in the orders, we must distinguish the positive factor, the call for a shift in emphasis and a change of proportion between the two elements in the dialectic referred to above, from a factor which is less acceptable, the idea, namely, that this change of emphasis must have an absolute application in the Church as a whole, and must take place in *every* Christian life.

and which needs to be sanctified is just as much a form of living the faith to the full. But it is in the act of renunciation, and in this *alone*,[28] that the element which specifies this faith, considered as the acceptance of divine grace from above, is made *explicit*.[29] The reason for this is first that every positive act which is applied to the world and what it contains bears its own intrinsic meaning and justification precisely as positive and '*this worldly*', and secondly that pure 'passion' as such, present without any free act being posited, can equally well be a manifestation merely of the experience that existence is absurd, or else can be interpreted and understood in this sense.

In order to provide a comprehensive evaluation of what has been said there is a further point to be considered. It is this: the basic difficulty in interpreting and justifying the evangelical counsels always consists in the fact that even without them the fulness of Christianity, i.e. love for God and man with one's whole heart, can be made real in a way of life which is not that of the evangelical counsels. And yet a life of this kind is not merely 'tolerated', but is the subject of a positive moral vocation.[30] But

[28] This renunciation is actualised *especially*, but of course not exclusively, in the evangelical counsels. From this it is clear that this word 'alone' is not intended in any *primary* sense to separate the life of the evangelical counsels from some other Christian way of life; rather it is intended to draw a distinction between the life of the evangelical counsels and other factors which belong to every Christian life. But it must be remembered that it is the factor of renunciation that does in fact characterise the life of the evangelical counsels, even distinguishing it from a life that is lived according to Christian principles 'in the world'. The term 'alone' here can also be used with the secondary significance of distinguishing the two Christian ways of life.

[29] This is not to imply that this 'explicitation' is *absolutely clear and unequivocal*, or that it removes at one blow those uncertainties and obscurities which faith (if it is genuine) entails. Those factors in the evangelical counsels which are directly evident to the onlooker might also be ascribed to mere 'human deficiency' or, to put it in biblical terms, they could constitute a 'circumcision' operated by human hands, and devised by a human ideology. Or else they could be due to physical or psychological weaknesses. But despite this the manifest way of life prescribed by the evangelical counsels does constitute the utmost which man can do on his side in order to impart to his faith, or to the factor of transcendence of this world which that faith involves, a palpable form which gives it a greater force of reality.

[30] In this connection, as we have already emphasized, it is no use attempting to evade the difficulty by saying that the 'spirit' of the evangelical counsels must be present in those who live 'in the world' as well. This may be true – though great great caution is required as to the sense in which it is taken. But what we are concerned with here is precisely not the justification of the evangelical counsels as such or in themselves, but rather the explanation of why it is that so many rightly refuse to content themselves merely with this 'spirit'.

this means that every kind of human life, human life as a whole in all its forms and possible variations ('sin only excepted'), can be integrated into the love for God and man, and can be made the means by which these are brought to their true fulness. But we only understand this statement aright when we recognise simultaneously that prior to any such process of integration, by which his love for God is objectified, man finds himself from the first involved in a multiplicity of 'worldly factors', earthly impulses, relationships' etc., and has already arrived at an understanding of himself (prior to this love of God) that is 'worldly'. And, moreover, this world has already all along been conditioned by sin.[31] From this it follows that (a) while all realities of the world in which human life achieves its fulness and enlarges its sphere of influence are indeed *capable* of being integrated into the love of God, they are not therefore already so integrated, and (b) the world is that in which man has existed right from the first, and which he has freely accepted as the sphere in which to objectify his own nature.[32] But not every element in this world, taken in isolation from the rest, is suitable for objectifying the love of God and neighbour *in the same way*. Still less is every element suitable as a *manifestation* either of the fact that this integration has taken place, or of the love which actually operates the integration. This is the existential and ontological background for the simple fact that it is true that normally speaking man does not choose marriage, riches, power, *because* he loves God, but already finds himself involved in these realities beforehand, or has already laid hold of them prior to experiencing the fact that in them he is explicitly confronted with the love of God. And then the concrete form which his situation in the world assumes acquires a significance which

[31] Though this does not necessarily mean that man, as being from the first a creature of this world, must also have sinned and fallen away from God by his own act before he has positively integrated everything into his love for God.

[32] It should be noticed that when an individual adopts, or alternatively decides not to adopt, the evangelical counsels, this always involves a conscious and deliberate choice of the finite and limited freedom which is his. But prior to this a comprehensive 'engagement' of his will has already taken place at the pre-conscious level, and from this it has already acquired a basic orientation in which it has come to a realisation of itself as 'belonging to the world'. On these grounds alone it is impossible that the life of the 'counsels', which belongs to the level of conscious deliberation and explicitation in terms of mental categories, could be, in the strict sense, a 'total offering'. Here too the original and all-comprehending 'engagement' in the world (in theological terms the factor of concupiscence, which is never wholly eliminated) is never totally permeated by the decision taken at the level of conscious thought.

could be called 'infralapsarian'. By reason of these prior orientations in it he experiences it not only as a confrontation with the love of God, but *also* as a restriction and a hindrance upon him (because of its power to absorb his energies, etc.), holding him back from the integration of his whole life into the love of God.[33] These characteristics of life in the world (not withstanding the fact that they can be integrated into the love of God) do not apply to the evangelical counsels. These, of their very nature, do not exist at all unless they proceed directly from the love of God. Their very nature is such that they entail a certain withdrawal which is the opposite of that attitude in which one strives to acquire a position in the world without recognising any of the problems which this involves. For this reason the evangelical counsels are, of their very nature, an expression and manifestation of *that* faith which, in laying hold of the grace of God, at the same time withdraws from this total and unreserved effort to achieve a position in the world.

7. The Status of Christians Under the Evangelical Counsels and In the World

The evangelical counsels, then, are the expression and the manifestation[34] of a faith that is reinforced by hope and love as well. In this they are

[33] Thus there is a *de facto* difference, but one which is also inherent in the nature of the case, between marriage as able to be integrated (Eph 5) on the one hand, and the experience of marriage as actually integrated on the other, such that the first does not lead on to the second without a certain process of transition (cf. 1 Cor 7). Moreover this difference does not apply to the unmarried state in the same way. It is this difference, therefore, and the process of transition it involves, which Paul has in mind when he recommends virginity as the 'more blessed' state. But this evaluation of the case must not be taken in an absolute sense, as though marriage were fundamentally 'divisive' in its effects, and not fundamentally designed by the love of God itself, and capable of being integrated into it; for on this view the unmarried state would always be the best one for every single one of us. But neither should we seek to eliminate or smooth out the real differences inherent in the situation. We should not pretend that the 'worldly state' which we freely accept from the first (and which finds its primary expression in marriage) is also always and *ipso facto* integrated into the love of God as well, or that it is easy so to integrate it. Nor should we pretend that it is our duty to love God 'together with' everything else, it being taken for granted that 'all else that we do besides God has already sufficient intrinsic justification in its own right, regardless of whether it is integrated into the love of him or not.'

[34] In all cases this 'manifestation' can only take the form of '*renunciation*'. For grace achieves a 'positive' manifestation only in the word of God and the sacraments. Even here, however, it is manifested only as offered and promised, not as accepted and triumphant.

distinguished from 'this worldly' goods (those of riches, power and development of the personality), though these two are capable of being integrated into, and subsumed under grace (through they do not make grace manifest in any direct sense). The evangelical counsels also represent an attitude of withdrawal as opposed to an unreserved striving for position in the world, for the world lies prostrate 'in the evil' of infralapsarian sinfulness. Now since the evangelical counsels do constitute an expression and a manifestation of a faith that hopes and loves in this way, the epithets 'better' and 'more blessed' as applied to them in that *objective* sense which accords them a pre-eminence over the opposite way of life, are altogether appropriate. The truth of this has always been acknowledged by scripture and tradition prior to any application of them to the merely individual case. In this sense, therefore, they have a relatively greater suitability as a means of exercising love for one who has been called to follow them.[35] Objectively speaking, therefore, the evangelical counsels do have a certain general pre-eminence over other ways of life. But this pre-eminence, taken precisely in the sense intended here, does *not* mean that the actual fact of fulfilling them in practice *ipso facto* and necessarily means or guarantees that a greater love of God is achieved than is, or can be, achieved even apart from these counsels. It does not mean that for every individual (or even for normal cases) the 'means' which is better for that individual constitutes the most perfect realisation of the love of God that is possible. It does not mean that one who practises the evangelical counsels is *ipso facto* 'more perfect' than the Christian 'in the world'. But it does mean that the evangelical counsels (considered as a renunciation, though admittedly such renunciation can also be present in other ways of life) constitutes an objectivation and a manifestation of faith in that grace of God which belongs to the realm beyond this present world. And this objectivation and manifestation *precisely as such* are not

[35] By this we do not, of course, intend to suggest that only one who is able to carry out this process of rational analysis of why the evangelical counsels should have pre-eminence can understand what this pre-eminence consists in. He who is called in the concrete to follow the evangelical counsels has a positive knowledge of this from scripture, tradition and the practice of the Church, and experiences this pre-eminence in an instinctive and non-speculative manner in the light of the grace of his vocation, when he accepts the evangelical counsels in a spirit of obedience. The emptiness and the pain involved in the renunciation is experienced as the openness of faith to the process by which the life of God becomes present in the death of man. And everything else which it is necessary to know in this connection is implicitly included in this.

achieved in any other way of life. Objectivation means – from the ontological point of view – that in the case of a being subject to physical and historical modalities certain ultimate and basic orientations have to be achieved, and these can be achieved only in an 'other being', though they are not identical with it. (For this reason this 'other being' can never show quite unambiguously what these basic orientations of the first being are.) This 'other being', therefore, has the value of an 'ontic symbol'[36] and is the expression of these freely adopted orientations. Again from the ethical point of view it is the 'means' by which these orientations are in fact achieved. 'Everything' (sin excepted) can be the 'material' which is integrated into a 'faith' orientation, and is constituted as such by it. But not everything is on that account *ipso facto* an objectivation and manifestation of faith itself in the sense intended precisely *here*, though, of course, it is also true that positively to opt for certain 'this worldly' goods as 'material for integration' in this sense can in itself be a 'means' of causing faith to grow.

We have not yet arrived at any clear and universally accepted terminology to give a satisfactory expression to this state of affairs with regard to the 'objective' pre-eminence of the evangelical counsels. If we merely say that the counsels are the 'better *means*' for achieving a believeing love, then this use of the term 'better' immediately raises the question of what this is intended to signify, if the counsels are, nevertheless, *not* the better means for the majority of men. It also gives rise to the further question of whether a satisfactory answer is arrived at merely by adding that these 'means' are better 'in themselves'. For when we use the term 'means' we imply a relationship not merely to the end in view for which the means are employed, but also to the subject whom these means are intended to help in the attainment of that end. If, therefore, we say that these means are not the 'better way' for the majority of men, what, in that case, can it still mean to say that they are the better means 'in themselves', seeing that we are nevertheless concerned to point out that this 'in themselves' does not apply to the majority of cases even when there is no question of acting contrary to their nature and so sinfully? The term 'means' is valid as an expression of the relationship between counsel and perfection only to the extent that this expression makes it clear that perfection is never formally constituted as such by the counsels, and that the counsels do not constitute a higher form of perfection (one which is

[36] Cf. K. Rahner, *Theological Investigations* IV, pp. 221–252.

inaccessible to the 'ordinary' Christian). Rather it must be taken as signifying that the counsels are ordered to *that* perfection to which all are
called; that the counsels precisely do *not* of themselves constitute a closer
form of following Christ, a more intimate unity with God, but rather are
there *for* these ends. But the term 'means' is inadequate because of its
nature it tends to suggest that there is an objective relationship between
perfection and counsel (the case is rather as if one were to call the body and
its actions the 'means' of the personal fulfilment of the spirit). If we really
say that the counsels are the 'objectivation' of faith and love then this
easily gives rise to the misunderstanding that they alone, and not every
rational activity of the Christian in this world, can be the concrete realisation of faith, that only the renunciation and sacrifice entailed in the counsels are able to constitute faith as lived in the concrete, of being faith
'spiritually', instead of realising that 'everything – including our worldly
activities – which we do' is able to become this if only we do it in the name
of Christ. We must therefore simply shift by saying that the counsels are
the sole mode in which faith achieves its objectivation *and manifestation*,
though when we say this what we mean is that in the counsels *alone* (in
contrast to other forms of renunciation, and especially to that which
consists in consciously and explicitly embracing 'passion') faith arrives
at a state of objectivation in which it becomes manifest precisely because
all forms of objectivation which entail a positive assent to the world also
conceal faith (where this is not thought of and practised as a mere ideological superstructure imposed upon one's ordinary life), since even
without faith they continue to be meaningful. Since they do constitute an
objectivation of the faith in this way, making it manifest (and thereby
bearing witness to it as well), the counsels are, of course, precisely *not*
mere empty manifestations of faith which have nothing to contribute to
the actual exercise of it because their nature is such as can only be realised
in the act of objectivation and manifestation. On the theory put forward
here, therefore, the evangelical counsels are of their nature the historical
and sociological manifestation of the faith of the Church for the Church
and for the world. But to proceed from this (this point must straightway
be added here) to a denial of the fact that the counsels also have an
'ascetical' significance for the individual would be an utter misconception.
Admittedly it remains true that this faith also achieves manifestation and
objectivation in the *freely accepted* inescapable 'passion' in the life of every
true Christian (not in 'passion' as such, but in the 'death' which we accept

in 'obedience' in that 'passion' as in the case of Christ himself). But it is precisely in order to inculcate this attitude of obedience that the counsels are given, to exercise man, by anticipation, and to prepare him for death. They are not intended to be anything more than this. And in freely accepting the element of 'passion' we are, materially speaking, achieving precisely the same effect as appears in the counsels: the free acceptance of a renunciation which, from the point of view of this world, is irrational.

The statement 'the evangelical counsels are the "better way"', therefore, is not an assertion that those who practise them have reached a higher stage of perfection. For the sole measure of the degree of perfection which the individual achieves is in all cases the depths of his love for God and his neighbour. This statement refers rather to the fact that the counsels are 'means' (an objectivation and a making manifest) of faith and love (a) *relatively speaking* in their reference to the individual called to follow them. Here a contrast is established between his situation under the counsels and the situation which would be his if *he as an individual* were to refuse them; (b) *absolutely speaking* to the extent that they alone, considered as a renunciation and a practising of the passion of Christ himself, can be said to have the character of an objectivation and manifestation of faith and love (not only as preached but as assumed and lived). Here there is a contrast between the way of life prescribed by the counsels and the other 'material' for a Christianity that is lived to the full, which is capable of being integrated into this fulness of Christian life because, as having positive existence in this world, it is the material in which the Christian can express his affirmation to the world. But even when it does this it cannot make manifest the 'transcendence' of grace and of faith.

8. The Ecclesiological (Symbolic) Significance of the Evangelical Counsels

The evangelical counsels are distinguished from other forms of renunciation and of accepting in faith the 'passion' of personal existence in that they have a *status* (in virtue of their unambiguously clear sociological orientation, their permanence, their clearly defined meaning and also the vows which are taken to follow them in the presence of the Church herself). This status which the evangelical counsels impart makes them (and those who practise them) an element in the 'visible' Church. In virtue of this fact they have an essential function to perform in the Church prior to any question of the 'useful works' which the orders perform on the

Church's behalf (by giving an example of moral living, by their apostolate, prayers, etc.). The Church is not only the fruit of salvation which springs from a reality hidden within her (the grace of the Spirit which quickens and sanctifies the Church herself). She is also a permanent and quasi-sacramental sign of salvation in her visible manifestations in history. But it is not only in virtue of her preaching of the word and conferring the sacraments that she has this significance of a historical presence. If this were the case she would only be the sign of the grace which is *offered* by God. But she must be something more than this. She must be the sign of the actual fact that grace has been accepted, that it is already at work eschatologically, and is already in fact triumphant. Now she is a sign in this sense not in her institutional, but rather in her charismatic aspects if, and to the extent that, this fact is objectified and made manifest for all to see on the sociological and historical plane. And this is precisely what is achieved in the life governed by the evangelical counsels insofar as these are visible in the Church's communal life. The evangelical counsels constitute that element in the Church which makes her a sign, a sign of the fact that in her eschatological faith she is reaching out for a goal that lies beyond this present world. They also constitute that element in the Church which makes her a visible sign of the fact (which is the real reason for the foregoing) that she is the community triumphantly possessed by the grace of God. Of course, the mere fact of observing these counsels being practised in the life of the *individual* for various reasons is not of itself, unequivocally, and in a way that objectifies it beyond all doubt, an existential symbol of the faith that really is present in the Church (which must be so present because the eschatological Church, in contrast to the synagogue, must be, as a whole, she who really is indefectible in her belief). But the reality of the evangelical counsels as lived in the Church taken as a whole does nevertheless constitute a sign in this sense. In terms both of material fact and of epistemological theory the situation here is the same (and in fact ultimately for the same reason) as with martyrdom considered as an objectivation of, and a witness to faith on the part of the Church, whose faith is, in a true sense, indefectible.[37] Like martyrdom[38] the evangelical counsels too are, in their fulness and totality signs in the Church of the

[37] On this cf. K. Rahner, 'Excursus on Martyrdom' in *On the Theology of Death*, 'Quaestiones Disputatae', 2nd ed.

[38] Which in *individual cases* it is difficult to distinguish from fanaticism, self-will, self-commitment to active opposition.

fact that God's grace is effectively triumphant in the faith of the Church. Now the Church must be a witness precisely in this sense. But she is a witness in this sense only (cf. above subsections 6 and 7) through the evangelical counsels (we are abstracting here from martyrdom considered as the active acceptance of 'passion' in the absolute, the state in which 'passion' and ascesis are brought together, for it is precisely *not* simply in 'normal' times alone that martyrdom can represent a rival to the Church's constitution in this function of being the sign of the real and effective faith that is within her). Thus it can be seen that these evangelical counsels belong (even if not in a form which is institutionally defined in any precise sense as a matter of the Church's law) to the essence of the Church because it is not only the official dispensers of the Church's truth and grace who constitute an essential part of her, but the grace that brings about her triumphant acceptance of truth and grace as well – this latter grace as received and as manifesting itself for what it is.

As witness of the fact that it is precisely the grace of *Christ* that is accepted in faith (cf. above subsection 3) by the Church this witness has a *soteriological* character. It attests the fact that the Church (as a whole) freely submits herself to the Passion of Christ to the extent that this constitutes a free acceptance of death in a spirit of obedience, and thereby brings about salvation. It also has an *eschatological* character, not strictly speaking to the extent that the evangelical counsels already contain the future life of heaven by anticipation already in the here and now. Rightly understood this can be said of grace itself and the fulness of it as attained on this earth. This is in accordance with the fact that in empirical terms it must be said that justification is already achieved 'in the here and now' (notwithstanding the fact that this concept applies primarily to the definitive consummation of salvation). But if this were all we were saying then it would be true of *every* kind of Christian perfection and every act of striving for such perfection. The counsels themselves as such, to the extent that they are distinct from that which constitutes their basis, the grace of justification and love, do not 'anticipate' eternal life as such. For they are, of their very nature, a renunciation, and this is no true characteristic of final perfection.[39] In particular when, according to many

[39] In the present article we are regarding the evangelical counsels as constituting a renunciation. In doing this we wish to draw attention particularly to the formal element in renunciation, the deliberate letting go of some good. Of course the concrete act in which such renunciation is posited is not simply one of letting go. The

Fathers of the Church, virginity in the earthly sphere is conceived of as an anticipation of life in heaven, as *vita angelica*, a life similar to that of angels, this is the outcome of a pietistic Neoplatonism, in support of which Mt 22:30 cannot be invoked. Marriage does not make a man 'earthly'. But the counsels can and must be understood as an eschatological witness to the extent that they objectify and make manifest that faith which reaches out in hope towards that future state which is the consummation of the grace which is received in this faith. To the extent that this objectivation and manifestation of the triumph of grace and of faith is the objectivation of that grace which embraces the world (even though this is achieved precisely through the Cross) and glorifies it, this 'sign' character of the counsels is essentially focused upon the Church, in which the consecration of the world takes place and the worldly becomes identified with the Christian. It is not only for practical reasons that there must be something

---

very fact that an act of this kind has to be *performed* is of itself enough to ensure this. A sheer negative act of letting go, without any positive element in it, is not possible. A further point is that if it is right to leave such an empty space in one's human life viewed as a whole (i.e. if one is not motivated in this by an attitude of reaction against the good that is surrendered) the resulting vacuum will inevitably and justifiably come to fill itself up with certain precisely positive modes of behaviour which are intrinsically connected with the good that is relinquished. These in themselves constitute an objectivation of faith and love, for it is for the sake of these that the individual concerned has chosen to make the renunciation. The poor man is in a position to acquire a *positive* attitude of detachment towards the earthly goods precisely from his position of deprivation, for in fact it is neither possible for him totally to renounce all use of worldly goods, nor would every attitude of withdrawal from them be reasonable. (Industry, a sense of social responsibility, concern for the worldly circumstances of the religious community, etc., are virtues which must be developed positively.) The unmarried man renounces one particular form of love between human beings, but does not absolutely renounce human love in itself. His renunciation is only Christian and is only permitted if it makes it possible for him, and actually demands of him, that he shall have a true love for his fellow men, a will to loving service of them and fraternal relationships with them. Religious obedience is not mere passivity, not a shrinking from self-responsibility and independence in the right sense. It does not entail the surrender of personal initiative and boldness. Rather it is that selflessness with which one places one's self at the disposal of others and subordinates one's self to the achievement of a higher common goal. And in all these positive aspects of renunciation, which constitute the formal essence of the evangelical counsels, there is, once more, a reference to that eschatological state which is the goal of all Christian striving for perfection: a proximity in love to a world in which God is present, because in the freedom bestowed by the Spirit we no longer have to choose between God and the world, a choice from which the man who is still making his way through an unredeemed world cannot remain exempt.

more in the Church than the *mere* practice of the evangelical counsels. Such a thing would actually be *unfitting*. The fact that some of the members of the Church live a 'worldly' life, that Christianity has also its 'everyday', and therefore almost anonymous aspects in the way in which it is lived, so that Christians act as the 'pagans' also act – this is something that belongs of necessity to the mode in which the Church manifests herself, and is inherent in her nature. The life of Christians in the world has a message for those who live under the evangelical counsels. It tells them that their actions too, do not compel grace, but rather that grace is bestowed upon those actions. The life of the evangelical counsels has a message for Christians 'in the world'. It tells them that they too are pilgrims, to whom grace comes from above and not *as a result of* their worldly activities (even though it does come *in* those activities). Both 'states' in the Church mutually contribute to one another according to the gifts which are given to each in particular precisely as proper to itself.

Of course, a further consequence of all that has been said is that the counsels must be lived in a manner (and that too precisely with regard to their sociological and 'institutional' aspects) which makes it clear that they have the force not only of objectivation but of a manifestation too of the faith of the Church. But at this point fresh questions are raised for today. The poverty of the orders seems often to have very little 'poor' about it. The evangelical state of virginity all too often vanishes into the vague indefinability and ambiguity of the attitude of contemporary society towards sexual love. Obedience appears as a way of organising the communities on the grand scale such as also occurs in other contexts and with greater severity. All this constitutes a threat today to the ecclesiological function of the evangelical counsels, and raises fresh questions concerning the contemporary forms of religious life.

10

THE THEOLOGY OF POVERTY

WE have here set ourselves the task of examining the poverty practised in the religious life and its nature, in other words the theology of poverty. We shall attempt, therefore, to establish what the theological basis is for what we call poverty and the vow of poverty as taken in the religious life. This means that we have set ourselves an extremely difficult task. I cannot hope, and the reader should not expect, to arrive at any very satisfying answer to the question we have set ourselves in this enquiry. We must content ourselves with throwing some light on the actual question itself and sketching in some partial answers here and there. When I say that I an unable to offer any total answer, such as would be satisfying even to some degree, I do not believe that in holding this opinion I am succumbing to the tendency which is so widespread and predominant today, to see only questions everywhere, and to be unwilling to entertain any kind of factual or down-to-earth answers. The reason why the question posed here, therefore, simply does not admit of any simple answer is that the subject of it, namely poverty, is a concept that can hardly be apprehended in any simple or unambiguous sense. Of course we might adduce doctrines which have a very profound basis in theology, and which, rightly understood, do express the theological significance of poverty. They tell us why, on what basis and for what end the members of religious orders embrace poverty in their religious life. We can, therefore, expound the 'ideology of poverty', if I may so express it, in a way that is theologically speaking very well thought out. But however right and important such an enterprise may be, in pursuing it we are attempting to speak of the basis and ultimate purpose of a matter which, in itself, is not clear or unambiguous. For prior to any question of the reasons why a man should commit himself to a life of poverty it is extremely difficult to obtain any one clear idea of what poverty is, viewed simply and straightforwardly as an objective phenomenon in its own right.

In fact this has always been the case. The history of religious life throughout the two millennia of its existence has been, one might almost be justified in saying, a constant record of shifts and variations in the interpretation of poverty in itself. It may perhaps be true that the actual motives and causes which lie behind the practice of poverty have also always been a matter of dispute. If we look into the matter more closely we find that at different epochs and in different religious orders very different motivations have been assigned for the practice of it. But the main point is that the actual ways in which poverty in itself has been practised and defined have been quite different from each other. Poverty considered as a concrete objective phenomenon is different today from what it was yesterday, and different in one order from what it is in another. This fact is recognised and conceded. It is even used as a criterion for distinguishing between the orders and their varying degrees of 'strictness'. And in canon law and ascetical writings *the* poverty of the religious orders is spoken of. Of course it is possible to devise a single formula standing for a unified concept of religious poverty such as would cover all these variations in the practice of poverty in the different orders and at different epochs, and which in spite of these variations would be applicable to all. But if we do this then the question still remains whether this formula really expresses what is essential in the poverty of any given order at all, or whether we can in any sense apply to this formalised concept of poverty those theological motivations which are assigned as the basis and the goal of religious poverty; of whether this formalised concept of poverty (it might be expressed as a total dependence upon the assent of superiors in disposing of material goods) in any sense corresponds to what is meant by 'poverty' in the bible and in tradition, and in the real motivation which initially inspired the various movements which led to the religious orders.

These problems concerning the reality of poverty have always been, and still are with us. But in addition to these certain quite fresh problems have arisen today. Today we find ourselves in the midst of a process in which an economy is emerging which forces us to alter the material content of what is meant by religious poverty. It is utopian to imagine that in applying the concept of poverty to the material of our concrete lives we can live and practise it in *exactly* the way in which an Antonius, Pachomius, Benedict, Francis, or, at the beginning of the new age an Ignatius thought that poverty should be practised in the concrete. Anyone who held this opinion would simply be closing his eyes to the realities of

the situation, and would thereby precisely be obscuring the real task
which awaits us, that namely of arriving at a materially new concept and
a materially new concrete application of the essence of what poverty has
been understood to mean in the new economic circumstances in which we
are inescapably involved. Precisely in the dimension of material values
and goods, and more here than in any other sphere, man is, with regard
to the shaping of the course of his private life, a subordinate cog in the
machine by which the shape of this dimension as a whole is socially and
collectively determined. The shaping of this dimension of life takes place
almost entirely independently of him, and so far as his individual life is
concerned it confronts him as an entity that is already given, and which it
is not in his power to determine. Whether one wears a shirt or has none,
whether one goes barefoot or wearing shoes, etc. – these are factors
which even as practised by the individual change completely from time
to time in different epochs and under different economic systems. And the
way in which such usages are actually applied in the concrete is almost
wholly determined by these circumstances of universal application. And
hence it comes about that the rules which determine the way poverty is
to be applied in the religious orders, as handed down from earlier ages,
which to a certain degree are intended to describe and to lay down the
actual material application of poverty in a particular order, are either to a
large extent no longer in force at all, or are no longer in any sense applicable to the realities which actually prevail. Hence it comes that poverty as
practised has become a reality which is, to a large extent, neither envisaged
nor catered for by the rules of religious orders at all. We shall have to
return to these matters at a later stage. Our only reason for putting
forward this consideration in the present context is that we wish to make
it clear that we cannot expect any answer which is really theologically
satisfying concerning the religious meaning and the theological significance of these matters, or concerning their religious motivation. For the
concept of poverty, so far as what is really meant in the concrete is
concerned, is no longer clear at all, and, moreover, is no longer capable
of being very clear. Also because we are no longer in any position to
obtain a clear insight into the phenomenon in which this is one particular
factor, namely the concrete economic situation as it exists today, its
nature and the lines along which it tends to develop. If we sought to give
the impression that we could provide an accurate and precise theological
interpretation, then the only way in which we could convey such an

impression would be to immerse ourselves in a sphere of abstract formalism in which everything would be true, beautiful and glorious, but the question of whether the subject of our discourse actually was in fact *that* poverty which we have to do with in our everyday lives would still remain open. The result of this state of the problem is that we must not expect to find any very clear and distinct arrangement of the materials in this essay. I shall speak first about certain traditional problems connected with the concept of poverty, and then about what can perhaps be said regarding the theological basis for poverty in view of the circumstances actually prevailing, and finally about certain questions which arise from the contemporary situation in the sphere of economics and political theory with regard to religious poverty. By way of reassurance we may reiterate once more that for men who are intelligent and wise a lack of clarity and a failure to solve all the problems at the theoretical level need not necessarily be extended to the sphere of practical action as well. There are thousands upon thousands of factors in human life as lived in the concrete which have proved themselves to be reasonable and valuable, beneficial and sound, by being tried and tested in the actual processes of living, and which, nevertheless, it is extremely difficult to speculate about so as to arrive at any clear theoretical conclusion. The practical knowledge which we gain in the spontaneous and uninhibited process of living our lives is always greater than that which we acquire through speculation, which can never adequately cover life in all its dimensions. And so we know that poverty too as practised in the religious life is reasonable and good because the living practice of it has been proved by the wisdom of the ancients through the experience of many centuries in the Church under the guidance of the Spirit with which she is filled. And we know it even before we have arrived at any theoretical clarity as to what we really are actively living out in this, and why it should be good in this way. This is not to say that there is no necessity for, or meaning in speculation of this kind, but it probably does serve to exclude a restlessness and a destructive force which such speculations might otherwise have.

I. SOME TRADITIONAL PROBLEMS

1. The distinction between the poverty of the individual in an order and that of the community as such is one that is well-known. Such a distinction is not without its significance, for there is no doubt that the

poverty of the individual does entail the factor of dependence upon the community in the disposal of material goods, and this factor cannot, in the nature of the case, be true of the poverty of the community as well. But dependence in the disposal of material goods and poverty cannot be identified one with another (however often the attempt may be made to do so on the part of the exponents of ascetical theology and canon law). And if there were no such thing as communal poverty, then it would be impossible to speak of the poverty of an individual either. Again the member who is totally dependent upon a society that is positively rich cannot seriously be called poor if the word poverty is to be allowed to retain any meaning at all. The consequence of this, therefore, is that the problem of religious poverty is primarily a problem of the poverty of the community to the extent that there is such a problem in the order concerned, and to the extent that it is presupposed that the way of life followed by the individual is determined by that of the community itself. This may be a platitude. Yet I have the impression that when the religious communities of today attempt to give new shape to the rule of poverty in the constitutions of their particular order, and one that corresponds to present-day circumstances, they are always tempted to think initially and primarily of the individual, and to allow the question of poverty, insofar as this applies to the community as a whole, to fall into the background. This is understandable. The question of communal poverty today is far more difficult to resolve than that of the poverty of the individual. But it must be solved. Otherwise the prescriptions concerning the poverty of the individual necessarily become mere casuistry designed for a particular set of circumstances, laying down how the juridical dependence of the individual upon the permission of his superiors in disposing of material goods can be maintained, simplified, intensified, etc., in this contemporary age. Such matters then easily degenerate into external formalities, which are still far from necessarily entailing any supernatural meaning designed to form the personality. And in any case dependency and poverty are not the same thing. This is an ancient problem which, nevertheless, still needs to be thought out anew today. In order to put the matter clearly once more: a rich order cannot have any poor members. It may have a well-lined purse even though it is strict in refusing the individual to draw on this at will. It may have members who in a juridical sense have no private possessions of their own. Orders can be poor in different senses. But an order that is really rich cannot have any poor members. At the most such an order can have members who are totally dependent upon the communal property reserved to the community in respect of the material goods which they need. Someone might perhaps say that these statements presuppose an idea of poverty which is at basis Franciscan, and which, for example, would be inappropriate to a rich mediaeval institution (a royal abbey founded by a prince). In reply to such an objection we would have to say that it is precisely this concept of poverty, the Franciscan one if we like to call it so, which is the biblical one, the one envisaged by the ascetical teachings of old, in other words the 'evangelical' one which is also envisaged in the mind of the contemporary Church even among laymen, when the demand is made that members of religious orders should be poor. Theologically speaking too, it is this idea that we must take as our basis. Otherwise poverty degenerates into a mere modality of community life and obedience (no wonder that in the ancient orders no specific vow of poverty was provided for at all). In this situation, therefore, poverty represents neither an evangelical counsel in the true sense, nor, in any effective sense, the material for a specific vow, not any real theological problem. In brief: the poverty of the individual and the poverty of the community are, in the last analysis, one and the same problem. It is because the community is poor, and to the extent that it is so, that the individual participates in the poverty of the community because he is a member of it, and therefore too, a sharer in its way of life. And it is because he intends to be poor that he attaches himself to a community which practises this poverty in its life. In all this it still remains an entirely open question, and one which still awaits our further exploration, what *degree* of poverty, and what *kind* of poverty a community has or should have.

2. In this the second point which has to be made here has in reality already been anticipated: What makes a man 'poor' in the sense in question here, where we are conducting a theological and ascetical consideration of the word 'poverty', is neither dependence upon others in the disposal of material goods, nor the juridical concept of the absence of private property. One who has no property of his own can certainly not dispose of material goods of his own power, and at the same time in a way that is legally valid. But if he belongs to a community (e.g. a family, a society, an order) which decides to set him in charge of the whole range of their material goods, and to allow him to control their use (a range which corresponds to that of an individual whom one would describe as

'rich' in relation to the general standard of living) then we cannot describe a member occupying such a position in a community of such a kind as poor. The most we can say is that he is economically speaking, totally dependent. Such a state of dependence may even be felt as thoroughly unpleasant. It may, at any rate in a certain respect (at least as far as outside appearances are concerned), 'deprive the individual concerned of his power'. And this dependence and deprivation of power in relation to others may even be susceptible of a wholly Christian and ascetical interpretation in harmony with the order's ideals. But this cannot be called poverty. If, therefore, the only cases in which we were willing to see offences against the vow of poverty were those in which it was this juridical dependence in respect of poverty that was offended against, then this would constitute a canonical or juridical distortion and diminution of the true concept of poverty, and in accordance with this even in those cases in which a superior has rights over property and is vested with legitimate canonical authority only as the authorised controller and disposer of the property of the community, he can still act in a manner which is absolutely contrary to the spirit of the poverty of the religious life. If, for instance, a superior attempts to employ all the arts of the business man, and to act like a ruthless capitalist in order to increase beyond all measure the resources of the order, he can offend against the spirit of poverty even when he modestly assumes the same 'ascetical' conditions for his private life as so many contemporary managers of great enterprises. In such a case he has not offended against the principle of dependence, because as superior he had a perfect right to dispose of the property as he had done. But he has sinned against poverty itself. When the superioress of a community of nuns exploits the individual sisters by laying excessive burdens of work upon them in order to make the order rich and powerful by establishing new houses, she has offended against poverty even though, precisely because of her acts the individual sisters have to live in an extremely 'poor' manner.

3. Religious poverty and poverty in one's *mode of life* should not be confused one with another. Certainly we must not sublimate poverty into a theory in such a way that it can be reconciled with any kind of usage of material goods. Otherwise we should be forced to arrive once more at that concept of poverty which identifies poverty and the relationship of juridical dependence with regard to these material goods. It is incontestable that a certain measure of real deprivation of material goods

does belong to poverty, even when we leave on one side the question of precisely *what* goods (as well as the standards by which we should determine this) poverty should lead us to do without. Poverty, therefore, has a thoroughly material content. Poverty as practised in the orders cannot simply be a 'poverty in spirit'. The subject's attitude to the world of material goods must be made actual in the concrete, and his withdrawal from that world (a point to which we shall be coming later) must likewise be made real in the concrete. Nevertheless we have to distinguish very clearly between poverty and specific modes of practising poverty. This is a point that has always been recognised from the first, and for this reason even those who took the 'Franciscan' concept of poverty as their common working basis still differed widely from one another in their applications of it. This is not the place to analyse the differing modes of poverty which have appeared in history, to describe the physiognomy of each or to define the differences between them. For our present purposes it is sufficient to establish that these differences do exist, because this is an important factor for the considerations which we shall later have to put forward. It is sufficient for us to say that we must recognise that these differences are justified in principle and theologically reasonable by the fact that the Church has recognised as legitimate the various modes of poverty practised in the individual orders. It may be that in earlier times an attempt was made too hastily and too facilely to draw an equation between the categories of the 'more strict' and 'less strict', and therefore a 'more perfect' and 'less perfect' kind of poverty. In this respect we of today are more cautious. We concentrate more upon the differences in mode and practice, and less directly and specifically upon the 'strictness' involved. We have to concede that here (as in many other matters) the differences in point of 'strictness' between the individual orders have largely disappeared, and that a movement has arisen which is still continuing even today, towards a fairly uniform mode throughout all the orders. Perhaps it is simply the fact that all in common are involved in the same economic situation, and the same general way of life in these present times that has to a large extent forced this state of affairs upon them. But if we concede that this difference between poverty (in its essence) and the mode of practising poverty is an already existing historical fact, then we cannot in principle simultaneously close our eyes to the fact that today a point that has to be thought out throughout all the orders and in each individual order is what form the mode of poverty should assume specifically today in order to be really convincing and really livable. Furthermore the man who concedes the initial point cannot simply hold rigidly and conservatively to the idea that the ancient mode of poverty inherited from the Fathers must be preserved, and imagine that this is enough to solve all the problems. In the light of contemporary ideas of social economy this is simply impossible. And if, nevertheless, the individual concerned is so uncreative as to attempt such a thing, what emerges is a lifeless mixture of purely external, but nevertheless unavoidable concessions to the new age (these may, perhaps, be formulated too hastily and with a lack of clarity) and the ancient traditions of the orders, which are no longer really meaningful from the point of view of ascetics, but only survive as relics of the folklore of the religious orders.

4. It cannot be denied that in the tradition of poverty too, and in the tradition of the theology of poverty various motivations and interpretations of poverty have been assigned. The poverty of the ascetics of the apostolic age and of early Christendom prior to the emergence of monasticism properly so called under Antonius and still more under Pachomius was a different phenomenon from the poverty of the coenobites both in its material form and necessarily to some extent in its motivation also. The poverty of the pure contemplative on the one hand, and of the active apostle on the other, cannot, in reality, simply be identical one with the other, and therefore neither can the motivations of the two kinds of poverty be identical. Poverty of life as practised in a given religious order, without diminishing its essential theological identity, derives a distinctive stamp of its own from the distinctive characteristics which apply to that particular order as a whole, and therefore the motivation of this poverty likewise has a different specification from that in other orders. Historically speaking, therefore, we have to recognise fully the existence of these very different motivations in the numerous movements towards poverty and controversies about poverty (all reform movements in the religious orders and all controversies have in fact always entailed disputes about poverty too, and these go far beyond the dispute about poverty in the Franciscan order). History, therefore, fully justifies us in refusing to strive for an absolutely univocal explanation when we come to investigate the theological meaning and motivation of poverty. It is to be expected *a priori* that the poverty practised in the religious orders is a relatively complex phenomenon, which, as practised in the concrete, is quite incapable of being reduced to any *one single* theological root.

II. THE THEOLOGICAL INTERPRETATION OF RELIGIOUS POVERTY

We have now to enquire into the theological essence of poverty. But two provisos which we must always bear in mind throughout our enquiry are first that what we have to say will be at an extremely abstract level, and second that we may perhaps not manage to lay bare *all* the roots of this extremely complex phenomenon. A further point is that any attempt at assigning the basic theological reasons for practising poverty must to some extent do justice to the complexity of the phenomenon. For this reason certain preliminary observations must be made concerning the limits within which we can and must attempt to find an answer to our question at all.

1. In any attempt at finding an answer to our question one point which we must bear in mind from the very outset may be stated as follows: (a) We are trying to ascertain the meaning of *evangelical* poverty, i.e. that poverty which is recommended by Jesus himself. However many forms religious poverty may have assumed in the course of history, however many modes and fashions of practising it may have been worked out, in all cases, wherever it has arisen, the intention has always been to fulfil the evangelical counsel which goes back to Christ himself. It is true that even in the teaching of the New Testament itself several different motivations are assigned for the practice of voluntary poverty, and these are themselves both susceptible of and in need of analysis. But however true this may be, it still remains a point of absolutely primary and overriding importance that religious poverty in all its forms is intended to be a following of this evangelical counsel, and that all forms of the religious life are conscious of being authorised in their practice of poverty simply by the very fact that Jesus has recommended it, even when they do not succeed in making clear the reasons which Jesus himself had for recommending this practice of poverty. In fact a point which can and must be made right from the outset is the following (and here we are already going beyond the preliminary group of questions which needs to be treated of here, that namely which is concerned with the problem of poverty in its total scope and ambience): *one* element in this poverty is precisely the inalienable connection with the Lord and his personal lot, a connection for which no more ultimate reason can be assigned. We can say that the practice of poverty is based, among other factors, upon

that theology which envisages the discipleship of Christ as a sharing in the lot of Jesus himself, and on this basis we can say that the reason for practising poverty is simply that this was, in fact, the lot endured by the Lord himself. The life of the Lord was, in its concrete realities, precisely so and not otherwise. And we cannot assign any more ultimate reason for this than the fact that it was so. Now this concrete reality is received and projected further into the life of the individual who loves Jesus and follows him. But there is a further point over and above this. Everything which the New Testament teaching on poverty assigns as a motivation for practising poverty over and above this central fact must be assigned a place in the poverty of the religious life.

(b) A point which must not be forgotten in the theology of poverty is that poverty as practised in the religious orders is concerned with a factor in communal living, and this communal living in turn makes manifest in historical and social terms factors which are inherent in the very nature of the Church herself. In fact the orders are not simply private confraternities of individuals who lead an ascetical life on their own account, and at their own risk, such that the Church still to some extent presides over these confraternities. The fact that these confraternities can provide useful assistance for the work undertaken by the Church's official hierarchy is not the sole reason that the Church concerns herself with them. For in fact, measured by the standards of the meaning and content of the religious life, insofar as the actual practice of this life is concerned, the giving of this help is a wholly accidental factor (as for instance when a bishop founds a community of sisters under vows because he needs to provide cooks for his seminaries and other institutions in the cheapest and most reliable way possible to him). Rather the orders constitute a concretisation, in social and communal terms, of the charismatic element and the element of enthusiasm in the Church which must always be present in her as an essential manifestation of her true nature. There cannot be any such thing as the Church of the final eschatological age in which the evangelical counsels are not lived and practised as a manifestation of the essential nature of the Church herself. Now such a life inevitably goes on to assume certain organised forms. And though the element in the Church which they embody is precisely not institutional but rather charismatic, still, in a certain sense, they do institutionalise even this charismatic element (with all the danger of misinterpretation which such a procedure entails). To this extent, therefore, the orders belong to the essence of the Church in the degree and measure that in them she, the Church, lives out certain aspects of her own nature, making them real and manifest to the world. The orders constitute an element in the process by which the fact that the grace of God has entered the world and has triumphed over it is rendered present. This is the grace that summons man to transcend the limits of his own natural powers as a 'this-worldly' creature, and draws him into the process by which that grace is rendered present which constitutes the very nature of the Church herself. In our attempt to say something about religious poverty this is a point that must not be forgotten. Religious poverty must be viewed in the light of this essential function of the religious orders themselves.

(c) Religious poverty has a function in these religious communities considered precisely as freely committed to communal living. This practical side of poverty, which we experience every day, does not constitute the ultimate essence of religious poverty, but it is one which we neither can nor may overlook. A certain measure of religious poverty (above all consisting in a certain dependence and equality in the mode of life followed by the individual members) is indispensable for the survival of a community committed to communal living down to the intimate details of life such as the orders are intended to be. From this point of view the meaning of poverty is determined by the broader and more comprehensive significance which such a community is intended to have. The significance of the community is also the significance of the poverty it practises.

(d) To the extent that an order has a task to perform for others outside itself, in that the life and work of the community and of each of its individual members is dedicated to promoting a task of this kind (apostolic, teaching, missionary or charitable work, etc.), the religious poverty practised by that order will also be affected by this aim. Alike in its essence and in the mode in which it is practised it will derive its concrete specification from this aim.

2. It now becomes clear not only that these various perspectives from which religious poverty can be viewed are legitimate, and that they make the concept of poverty complex, and therefore rich in overtones, but also that from these various perspectives various explanations of the meaning of poverty can be put forward so that a fresh problem arises once more with regard to how all these explanations can be unified. For it is far from being immediately clear from the outset that these various motivations

of themselves lead smoothly and without interruption to the same concept of poverty and to the same mode of practising poverty. Poverty as an evangelical counsel, poverty as an individual following of Christ the poor and the suffering, poverty as an element in the process by which the Church, considered as the eschatological presence of grace in the world, is made visible and palpable, poverty as a principle in the organisation of a community, poverty as a means for drawing the powers of a community together for the fulfilment of its common task for others – all these do not necessarily or *ipso facto* lead to the same concrete 'poor' mode of life. It may even be the case that they constitute absolute threats or obstacles to one another. Poverty in a radically ascetical sense, for instance, can represent an actual threat to the possibility of living a common life, or take away this possibility altogether. The fact that poverty is subordinated to the interests of apostolic work can appear to make it necessary for the community to be rich to an extent which makes it impossible to speak any further of any real poverty on the part of the individual member of the order, and so of poverty in any ascetical sense.

From this point of view, when we come to consider how the various aspects are to be co-ordinated and reconciled, remembering that no one of them needs to be absolutely excluded, the following point must be laid down from the outset: the poverty which consists in following Jesus and sharing in his lot, in a kind of mystical identification with him, on the one hand, and poverty considered as recommended in the New Testament as a counsel to leave all things, to sell one's goods and give the proceeds to the poor on the other, neither need to cause, nor are capable of causing any difficulties one for the other. Even if they are not absolutely reducible one to another (the uniqueness of Jesus even in the concrete historical realities of his life, in which, nevertheless, this uniqueness still becomes our *nomos*, is not capable of being adequately resolved into principles which are intrinsically comprehensible and for which *a priori* ethical explanations can be assigned), still these two ideals of poverty constitute two intrinsically related entities, a fact which will become clear in what immediately follows. A further factor is introduced into poverty in virtue of the fact that the orders constitute elements in the essential meaning of the Church. But this too cannot come into conflict in any way with the two first-named constitutive elements in poverty. For the Church must, in fact (a point which must be demonstrated at a later stage), make manifest and visible in the world *that* grace in which the essential content of the *basileia tou theou* consists. For it is for the sake of this that it is required of the disciple of Jesus that he shall be poor. But on the other hand it must also be clear from the outset that the further shade of meaning in poverty, its function, namely, in making a technical contribution to the organisation and work of the order concerned (if we may so express the two shades of meaning mentioned above under a single heading) can only be proved to have a right to be taken into consideration insofar as it is dependent upon, and subordinate to, the two shades of meaning which we have just indicated. In cases in which it came to be so emphasised that it derogated from, or suppressed altogether the more original and essential meaning of poverty, it would have to be denied and resisted. If an order intends to be and to remain an order following the evangelical counsels, then any apostolic, missionary, pedagogic, charitable, etc., aims which it may have can never be put forward with such emphasis as determinative elements in the communal way of life proper to that order that for practical purposes they can cause the order to turn aside from the ideal of evangelical poverty. If certain aims, in themselves perfectly legitimate, were to demand a mode of life which could no longer in all reason and honesty be described as poor, then such aims would have to be pursued and realised outside the religious community concerned. Indeed it is in principle true that we cannot take *a priori* as our starting-point the axiom that all the aims which are reasonable and necessary for the Church must for that very reason be capable of realisation in religious communities. The modern tendency to see a connection between the religious life and more or less every conceivable kind of enterprise in the Church has in fact given rise to the supposition that this axiom does apply. But it is, and remains, false and unproved, however much it may exercise an implicit influence as something that is taken for granted.

3. What then is the meaning of poverty in the evangelical sense in the teaching of Jesus? Here we are abstracting from the fact that poverty is first and foremost simply a sharing in the life of the Lord, who was, for all practical purposes, a poor man, or better, lived poorly (Lk 9:57; Mt 8:20; 2 Cor 8:9). We are also abstracting, for the purposes of the question which we have now posed, from the fact that we only encounter poverty in the New Testament as a recommendation of a way of life which the individual can lead as an individual, in other words, that in the New Testament the idea of a communal life lived by those dedicated to poverty in the evangelical sense, and united in a community which is itself poor, has

not yet become apparent. A further point from which we are abstracting is the 'communism' of the early Christians of the primitive community in Jerusalem (Acts 4:32–37). We do not propose to include this in our consideration because this would have the effect of broadening the field of investigation to an excessive extent. But we have the right to reflect upon the fact that as the Lord himself conceived of it, it is evident that the virginity recommended by him 'for the kingdom of heaven's sake' (Mt 19:12) and the poverty likewise recommended from the same motive (Mt 19:21; Lk 18:22) derive from a single basic presupposition. It is true that no compelling reason is *a priori* apparent from the first for explaining that this moral requirement or recommendation here put forward by Jesus never existed before his time. From the point of view of dogma and history, therefore, we can actually *reckon a priori* with the possibility that in his recommendation of poverty Jesus was making his own a programme which was already available in the traditions of later Judaism prior to his advent. But while all this is true, we can say, nevertheless (albeit with a certain caution) that the poverty which Jesus has in mind, and which he recommends to his disciples, is found neither in the Old Testament nor in the traditions of later Judaism, which constitute the religious environment in which Jesus worked. Nor, properly speaking, is this ideal of poverty to be found in the traditions of Qumran. This is a point which cannot be explicitly demonstrated here. But neither is it one which is of decisive importance for the problem with which we are concerned. We also presuppose (to prove this would likewise carry us too far afield at this point) that when Jesus summoned his disciples to poverty he did not intend to inaugurate any social programme. The idea of bringing about a *universal* economic and social transformation in the world was never in his mind either as a concrete demand or as an abstract idea.

With these provisos we can say: Jesus is conscious of the fact, and explains, that with him and in him the *basileia* of God has arrived and is being offered to men, that by this coming of the *basileia* men are placed in a situation of absolute and radical decision of the utmost acuteness and urgency, in other words in an eschatological situation. What is in question here is not the fact that man is, of his very nature, a moral being, and as such always, and in a manner that is constant and unvarying, confronted in all that he does with a decision between good and evil, between assent to and refusal of God himself. Rather it is that now in Jesus the supreme offering of salvation by God has been made present as a supreme moment of opportunity in history. It is that of his own nature in Jesus God compels man to take his ultimate decision. It is in virtue of this fact that, according to Jesus' teaching a situation of radical decision has arisen in the *kairos*, the time of opportunity, which the life of Jesus represents for man. Now according to Jesus the advent of the *basileia* of God as understood here means that human riches have become a danger and an obstacle to the acceptance of this kingdom of God in faith to such an extent that it is easier for a camel to pass through the eye of a needle than for a rich man to enter into this kingdom (cf. Mt 19:23 f; Mk 10:25; Mt 13:22; Lk 1:53; 6:24; Mt 6:19–24). This is not to say that possessions as such are *ipso facto* immoral in themselves, or that the absence of such possessions *ipso facto* constitutes a moral value in itself. 'A radical rejection of possessions, such as we meet with in Buddhism, in the tenets of the Greek Cynics, and among certain adherents of Stoicism, is foreign to Jesus' (Schmidt, *LTK* Vol I, 2nd ed. col 880). Jesus' attitude to the rich is not that of one sociologically opposed to them as a class. But what Jesus does say is that riches, the accumulation of possessions, signifies the direst peril for man in that once he becomes involved in the cares of this present world he becomes blind to the advent of the kingdom, and deaf and unresponsive to the radical summons of God. He does not have at his command that radical freedom of spirit, and of all the powers at his command, which is necessary for him whole-heartedly to receive the kingdom. And for this reason Jesus requires of those who decide to follow him with special closeness in order to receive this kingdom that they shall give their possessions to the poor and become poor themselves (Mt 19:16–30; Lk 9:3; 9:57 f.; 12:33; 18:22).

To the question of why, under which aspects, and because of what qualities inherent in it, riches should constitute an obstacle in this sense, holding men back from preparing themselves for the *basileia*, Jesus supplies hardly any explicit answer. He seems to regard this as self-evident. He who is rich is full of cares (Mk 4:19; Lk 8:14), wants to have more, gives himself up to enjoyment, takes pleasure in the power, enjoyment and security which his possessions give him (Lk 16:19; 12:15–21). He has his 'treasure' on earth instead of in heaven (Lk 12:33 f.). Jesus' appraisal of the danger which riches entail, therefore, is simply based upon the observation of ordinary everyday realities such as are borne in upon any man of good sense who faces up to them whole-heartedly, does not idealise them, and does not allow himself to be beguiled by them. Taking this as our starting-point it is immediately evident that anyone who sets out to systematise this condemnation of the rich and riches on Jesus' part (cf. Lk 6:24 f.) must constantly bear in mind the *genus litterarium* in which these words are uttered, which is prophetic and was initially inspired by the concrete realities of everyday life as Jesus encountered them. If we fail to do this we may fall into a state of mind in which we apply these words in a doctrinaire and universal sense, and erect them into an axiom admitting of no exceptions in a way which is quite foreign to Jesus' intention, seeing that he explicitly disassociates himself from any such attitude (Mt 19:26). A further reason for avoiding this is that the ethical ideals which he taught were intended for the heart, whereas to adopt this approach would be, once more, to reduce them to a sort of univocal ethical pragmatism by which we could check and control our actions in all cases, in other words to a kind of pharisaism. A further point is that in spite of Mt 8:20 the impression is borne in upon us, that Jesus was not strictly speaking in a state of abject destitution or really threatened by hunger. He did have money (cf. Jn 12:6) and quite clearly opportunities enough to obtain support from his rich friends when he had need of this. It should be remembered that the opinion of the Old Testament (Prov 30:8 f.) is that the optimum average conditions for the service of God obtain when man is in an intermediary position between the extremes of a degree of wealth on the one hand that satisfies every possible need, and abject poverty on the other. It cannot be said, therefore, that this opinion is simply invalidated by the example of Jesus.

It is immediately evident that the motivation underlying the poverty inculcated by Jesus is identical with the motivation he puts forward for voluntarily remaining single for the sake of the kingdom of heaven. In the evangelical counsel of poverty Jesus requires of those who decide to dedicate themselves to following him in an especially close way, and so to being 'perfect' (Mt 19:21) that by their own personal decision they shall bring their own personal lives into a situation which is that of those 'poor' whom he himself pronounces blessed in the Sermon on the Mount, in other words the situation of the 'anawim' who are really poor, socially underprivileged, threatened and suffering, but who at the same time bear their lot 'meekly' and in a spirit of resignation to God, imposing the imprint of their faith upon their external lot and so transforming it to that state to which, in Jesus' intention, the voluntary poor should bring their lives: one in which they totally dedicate their freedom to fulfilling the demands of their interior faith in such a way that it shall be imposed upon their exterior situation, and so responding to the summons of the *basileia* of God in Christ.

There is yet a further aspect to be considered in addition to what has already been said. Jesus requires of him who voluntarily decides to become poor for the kingdom of heaven's sake that he shall give his riches to the *poor*. Manifestly for practical purposes this is not the easiest way open to him of becoming poor. Thus, for instance (provided that technically speaking it was just as easy to carry out), the man concerned might just as well burn his possessions in order to become poor. It is clearly envisaged and intended that the poor *neighbour* shall be the goal and object of the individual's act in surrendering his personal riches. It is the poor neighbour who must be helped. Certainly it is not the mind of Jesus that this neighbour should be regarded as one who has been 'deprived of his rights' and 'disinherited', one who, in other words, has a social and political right to riches. Rather it is because he is a brother in the kingdom of God, because as such he is beloved, because the message that must be conveyed to him in this gesture of faith in the coming of the kingdom of God from above is that this kingdom of God is already there. This kingdom, in fact, unites and combines those men who have fallen into disunity and disharmony through the presence of sin in the world. When, therefore, belief in this coming of the kingdom of heaven is lived out in the concrete in the form of voluntary poverty, then this faith must be expressed in the concrete as faith in the unity in love of those who have been united by God's grace. The individual no longer defends that sphere of his life which is occupied by his worldly goods as the bastion of his own egoistical self-defence against others, but rather gives them a share in these goods because he can regard them in a spirit of trust and love them as fellow citizens in the kingdom. The holding of property in common in some form (though of course this can take the most diverse forms and need not necessarily appear precisely in the form which we encounter in the primitive community of Jerusalem) is an intrinsic element in this poverty considered as the gesture which expresses in concrete fact the new brotherhood of men in Christ (the spirit of brother-hood in the orders, one of the conditions of which is likewise the holding of goods in common might also be viewed from this aspect, for by being placed at the service of these, what was once private wealth is placed at the service of the Church as a whole. Admittedly this is only the case provided that that private egoism which seeks its own personal possessions is not replaced by a collective egoism on the part of a greater community precisely with regard to the Church or other Christians, e.g. with regard to domestic servants employed in monasteries, convents, etc.). This aspect of evangelical poverty is one of the factors which once more must be borne in mind whenever we seek to interpret poverty in a manner which is, theologically speaking, more systematic, considering it namely as an eschatological gesture of faith in the coming of the kingdom of God by grace from above. A fact which must never be overlooked in all this is that this kingdom, which is the unity of the brotherhood in love, is also intended to be received precisely by the gesture of voluntarily becoming poor.

Jesus regards the disciple's act in attaching himself more closely to his person, and the voluntary poverty which this entails, as enjoined also, and especially, upon those who dedicate themselves to responding to his call for missionary service (Mt 10:9 the missionary discourse).

We may, perhaps sum all this up by saying: for Jesus voluntary poverty in the evangelical sense is not a sociological programme for the reform of economic circumstances as an end in itself. It is not an element in some system of merely natural ethics which is of universal and unvarying application (to that extent, therefore, not 'ascetical' if we understand this to involve requirements of abstemiousness of a radical kind). It is the outcome of the situation of eschatological salvation. It has meaning, therefore, only to the extent that it requires us to be in a state of radical preparedness for the kingdom of God. But neither the state of being totally devoid of possessions nor that modesty and frugality which is associated with the petit-bourgeois enter of themselves into the meaning of the poverty which Jesus inculcates. This poverty has not yet arrived at the stage at which it is regarded as a way of life for a community. But it probably is regarded as a means of setting the individual free and enabling him to devote himself to missionary activities. It is primarily and essentially a renunciation of riches in that form in which they figured in the historical situation which Jesus knew, together with the ordinary effects which riches had in that particular situation. Thus a 'transference' of the counsel of poverty into all subsequent economic situations, the circumstances of which are constantly changing, is inadmissible. But the poverty which Jesus prescribes is not intended as a mere attitude of mind and conscience, as (in this sense) 'poverty of spirit'. On the contrary it involves, as one of its intrinsic material elements (this still remains true in spite of all the emphasis on the mental attitude of liberating the heart and spirit for the kingdom of God) a renunciation of material goods which is actually put into practice in the concrete.

4. Now when we attempt (passing over the teaching of Acts, Paul and James) to evaluate and to systematise the results we have achieved somewhat more in terms of theology (this will at the same time have the effect of carrying our findings still further in that they will be brought into connection with more general theological insights) then we arrive at the following conclusions:

(a) Christian morality is always a morality of mind and conscience in the sense that the attitude of the heart must be objectified and realised in the dimension of concrete and apprehensible reality which is distinct from this interior dimension of disposition and attitude – in other words it must be realised in 'works'. Now since these works are different from the mind and conscience, which embrace all things, they do not admit of any ultimate assurance that the innermost attitude of the heart is pleasing to God. Yet at the same time these works do constitute the necessary and indispensable material, the material willed by God in itself, in which this innermost attitude (that namely of faith and love) can alone be realised. This remains true however many different forms this objectivation of the interior dispositions may assume, and however much the degree of clarity achieved in this objectivation may vary. All this, therefore, applies to poverty too. Poverty is a combination of interior attitude and exterior 'work', and the dialectical difference which we have found between disposition and 'work' applies to it. The attitude of detachment with regard to material possessions is in itself not yet faith and love, the sole standard by which all must be measured, and yet for those of whom it is required this same faith and love cannot be made effective and real otherwise than by the fact that they are realised in poverty as their manifestation, their 'work'.

(b) Evangelical poverty (considered as the unification of two distinct elements as explained above) is simply intended as a response to the situation in saving history in which man stands by the very fact that the kingdom of God has been made eschatologically present in Jesus. Poverty, like all renunciation (the attitude of 'allowing the world to pass one by' – cf. Didache 10:6 –, the attitude of having as though one had not – cf. 1 Cor 7:29–34 –, the unmarried state, etc.) as conceived of in the New

Testament is the realisation of faith in the coming of that grace of God which is God himself, and which transcends all 'this worldly' fulfilment such as can be achieved by man himself. Now because this grace is the absolute self-bestowal of God as he is in himself, and because it has only now been revealed in Christ as the glory of God himself which exceeds all earthly measures and all values available to human experience, therefore it is only now that man can respond to this coming of God. He can so respond in virtue of the fact that he (who, so far as his purely natural state is concerned is, once more, one who is held captive within himself by sin, and therefore can only experience his openness to the glory of God, which transcends his own nature, as a deadly pain) suffers the 'this worldly' values to fall away from him in the act of faith (which God himself, and not his own autonomous powers, inspires him to make) yet to make this same sacrifice *without* being called to it by God in this way would be meaningless, immoral and contrary to his own nature. The act of faith is realised and made concrete, i.e. in a manner which embraces the *entire* reality of man, his physical nature, his social relationships and the place he occupies in history, in virtue of the fact that he gives up realities and values when to sacrifice them is either an act of despair (or surrender) with regard to the meaning of existence, or else a transcending of the 'this worldly' order so as to attain to the reality of God himself which comes to us from above in the form of grace.

On this showing the meaning of poverty is that it is the act of faith in that grace which comes from above as the unique and definitive fulfilment of human existence. From this it follows that if faith means salvation, and if it is true that faith must always and necessarily achieve its own concretisation (cf. (a)), then such an attitude of withdrawal and allowing the world to pass one by belongs to every act of faith, whatever the context and whatever the manner in which it is posited. Thus the 'poverty in spirit' which all Christians must have necessarily entails a poverty that is made effective in the sober realities of life even though we may not be able to determine in material terms the limits within which this poverty should be applied. In the very nature of the case, therefore, the boundaries between the poverty of the religious orders on the one hand, and the riches or poverty in the lives of the rest of Christians on the other, must necessarily be fluid. No absolute dividing line can be drawn between the two such as would define them as two essentially different ways of life. And conversely the attitude of detachment and renunciation of the 'world' and of any attitude of absolute self-assertion is an act of that Christian faith which is conscious of the world as that which in all its dimensions *positively needs to be redeemed.* As such it must also be an act of faith in the fact that the world is capable of being redeemed. It is quite impossible, therefore, for one who makes an act of faith in this sense, and thereby becomes poor, to regard the absolutely essential form in which this faith must find its fulfilment as consisting in a state in which, as far as such a thing is physically possible, he possesses absolutely nothing at all. This would, in fact, be tantamount to saying that freedom from the world is *ipso facto* and in itself possession of God. Now this is not true. The attitude of transcending the world is only a gesture of faith made possible by the grace of God himself in virtue of the fact that by his grace God bestows himself upon the world, and in doing so actually glorifies it. And this grace cannot be obtained by force, either by seeking for the fulness of the world itself or by fleeing from the world, taking either of these approaches simply in themselves. And furthermore in making the act of faith we can only allow for the fact that the world has a positive value of its own if we maintain a positive relationship with it. The petty-minded man, the man who is timid, undeveloped, frugal in the demands he makes upon life, the man who right from the outset has the standards of the petit-bourgeois only because his own nature is too paltry to make many claims upon life, is certainly not the man who is capable, to any notable extent, of bringing the meaning of the act of faith to its fulness in poverty. The 'ideal' of religious poverty, therefore, can never consist in the fact that the realisation of it is regarded as increasing in precisely the same proportion as the act of externally ridding one's self of material goods. Nor is it the ideal of those who are too easily satisfied with commonplace things, or that of those who, in a spirit of narrow-minded pedantry mount guard over the standards of a petit-bourgeois way of life of this kind and legalistically try to ensure that the rules of the game are kept for their own sake.

(c) The Church taken as a whole not only has to be the Church of the faithful, but has to be seen to be such as well. She has to be the sign of faith in the world. To this extent the concretisation of the act of faith as realised in the act of renouncing 'this worldly' fulfilments (of the most varied kind) belongs necessarily to the mode in which it is manifested, and which it can never be without. It is the mode in which, existentially speaking, witness is borne to the faith, which likewise belongs to the Church's nature as holy, together with the function of authoritatively proclaiming the faith. From this point of view it becomes understandable that the task of ensuring that witness is borne to the Church's faith and in the Church through asceticism of this kind is to be numbered among the essential functions of the Church herself. The Church herself must again and again show herself and present herself as a Church in which the truth is actually lived, the truth, namely, that grace is in the very act of coming and the form of the world passing away, that the Church herself is she who looks for the return of her Lord, she who waits with hope for the eternal kingdom of God as that which is still in the very act of coming – all this in a spirit of faith, hope and love. It is the 'ascetics' of the Church and in the Church who have the duty of ensuring that eschatological witness of this kind is borne to the faith. And because of the fact that this witness belongs essentially to the Church there is always a 'class' in the Church constituted by this element of asceticism. Now the duty of ensuring that witness of this particular kind is borne is achieved in the nature of things more easily and more effectively when the Church has not simply individual ascetics living in isolation to turn to, but an actual corporate body formed by these ascetics in order to give effect to their charismatic mission and function. It is also facilitated and made more effective when this corporate body, together with the individual ascetics in it, is formed and led by the Church herself, endowed with the salvific powers of the Church herself, and constantly directed anew to the task to which they – the individuals in these communities and the communities in themselves – are called by God. Poverty as a 'situation' in life which has been chosen voluntarily, which proclaims and expresses the Church's belief in the coming of grace from above, is therefore, of its very nature, an ecclesiastical function, as also is the whole ascetical movement, and is the outcome of an eschatological vocation as well as of this faith. From this it follows that we must do our utmost to give the practice of this poverty a form such that it can maintain this function of bearing witness to the faith of the Church and in the Church, both internally and externally.

III. ON THE CONTEMPORARY SITUATION WITH REGARD TO THE FORMS ASSUMED BY RELIGIOUS POVERTY

We now arrive at the third and most obscure stage in our considerations. The question which presents itself to be treated of at this point is whether this evangelical poverty should be made real and actual in one specific age, namely our own. Poverty and riches are, in fact, right from the outset relative concepts. They always presuppose the whole range of material goods which an individual has at his own free disposal, instituting a comparison between these and the range of similar goods which are possessed by the average individual in the relevant periods of history considered from the economic and social point of view. There is not much point in calling a pigmy in the forests of central Africa 'poor' on the grounds that he does not have a shirt. It may be that at the time of Jesus a man living in Palestine was 'poor' when he possessed only one instead of two coats (cf. Mt 5:40; 10:10). Today we rightly call an individual 'poor' when he can only call two shirts his own. Poverty, therefore, is a relative concept, bearing upon a specific economic situation. Nevertheless it is not *absolutely* relative. For in spite of what we have said there is a certain constant factor within the continuous alterations in the economic situation which take place throughout history. As applied to the basic biological act of human existence there are certain upper and lower limits defining the absolute minimum necessary for this existence. It is possible to define in figures which are more or less absolutely constant how many calories a man needs in order not to starve. Because of these constants it cannot be said that the concepts of poverty and of riches are solely and exclusively to be defined from the particular economic situation prevailing at any given time, and it is certainly not legitimate to doubt whether, for instance, 'poverty' as we know it today still has anything material in common with the 'poverty' of the time of Jesus. But on the other hand, because man is not only a purely biological being, in other words because he has needs which are not merely determined by his 'bios' but are rather subject to historical changes without for that reason being simply arbitrary, and because these cannot be established solely by the individual according to his own personal decision – because of all this there enters into the concept of poverty a factor which is variable, subject to historical alterations, and to a large extent beyond the powers of the individual to establish or control. From this a further question follows: What does religious poverty really mean today? And this question will lead us to recognise the fact that in poverty, and in the mode of practising poverty, the mere fact of the changes which have taken place in economic and social relationships has brought about transformations which are not insignificant, transformations which we have not yet sufficiently taken cognizance of in the Church's laws relating to the poverty of religious communities, and which we are still far from having been sufficiently realised and worked out in terms of the constitutions of religious orders. A further conclusion is that there has been a not insignificant shift of meaning in the concept of the poverty of the orders for the Church and her witness in the world, and that we are called upon to make fresh efforts to develop a mode of poverty which is more effective in enabling poverty to fulfil its constant and abiding function in the religious life of the individual, of the order and of the Church herself both internally and externally.

It is very difficult to give any satisfactory reply to this question in a manner which is systematic, clear and comprehensible, and which at the same time is, even to some extent, satisfying and constructive. The reader is therefore asked to excuse the fragmentary and disorderly presentation of the considerations which follow.

1. Our first observation is one which is, perhaps, calculated to meet with that feeling of mistrust and irritation which is occasionally experienced today among members of the orders in dealing with religious ideals; the feeling, namely, that it is a clear and established fact that in the question of poverty the contemporary members of religious orders are only threatened with the danger of becoming more lax, and the sole task of superiors in the orders is to set thèmselves firmly against any such falling away. If poverty means economic insecurity and a renunciation of that power in society which is associated with possessions then we shall be able to say that the orders considered as corporate bodies, and viewed as a whole, have never been so poor as they are today. If it is true that the individual member of an order shares in the riches or the poverty of his community then this conclusion has implications for the position of individuals in the orders. But surely this conclusion does prove to be unambiguously true. The united resources of a foundation of the Middle Ages, or even of a house of Mendicants of the period or of a Jesuit house of studies of the seventeenth century, and the power which these gave to their holders, represent, when measured by the general economic standards of the relevant periods, a far greater percentage of the total amount of goods available for all than is the case today. But presumably this would still apply even if it were sought to reconcile the proportions between the two sets of figures by pointing out that the proportion of religious to the population as a whole was different then from what it is now. The religious houses have all become poorer than they were, even if the degree of

poverty involved is determined by another principle, that is, not merely by the amount of goods available in the absolute, but also according to the proportion these represented of the total amount of goods available to the community as a whole at any one particular period. The fact that this increase in poverty has not been accompanied by a corresponding increase in the degree of economic insecurity experienced, whether with regard to the needs of life at the biological level or otherwise, is simply a consequence of the general economic situation. In other words it may be that even a member of a religious order stood in greater danger of going hungry in former times than he does today. But this is simply due to the fact that this danger has become less for everyone than it was in former times. Again a relatively smaller increase in the degree of economic security enjoyed has probably been achieved for members of religious orders than for many other social groups in comparison with the degree of security which these would have enjoyed in earlier times. This finding is not invalidated by the fact that the decrease in economic security for the member of an order is not, strictly speaking, due to economic factors (as in earlier times) but rather to other causes, for instance the threat which political forces hostile to religion and the Church represent for religious communities. From certain points of view, therefore, it can absolutely be asserted that in guiding his Church God has so arranged matters that the Church and her orders have become poorer than in earlier times. To that extent we do not, strictly speaking, have any need to suppose that we are greatly inferior to our fathers in this question of poverty, even if today we have a typewriter and a wristwatch and other things as well which they did not possess. Of course it is right that the absolute quantity of goods which are available to a member of an order today has increased to a quite extraordinary extent in comparison with earlier times. But that is the outcome not in any sense of a development in the orders as such, or even of a decline from the ideal of religious poverty. Rather it is the consequence of the general economic development. Yet even as such this fact constitutes the basis of the present-day problem of poverty in the orders.

2. The first problem confronting us is the security of modern man (and so of the member of an order too). In our present-day economy, in contrast to that of earlier times, everyone, and so the member of an order too, can count with relatively greater security, on the availability of that absolute minimum necessary simply for maintaining life at the purely

biological level. Today in the areas governed by our present-day economy the probability that we shall starve is minimal. But strictly speaking it is precisely this security that poverty in its original form, and as practised in earlier periods of the economy, to a large extent gave up. Then a man became poor when in a literal sense he was reduced to begging, and not only starved when he did not succeed in obtaining alms (and there was no guarantee of this), but also, when a general situation of need arose (a failure of the crops, pestilence, etc.), he felt its effects most directly and most severely of all. And again this situation itself arose far more easily and with far less possibility of escaping from its effects. Even if we can say that in spite of this present-day economic situation the elemental anxiety (*Angst*) and insecurity underlying human life are a characteristic of man to a greater extent even than formerly, still this does not alter the facts as we have found them to be. For this insecurity in our basic personal life, even to the extent that it should be present at all in the lives of members of orders, is not in fact increased by the religious poverty which they undertake, as was the case with religious poverty in earlier times. It would not even be intensified if the members of orders were to practise a more radical form of doing without than they normally do, for even by a more strict withdrawal from goods of economic value both in point of quantity and kind they would not really be coming any nearer to those limits which define the minimum necessary for existence, and so the point at which this radical insecurity of existence arises. Their way of life would indeed be more severe and richer in point of detachment from worldly goods, and we can whole-heartedly defend and praise such a way of life. But even so, when they had reduced their level of consumption to this extremely modest level they would still be wholly secure. For it is precisely this abstemiousness with regard to material goods that is easiest to acquire and to maintain. This is due to another circumstance which also radically alters the situation within which the phenomenon of poverty, including religious poverty, has to exist today. In industrial societies everyone who has the power to work can in fact put it to fruitful and profitable use. But this means that mendicancy has been reduced to a mere peripheral phenomenon. As a means of maintaining the minimum necessary for existence the question of alms only still arises for all practical purposes for those who are incapable of work. Money is a symbol of the power to work productively. It is no longer what it was in earlier times, in the first instance a counter representing some consumer good which is not simply any kind of possession. This means that begging (especially as the resources of the welfare state are also available) is regarded to a large extent as unnecessary and therefore as inadmissible. Even if it can be said with a certain justice that the present-day orders are perhaps compelled to 'beg' more than in earlier times to sustain themselves and to educate their younger members who have not yet been put to 'productive' work (because these are still not equipped for the apostolate, and those who are so capable do not 'earn' enough for their part to maintain the younger members) still this is 'begging' of a kind which other cultural institutions too avail themselves of today to assure themselves of a sound financial basis (by 'donations', 'contributions', financially powerfully 'associates', 'promoters', etc.). All that this kind of 'begging' therefore has in common with what was earlier understood by begging is simply the name, and perhaps a 'nature' too, in an abstract and metaphysical sense, but otherwise nothing more. The members of religious orders in our countries do not, viewed as a whole, really need to beg in the old sense any more.

Because we live in a productive economy in terms of work and money, spiritual and intellectual achievements too can be regarded as work which can be turned to profit, and so we can, if we wish, take this fact into account in formulating a theory to cover the rules of poverty. We can say that for all practical purposes, and as a matter of concrete fact, the members of orders too live to a large extent by the just remuneration of their activities, which can be considered as work. Just as with doctors the honorarium which they used to receive in the old days has given way to a straightforward payment for their work, so too it is with the activities of members of religious orders. They find their reward. But precisely because of this their contemporaries in modern times have come to think of them from the economic point of view as having passed from the class of the poor in any ordinary sense into that of those who receive recompense for their work, with all the advantages or disadvantages which the economic situation of such people entails. At any rate the members of orders are no longer classed in men's minds among the genuinely poor, the class to which many orders at least were still thought of as belonging in the Middle Ages. At the most they belong to those who have to satisfy themselves with a relatively modest way of life. In view of this situation it is of no avail to console ourselves with the thought that in spite of this we who are members of orders still live on a modest and simple scale (even though inevitably our standard of living too has been raised together with the general standards prevailing outside the orders). This may be true but it cannot be denied that because of this development, however inevitable it may be, the character of religious poverty as bearing witness has to a very notable extent been deprived of its clarity and its power to convince. With regard to the juridical aspects of our religious poverty, which lay down that all property shall be communal property, this is regarded as a measure which is serviceable from the point of view of technical organisation for a common way of life and for an organisation the members of which have set themselves a common goal (the more so since they are committed to celibacy, and therefore from this point of view alone are destined to live in a restricted community of this kind). But this life in which property is held in common is not thought of as that poverty which is designated as such by the gospel, and which, in virtue of the fact that it involves committing oneself to insecurity and defencelessness, is estimated as an act of faith and as a palpable attestation to faith. It is still conceded that the lives led by one or two individuals among us do have this significance, namely in those cases in which the impression is very clearly borne in upon the onlooker that this individual in particular would be 'earning' far more if he had not become a member of an order. But in general we are not credited with such capacities at all and, moreover, in the majority of cases, it simply is not the case that we would 'earn' far more in the world.

And so the fact remains. Religious poverty as it is still practised now has very little to do with any kind of insecurity (voluntarily undertaken) in one's earthly life beyond that insecurity to which all men are subject. And, furthermore, by reason of the alteration in the nature of work in industrial societies it can have very little to do with insecurity in this sense. And for these reasons religious poverty has forfeited much of its character as witness, which it is radically necessary that it should have if it is to retain its religious and ecclesiastical significance. The insecurity of life which arose from poverty as practised in earlier times has, from the economic aspect, given way to a special kind of security which belongs to life in religious houses, and this security becomes particularly intensified in those cases in which a member of the order identifies himself with his community and modifies his own personal claims to fit in with the economic possibilities open to his community. If he does this then it is hardly possible to speak any longer in any real sense of an insecurity and lack of safety in one's earthly life arising from poverty. If, and to the extent that, insecurity of this kind is still present in the religious life it arises not from poverty but from the threat which forces hostile to God and the Church represent to the way of life followed by religious and clerics. This may be God's way of providing a substitute for this particular kind of insecurity which the poor for Christ's sake are inspired by faith to take upon themselves. But for all this this new kind of insecurity is precisely not poverty.

3. A further problem to which this new economic situation has given rise is concerned with the technical procedures by which the canonical dependence of the individual upon the permission of his superior with regard to material goods is put into practice. There have already been frequent opportunities for drawing attention to the fact that the merely juridical dependence of the religious upon the permission of his superior in the disposal of material goods cannot, of itself, constitute the essence of evangelical poverty. To suppose that the state of being propertyless in this formal and juridical sense, and the dependence upon superiors arising from this, constitute of themselves alone the whole essence of poverty, would mean the destruction of poverty in the true sense. But abstracting from this, a not inconsiderable difficulty arises, and one which cannot be overlooked, from contemporary economic ideas precisely in their bearing upon this dependence. I would not for one moment maintain that it is impossible in formal and juridical terms to put such a construction and interpretation upon all the deeds and omissions of a religious that each of these deeds and omissions on his part with regard to material goods could count as authorised by the superiors of his order. In other words these deeds and omissions of his would not mean that he had any ultimate control over these goods as over private property. But the question is whether this is of itself enough to guarantee that the religious is actually living a life of 'poverty' thereby, and whether this poverty is fruitful in those religious consequences without which, whatever form it takes, it is meaningless. And at this point a special difficulty arises for the times in which we live.

We are all living in a world of material goods which is extraordinarily rich and extremely complex whether we wish to or not, whether we live on a modest or a grand scale. Now it necessarily follows from this that we are all the time positing and having to posit acts controlling the disposal of material goods. And these acts are extremely numerous, extremely varied in character, and constantly being adapted to meet the new and different situations which arise in the material world. But by very reason of the immense number of, and the great differences between, these acts the idea that they are controlled by the permission and agreement of superiors can, for purely technical reasons very often still be upheld only in a formal and juridical sense with no effective basis in reality (so at least it appears to me). In other words in fact, even if not in a formal or juridical sense, the religious of today, whether he admits it or not, has a not inconsiderable range of material goods at his disposal, which for all practical purposes he controls in exactly the same way as if they were his own private property. It may perhaps be rejoined that this has always and inevitably been the case because already even in ancient times the disposal of the handkerchief in the pocket of a religious was provided for and managed in exactly the same way as if the handkerchief belonged to a private individual, and because even in those earlier times it had already become more a joke than a legal fiction which had any effect when a nun spoke of her false teeth as 'our' teeth instead of 'my' teeth. This may all be very true. But the important point is this: the effect of modern economic developments and of the abundance of goods with which everybody today surrounds themselves and concerns themselves as a matter of necessity has been to cause a notable increase in the whole sphere of what is for practical purposes, if not in juridical and formal terms, one's private property to dispose of as one pleases. Thus a problem does exist with regard to how the economic dependence of the religious upon the assent of his superior can be put into practical effect in the concrete. It seems to me that if we conceal these difficulties beneath formal and juridical façades consisting of permissions which are mere fictions it becomes meaningless and does not promote, but rather derogates from poverty in the true sense. For if we do this then there is a very great danger that the acts by which we dispose of material goods are likewise hidden under the same legal fictions, whereas in reality these acts must absolutely be subjected to the yoke of a genuine dependence if religious poverty is to remain poverty in any real and effective sense at all. If we maintain legal fictions of this kind then we are forcing the modern religious to busy himself with a whole host of superfluities of a bureaucratic kind, for which there will be very little understanding on the part of those who have to work hard.

This is not the place to undertake the task of developing these considerations further in the direction of practical proposals. Here we shall confine ourselves to asking whether the resources actually used, which for all practical purposes already have a permanent value of their own, should not in reality (if not in terms of formal canon law as well) proceed a stage further and come to be openly regarded as goods that are to be treated of as the individual's private property. The reason is that the opposite attitude is merely formal and legalistic bureaucracy, and so far from promoting frugality in one's way of life – a frugality based upon one's personal decision, and for which one makes oneself personally responsible – actually contributes to the opposite effect, and leads again and again to the temptation of believing that poverty is preserved in other acts of disposing of goods as well, because such acts are covered by a show of legality.

4. Attention must likewise be drawn to a further change which has to be made in the concrete mode of applying the ideal of poverty, a change which is forced upon us by the manner in which modern economy has been developed. The quantity of those goods which are *productive* (taking the term 'productive' here in its broadest sense) has also undergone an extraordinary increase in the life of the individual religious. Naturally there have always been such goods from the first, goods which are designed not simply to be consumed for the maintenance of life in the biological sense, and which are agreed not to be means of increasing one's enjoyment either, but are rather 'instruments of work', the tools necessary for the active pursuit of those aims which an individual religious or an order set themselves. Francis himself must already have realised that even his poor men had need of books, breviaries and churches. But today the quantity of such goods has grown quite immeasurably – almost, one might say to an extent which alters their whole nature. If we abstract from the actual basic essentials the typical instance of a material good in former ages was the consumer good. In order to understand this we have only to recall the controversy about whether it was legitimate to take interest, a controversy stretching over a thousand years. Today the typical instance of a material good is neither the basic essentials of life nor the consumer good, but the machine, the instrument of work, the good that is productive. As a result, therefore, and on the basis of this, the concept of the 'rich' in earlier times immediately evokes the idea of a man who is in possession of great resources for his own enjoyment, one who can live as a 'reveller' (and because he is in possession of the necessities of

life which another needs is also in this sense powerful). But the effect of this new concept of the typical material good is that the concept of the rich man has also changed. He is no longer so much the man who has great resources for his own enjoyment (firstly these are, in fact, extremely limited for all men simply from the biological point of view, and secondly in the economy of the modern mass-consumer society the 'poor man' has in this respect no longer so immeasurably less possibilities of enjoyment than the rich as was the case in earlier times), but rather the man who can dispose of a whole quantity of instruments of work, of productive goods, and in *this* sense possessive power is of a quite different kind from the power of former times. At the same time, however, it must admittedly be borne in mind that there are many goods which can serve both as instruments of work *and* as means of enjoyment (taking both in the broadest sense). A radio receiver can serve both purposes. A further point to be borne in mind is that the fitness of the means for a specific end within a society depends on the circumstances of that society considered as a whole. In the time of Jesus an ass was a useful means of transport. Today it is so no longer.

On the basis of these observations a fresh problem now arises with regard to the ideal of religious poverty and the mode in which it should be practised. When an order and a religious pursue specific spiritual, apostolic, etc., ends they have today to avail themselves of a far greater number of instruments of work and productive goods than in former times. A serviceable library such as can provide a starting-point for research costs at least ten times as much in the purchase of books as any comparable library in the Middle Ages. And if we should wish to travel in pursuit of such aims we have to go by express train or aeroplane. We use clocks, dictaphones, photocopying equipment, we have electric shavers (because otherwise we would lose too much precious time). It is taken for granted that we have a typewriter and a telephone. Many will actually declare (and they may actually be right in this) that a television set, and not merely a radio receiver, is part of the equipment which is necessary or useful for their work. In the missions a private plane may even be regarded as necessary. Because of the lack of labour forces and for other reasons an immense quantity of technical equipment is already available in every modern religious house. Lifts, oil-heating, hot and cold water laid on, electric stoves, etc. We may go on explaining that in spite of all this everything belongs not to the individual but to the order, and so that poverty is preserved. This is not true. An order that is really rich cannot have any really poor members. But is an order not rich in the modern sense when its members can and do have at their disposal so significant a quantity of equipment of this kind?

Of course it might be said (and there may even be a certain consolation in this) that the amount of such goods in comparison with the amount of productive goods held by other people in the present age is very modest indeed, in other words that today, too, in relation to the rest of society an order is still poor (indeed that from this aspect – in accordance with what was said in subsection I – the orders have actually become poorer). It might be said that this increase in the number of instruments of work employed brings about effects that are absolutely ascetical, in that they compel the tempo of work (at least for those who are conscientious) to be greatly increased, and thereby force the order too to subject itself to the ascesis of modern work to a point where all the dangers entailed in a manager's position are present in it too, because today the individual religious is stretched to his limits by his work to a notably greater extent than in earlier and more comfortable ages. Perhaps this too, is something that God has arranged to compensate for the loss of poverty. But in this type of penance too, which consists in being worn out by sheer work, the factor precisely of poverty plays no part.

In any case the great majority of such instruments of work always represents, in the eyes of those outside the order, a possibility for greater enjoyment, and can, indeed, very quickly come to be used for such a purpose. And therefore this increase in the amount of productive goods in the life of orders in the present day, however unavoidable it may be, is liable, at least according to the general view of those outside the order, to make them appear not poor but rather rich. For practical purposes, therefore, this derogates from the function of representing the Church which belongs to the essence of religious poverty. A further factor is the influence of this state of affairs upon the mentality of the individual religious himself. He regards goods exactly as other men regard them at the present day, not so much, and in the first instance, as goods to be enjoyed; he does not want to have goods in order to lead a life of ease and to enjoy them (any more than the modern managing director does this, who, in spite of his great 'private resources' has such a burden put upon him, and such difficulties to cope with that a smaller man would be quite incapable of being a managing director because this would mean too much work and responsibility for him). The modern religious (who genuinely is such) also belongs to the modern type of 'man of ambition' who wants to increase the output of his work at an ever-increasing rate, and therefore wants to have an every-increasing amount of goods at his disposal to serve as instruments for his work. On this basis, however, it is far from easy for him to find any connection with poverty within himself at all, at least such that what he means by poverty can be brought under the heading of 'poverty' as it is normally understood. He is subject to one of the severest forms of asceticism (the 'this-worldly' form), and this demands of him that he shall organise down to the last detail the use he makes of his time, his powers and his work. All this he understands. He does not want to 'take it easy'. On the basis of this will to work and to achieve he will absolutely expose himself to a very considerable degree of ascesis at the hands of those who use what he produces, a degree which is, perhaps, significantly greater (measured by the relative standard of the possibilities open to him at the particular time) than that practised by the orders in earlier ages, when the religious could, and in fact had to spend much time in conversations, slow journeys, setting aside time to care for his daily needs, when life was maintained by the most primitive means by the use of wine, etc. He will say that if that is what poverty means then he has the greatest sympathy with poverty. But not if poverty means a *petit-bourgeois* mode of living and working in the style of the eighteenth century, and not if it makes it seem as an ideal that a religious house, even today, should as far as possible be made to appear in its interior dispositions to have the same style as houses of a hundred years ago, when such houses were certainly not built by le Corbusier, the architect of the new study-house of the Dominicans in France. The question, therefore, is this: According to the meaning of the ideals of the religious life, is one still poor if, while maintaining a strict ascesis in terms of consumption or enjoyment, one is unembarrassedly 'rich' in all that can fittingly be demanded for the other aims of the order and of the individual religious? Or must it be the case that the amount of instruments of work employed must be on a modest scale even if this imposes a certain restriction on the effectiveness of the work achieved, and must be so arranged that these instruments of work in themselves can also be brought under the concept of poverty? Should we hold this latter view in spite of the fact that it is far from being generally agreed that an order can, or should pursue a legitimate aim with *all* means which are not actually illegitimate in themselves? Is this question a genuine question? Can any unambiguous theory be found to solve it? Is it not solved in that compromise which life entails in the concrete, and which can never wholly be resolved by any theory? At all events we must certainly be more precise and more honest in viewing from this aspect the practical problems and concrete cases which arise in the practice of religious poverty in the present day.

5. Again even at the peril of repeating much of what has already been said in a different form we must put the question explicitly: Can poverty in the form which it inevitably assumes in the present day, and under the economic circumstances which prevail at present, still have that meaning and those religious effects which it had originally, and which constitute the basis upon which its existence is justified? Or, to formulate it in another way, does present-day poverty still possess that formative power for religion which it once had? We have already pointed out certain aspects which do not make it easy for us to answer this question in the affirmative. Poverty used to mean exposing oneself to a certain elemental insecurity in one's existence. Today it affects fewer areas of our lives in this way, and the depths of the insecurity involved have been diminished. Again this insecurity, undertaken for the sake of religion, raised men to the very heights of faith, making them cleave to the eternal goods of grace and entailing an existential self-commitment in hope and trust to God himself. Today in practice (if not juridically speaking as well), a significantly greater area of life is open for the individual to dispose of as he will and as he thinks necessary. And this is in contrast with earlier ages, and once more makes the religious of today a figure far more similar to the man of the world who possesses private property of his own, the more so since the freedom of the man of the world to dispose of his goods as he wills has become notably more restricted in comparison with earlier ages by reason of the greater social intermingling of private property with the economy as a whole as guided and controlled by the state. From this point of view too the formative power of poverty for religion must seem to be diminished. The religious cannot now think of himself as much as he did formerly as one of the *anawim* of the New Testament in the sense of the small, the humble, the socially weak, with all the religious effects which such an experience was able to have earlier. We have already seen that from the attitude to material goods which prevails today modern man finds if difficult to recognise any meaning in poverty considered as a means of obtaining certain preconceived and legitimate ends, if it is to be

anything more than an ascesis in respect of goods consumed. Because in any other kind of poverty he can only see a renunciation of a possibility of attaining to these ends, which are legitimate, and even, under certain circumstances, to be regarded as having a positively religious value, together with all the means necessary for those ends.

There are still further and different considerations which make it appear that the religious effectiveness, and therefore the evangelical meaning also of religious poverty, as able to be practised in the economic circumstances of today, have been lessened and have therefore become questionable. Today for all practical purposes poverty as practised in religious houses no longer really signifies any 'deprivation'. Today too it can indeed demand a not inconsiderable degree of renunciation of enjoyments and similar things, which in other circumstances we could immediately approve of and feel inclined to. But almost all these renunciations are concerned with things which can be renounced *in such a way that* not possessing them does not signify any real deprivation. When, for instance, I *will* not to make a journey round the world by aeroplane the fact that it is impossible for me to reconcile this with poverty does not signify any 'deprivation', any pain, anything which affects the way I like to live. But those deprivations which are worthy of the name, and which in earlier times were still quite often entailed by poverty, and which always and everywhere, independently of what attitude we freely adopt, are felt to be such, no longer exist for practical purposes in religious poverty as practised in the present day. Such are hunger, cold, sickness, which for want of means cannot be warded off, the feeling of being thrust down to the lowest social levels and despised, ill-treatment, and being reduced to begging in the true sense. It might be said that by force of present-day economic conditions our modern practice of religious poverty has become so emancipated from practical living that it is in danger of no longer existing in its original sense at all. What happens again and again in life in human society takes place here too in its own way: the earlier nomenclature and the earlier juridical form is still retained, but underneath them something which is, in reality, quite different comes into being. The question arises whether the present-day practice of poverty in religious orders now amounts to anything more than an ascesis with regard to the consumption and enjoyment of goods, as well as to that practice of holding goods in common which must *inevitably* be maintained wherever a number of individuals live together closely, intimately and on a permanent basis after the manner of a family, if this common life of theirs is to function at all. If we had to concede that the real meaning of poverty, for all practical and effective purposes, did in fact consist in these two elements, then we would have to reconstruct, on the basis of these two elements, the theological and ascetical basis for poverty both in terms of theory and in terms of the concrete mode of poverty too, in a clear and decisive way, and in doing this we would have to renounce many of our ideological ideas upon the subject as out of date. It may indeed be the case that we actually need to embark boldly and unflinchingly upon such an undertaking as this would imply. For it might be said that the ultimate theological essence of evangelical poverty is still preserved even in an ascesis of consumption and enjoyment, though admittedly this is a statement which would need prolonged testing and examination. It might be said that from these two elements in present-day religious poverty (even if no others were present, whereas in reality they are present though less clearly and prominently than formerly) forces could be brought to bear which are religiously constructive and still retain an importance which is absolutely decisive. These would make even this kind of poverty still appear as the basis and rampart of religious life.

6. No ultimate and wholly satisfying answer to this question can be put forward here, but the way in which we answer it depends to some extent upon the answer to another question. This is a radical question which can be stated as follows: Is the mode of life which, for practical purposes, all the orders practise today, with only relatively minor variations, *really* forced upon them by the concrete structure of the economy, or could this mode of life still retain a form such that it constituted a manifest approximation to the old mode of practising poverty without thereby falling into an anachronistic romanticism? In fact there can be no doubt that in very many matters and in many respects we have simply and unmistakably been forced to adopt a different mode of practising poverty than that which formerly prevailed. And all attempts to break away from this compulsion, however ideal the motivations might be (or however reactionary they in fact are) that lie behind such attempts, would simply be acts of material disobedience against God and the dispositions he has ordained when he imposed the particular situation upon man by sheer force of the changes which have taken place in history. If a Capuchin does not enter the city barefoot today, then he is in no sense being untrue to his ideal of poverty. For his forebears did not go barefoot into the cities

(and this means that even if he did do this today he would not be doing what his forebears did). Nor can he feel obliged by the ideal of his order merely to wander in poverty through the plains of Umbria in the footprints of the Poor Man of Assisi. Nevertheless the question can be raised of whether we members of religious orders, as a result of these changes which are so clearly necessary, have not taken much into our mode of life and mode of practising poverty which has no place there, and which renders our mode of poverty of today *unjustifiably* remote from the ancient mode. Have we not done this without reason and without drawing the necessary distinctions correctly? Have we perhaps allowed ourselves to be influenced by a reactionary traditionalism on the one hand, and an imprudent eagerness to fall in with the spirit and mode lif life of our times on the other (this spirit is always a spectre too), and so neglected to reconstruct our mode of poverty in a manner that is really creative? And is not the result of this that our practice of poverty too often appears as a makeshift and indefensible compromise between the modern mode of living as practised by 'Mr Everyman' and the ancient and traditional monastic forms of life? The fact that something of this kind has in fact taken place *in some degree* among us religious will only be contested by those who suppose that the mentality of the average religious and the average religious house is totally immune to the general blindness, sinfulness and state of 'thrown-downness' in the world. But the question remains *how great* the degree is of this false and uncreative compromise among us. And the further question is that of whether overcoming these deviations in the contemporary mode of poverty would not lead precisely to the development in clear and manifest terms of an ascesis with regard to goods to be consumed or enjoyed and the institutionalisation of this in terms of modern community life. These are questions which we cannot spend any further time in answering at this point. We cannot do this for the very reason that they would require a detailed analysis of the concrete forms assumed in the mode of poverty envisaged which were adopted in each individual order to answer its own particular requirements.

7. Finally our problem must be viewed from yet another angle, that namely of the social and ecclesiastical function of poverty in the Church, and of the Church herself for the world, which, as we have explained, pertains to the very essence of religious poverty. This too, by reason of the modern structure of the economy, has been brought into a unique state of crisis. Voluntary poverty as lived in a clear and exemplary manner in

the Church carried a message and witness for the man of earlier ages who was poor by force of circumstances that there are higher goods than those which we merely consume, that to strive for the possession of these latter must not constitute the true or ultimate aim of human existence, that even he who is poor in the economic sense can make precisely this situation which is imposed upon him, with all the dangers, insecurities, humiliations, etc., which it entails, into a concrete form for expressing his faith in the God of grace that comes from above and of eternal life. The message of voluntary poverty, therefore, is that if rich men become poor of their own free will, when they really do not need eternal life as a palliative for the pains and miseries of human existence, then eternal life is not simply the opium that is offered to the poor. It is a self-evident fact that the function of holding up an example in a world which, economically speaking, was poor in consumer goods and materials, had a greater and more universal range of application than it has in a world which, economically speaking, is rich in these goods and developed intensively in terms of material production. The task of giving a religious meaning to *in*voluntary poverty by providing an example of *voluntary* poverty is more relevant in a society of those who are poor in material goods than it is in one which is rich in them. If, apart from a very small upper class, the *great majority* of men is really poor and deprived, then voluntary poverty acquires the function of providing an example which is of *universal* application to the religion of all. Now if today society is inevitably pluralistic in character, and if for this reason those who are still really poor and deprived constitute only a small group in this society, then it becomes inevitable that poverty no longer has the same *universal* function to perform of bearing witness as in former ages. The Church has to hold up quite different examples in her preaching and life to cater for other groups in the society. The experience of radical contingency is one which is always present in human life. In earlier times this experience took the form precisely of a threat to life through poverty and the hunger arising from it. Today this same sense of radical contingency manifests itself in areas of human life which are 'existentially' other than those affected precisely by material deprivations, and it is these other areas which now have to be interpreted by the Church in a religious sense and in terms of her faith. A question which might be put forward as extremely urgent, therefore, is this: With regard to the radical contingency proper to man and the fact that he is thrown upon God, what is it that really

makes this present in the contemporary industrial society of the masses
in this world that is rich in consumer goods, and in the planned economy
of our time? Man as he exists today can no longer experience with the
same directness and the same urgency as formerly that he has to ask God
for a piece of bread. Of course man in himself is constantly in a state of
that 'need' which teaches him to pray. But in the concrete this state of
existential need has nevertheless a history of its own and undergoes
changes. And for this reason, at the present at least, the old mode of
poverty is no longer capable of providing an all-comprehending example
of the religious meaning to be found in existence for all with such unambiguous clarity as formerly. For this reason religious poverty, considered
as the palpable expression of this significance to be found in human existence, has inevitably ceased to have the function which it had in earlier
times of providing *the* universal example of religion for society as a whole.
For the same reason too it is no longer capable of providing this in the
same degree as formerly because those poor who are still with us even
today are presumably for the most part far poorer than the members of
orders, and in other words for them the orders as a whole are quite
incapable of providing an example of the meaning to be found in poverty
precisely as it applies to *them* (perhaps here we should abstract from the
instances of the Little Brothers of Jesus of P. Charles de Foucauld and
new confraternities of a similar kind). Does this imply that religious
poverty as practised today has – albeit inevitably – simply lost its function
of providing an example of religion in the Church, and so too of bearing
witness to the faith before the world? This cannot be, seeing that in other
respects poverty is an essential characteristic of religious life, and this in
turn sustains an essential function in the permanent life of the Church.
But even if we concede the fact that this function of religious poverty as
providing an example still persists even today, in what *precisely* can this
consist? Here again, in answering this question we find ourselves compelled to invoke the key concept of an ascesis in respect of the consumption and enjoyment of goods. It might be said that the high level of
consumption enjoyed by the masses today constitutes a threat to the
Church, because she has not yet succeeded to a sufficient extent in con-
structing examples showing how this consumption can be made to
conform to the principles of human ethics and morality. (The most we
can say on this point to console ourselves is that the trend to an ever-
increasing rate of consumption also at the same time, and in the long run

constitutes a far more decisive threat still to communism.) Here religious poverty might discover a new function which is (in its essence) at the same time an old one: that namely of living out an ascesis in respect of consumer goods which is both comprehensible and convincing;[1] not, in the first instance, in the sense that the members of religious orders represent in some degree the finger of the Church raised in admonition as though she were saying 'You must not proceed with a constantly rising standard of living, there is something still higher than this'. Religious poverty has this function, rather, in that the orders, through what we call poverty, provide an example to modern man of that consumer ascesis which shows itself to be the only possible genuine and effective 'hygiene of need' which exists, and which cannot be replaced either by merely 'this-worldly' social techniques (the manipulation of needs on the part of the community and the powers it has at its disposal to enforce its ideas) nor by merely functional but meaningless techniques of psychology. Consumer ascesis exists simply in virtue of the fact that man straightforwardly and manifestly renounces a thousand possibilities of consuming goods (even if this is the outcome of a policy that has been planned and institutionalised precisely in religious poverty) because he has a genuine and living relationship with God, Spirit, person and love, and does not have to conceal and suppress those experiences of his own radical contingency which are always with him, by the narcotics of enjoyment and dissipation in forms which become ever more intense and more refined.

Of course this mode of poverty would have to be developed in such a way that it became noticeable and convincing at the same time. If we are to let our works shine before men (although we keep our hearts hidden in the intimacy of our relationship with God), then there is nothing to prevent us also from devising ways to ensure that our consumer ascesis really makes a strong and living impact and is in the best sense of the term radical (though this does not mean renewing and reviving the mode of life followed in earlier ages). We must also ensure that this consumer ascesis of ours is lived out as such as an example to men, and shown to be a source of invigoration and happiness for the tasks which men have to perform in their lives in this world. The members of religious orders would have to be characterised by a sort of non-conformity with regard

---

[1] On the problems of consumption and on 'consumer ascesis' cf. the observations of K. Lehmann in *Handbuch der Pastoraltheologie* II/2 (Freiburg 1966), pp. 130 ff.; 175 ff. (cf. also above pp. 27 ff.).

to those forms of consumption which are typical for modern times, with their techniques of artificially stimulating needs, controlling and manipulating the processes of consumption and making it desirable to indulge in consumption in order to demonstrate one's position. They do this by deliberately laying emphasis on the factor of social position instead of making consumption serve to satisfy any genuine need. (Even a provincial might believe that he owed it to his position to have a Mercedes 300.) But in all these observations one point on which we must be clear is that the members of religious orders are still far from having worked out any concrete example of how such consumer ascesis ought to be practised as a form (though not the only one) of the religious poverty to which we are committed. The mere fact of developing a few abstract ideas of the kind which have just been presented here is not enough. We are still far from having achieved a concrete and formative example for this modern way of living which we call consumer ascesis. Abstract ideas, general principles can be very true and very important. But they are no substitute for concrete example, which is the outcome of a creativity that is applied in practice. To suppose that abstract principles could be a substitute for concrete example in this way would be just as absurd as to imagine that the principles of pedagogy could be a substitute for the personality of a genuine teacher, or to suppose that this personality itself is simply the sum total of these abstract principles. And even when we have worked out in this creative way a concrete example of a modern man whose life is governed by consumer ascesis, who is able freely to abstain from much which he might do physically and technically, still even then we have not advanced so very much further. We still remain, so it appears, at the stage of an uncreative compromise between the old mode of poverty and the new modern mode of living, for even the orders are invaded by the unbridled lust for consumption, while those in charge of the orders are seeking in a negative and timid way to check and restrain developments of this kind.

8. The considerations which are still to follow are proposed for discussion in all modesty and simply with a view to stirring up the spirit which will lead us to seek for a new and concrete mode of applying the ideal of poverty in this way. We live in the age of the masses, and therefore in the age of organisations and of great mass groupings as well. Even the Church and the orders will appear, and will actually come to be such in the eyes of modern man because even they have become, in point of

actual numbers, extremely large and so subject to the sociological laws applying to all such major groupings in society. In its bearing upon what we have to say here this has a two-fold significance. Humanly and morally speaking the impression which the Church and the orders as a whole make upon modern man is one that is extremely profane, one that has been 'demythologised'. His estimate of them is almost the same as his estimate of the national health, the unions, the state institutions. They are inevitable, they are heartless, they are hard, egoistical, groupings of men combined for a common interest. The morality of them is extremely problematical. They have very little influence upon him so far as his personal way of living is concerned. Precisely because they take such great pains to penetrate right to the innermost recesses of his private life with their attempts at regulation and standardisation, they have to be regarded with caution and mistrust.

And in fact the greater such mass organisations become the more difficult it becomes for them to succeed in bringing something new and creative into being in, with and in the midst of the inexpressible complexity of the institutional factors, the responsibilities which cannot be pinned down, the effects of bureaucracy (which are inevitable for governing and controlling any major grouping in society). I suppose that all religious confraternities which have any antiquity are proud of the fact that they have not had any need of any movements of reform and fresh formations of a reformist character such as were customary and traditional in the middle ages and at the beginning of the new age, amongst other things precisely with regard to the way in which the ideal of poverty was applied. The question can be raised whether this pride is really justified, or whether the fact to which we point with such satisfaction is not rather an indication of the fact that in this age of mass organisation emphasis has been laid upon the element of the uncreatively traditional in all our major groupings in society to such an extent that it must seem that every attempt at altering the mode of living in religious orders in general and the mode of poverty in particular to any extent can only achieve its object by the founding of fresh communities. It has to be admitted that both observations have some truth in them, and the result of this for our enquiry into poverty in this present age as practised in the religious orders may be stated as follows: In working out a mode of poverty that will be convincing to outsiders as well, the individual and the small units are the more important and have more chances of succeeding than the major religious communities as such. This is not to say that these individuals and minor units could only exist and develop their own mode of poverty *outside* the groupings of the major orders. But it certainly is our opinion that the mode of poverty practised in these major communities of religious is liable to give an impression of ossification, or else is weakened by compromises with the new age which are regrettable. The result of this is that it becomes inevitable that the continual creative force present in any genuine idea of evangelical poverty creates fresh forms outside the communities of the traditional orders, since these orders fail to give the individual and the smaller unit scope and opportunity to exercise their creativity in working out a new mode of poverty without straightway attempting to bring everything in these developments under their own authority by applying the rule of their order to them. The question, therefore, is this: could not the orders, without prejudice to the discipline of the common life, give more scope for such creative attempts at developing a mode of poverty suitable to modern times? If the appeal of religious poverty is *effectively* to retain its force is it not absolutely necessary for different modes of poverty to be developed within one and the same religious congregation or order? When we reflect that Ignatius of Loyola actually provided for variation of this kind as a matter of firm and permanent institution in his order (even if in practice not many survivals of this remain today) then we cannot reject a question of this kind from the outset as meaningless. For instance ought not poverty as practised in a modern parish house belonging to an order, with its small family-size unit of religious, to have another form from, and should not its appeal radiate out to different sectors of the population from the poverty of a major study house of religious, which is, and necessarily must be, a little like a barracks of God's love, and therefore should also be different in its mode of poverty, and appeal to a different type of people? Ought we not to have a clearer idea of how the popular missioner, the student chaplain, the missionary to pagan peoples should live out and exemplify religious poverty, each in his own way? When, for instance, we remember the fact that the way of life in the religious orders today is followed more or less in the same manner in Europe as it is in Asia, and that even today it does not for one moment make a convincing impression of asceticism on the Indian, even when, by European standards, it is thoroughly 'poor', then perhaps it becomes clear that these questions cannot simply be rejected with the demand that each order shall require all of its members to follow a single uniform way of life. But it also becomes clear that such questions cannot be solved straightway and right from the very outset by the order making laws to cover them. Rather the individual members and the small units should be encouraged to make attempts of this kind even within a religious community that is already in existence.

9. In concluding at this point, the impression must not be given that we are doing so in the conviction that we have now dealt with all essential questions regarding religious poverty. On the contrary some of these questions have not so much as been mentioned. To provide a comprehensive treatment of this kind we would have, for instance, to reflect in greater detail upon the fact (to name at least one point beyond what has been mentioned here) that the division of labour in the modern economy also has its effects upon religious poverty. Life in the religious orders, too, inevitably falls under the influence of this economic system, which is based upon a highly sophisticated division of labour, and one which in fact even extends to the sphere of spiritual labours properly so called. As late as the eighteenth century any intelligent member of an apostolic order was in a position to understand more or less every enterprise included in the activities and works performed by his order (so that, for instance, a superior was *ipso facto* able to act as a 'specialist' in each department, and as such able to judge the various kinds of work in which his subjects were engaged). Today this is no longer the case. In none of the active orders is there any one individual who really understands *all* the 'special avocations' which are included in the work of his order: preacher, professor, financial expert, youth chaplain, etc. – each of these has become a separate calling in its own right, so that each individual can have a real grasp only of one of these callings. The consequences of this not only affect the practical application of leadership and obedience in a religious community, but also have a bearing on poverty. The differences in these particular callings, and arising concomitantly with them, affect not only the education, way of life and mode of fitting in with society in the world as a whole, but also the nature, quantity and value of the instruments of work which are the necessary prior conditions for each of the individual callings to be pursued in an order. These differences in the instruments of work (we might take them in the broadest sense so as to include also the special journeys which scholars have to make for their researches, the need for the specialist to associate himself with specific groups in the secular community, expensive instruments and especially libraries) again have further

effects bearing upon the way of life and mode of poverty practised by individuals. From this point of view too it is impossible in practice altogether to prevent different ways of living and working from developing, even within one and the same order. These still persist even if we look realistically, and to some extent with the sharpened perceptions of the sociologist, at life in religious communities. But not much thought has been given to these variations. If we still persist in trying to formulate legalistic rules in our attempt to overcome them then we have not yet really and whole-heartedly come to grips with the reality itself, and the difficulties which it entails. From this point of view also there would still be much to consider on this question of religious poverty, and there are other questions still, especially those more concerned with the sphere of moral theology, which have not been treated of: questions concerning the nature of the vow in general and of the vow of poverty in particular. On the other hand these questions, which pertain in the narrower sense to moral theology, are so well known that for our present purposes we can take the answer to them as read.

PART THREE

The Veneration of the Sacred Heart

I I

THE THEOLOGICAL MEANING OF THE VENERATION OF THE SACRED HEART

WHEN a dogmatic theologian is called upon to speak of the veneration of the Sacred Heart from the point of view of his particular discipline he can, in a certain sense, make it easier for himself to do so simply by referring to Pius XII's great encyclical, *Haurietis Aquas*, of 15th May 1956. This contains a particularly comprehensive treatment of the subject, one that goes beyond those of Leo XIII and Pius XI, and which includes everything connected with this particular devotion. But precisely for this reason the converse is also true: the very fact that there can hardly be anything left to add to this treatise, which comes from the hand of the supreme teacher of the Church, and the further fact that the actual text requires to be studied again and again in order to grasp the full depths of the doctrine it contains – these two facts together justify us in presenting a few ideas at this point which are intended neither as a summary of the treatise itself, nor yet as a supplement to it, but rather, unencumbered by any such ambitious aims, simply offer a few observations of an extremely subjective and peripheral kind bearing upon this subject.

Man is not God, but rather stands in a relationship to God in his uniqueness. Two points follow immediately from this: first, neither in his being nor in his thinking and loving can he be all in one or have all in one (otherwise he would be God); second, while the mode of his being and the mode in which he achieves the due fulness of his existence is necessarily complex he cannot withhold himself from constantly striving anew to achieve anunity in the midst of this complexity, and from actually attaining to the unity for which he strives (for otherwise he would not be the spiritual being who stands in a special relationship to God in his uniqueness). Because of this his movement outwards from himself into reality is always and necessarily a movement from unity into multiplicity, and this applies to his religion too. His 'credo' comprises a series of articles. The expression of his worship in the liturgy assumes manifold forms. An extreme diversity is to be observed alike in the nature of his religious acts and in the objects to which they are directed. He must love God and man, direct his spirit outwards into a whole range of activities, and at the same time retain his interior life, returning to the innermost centre of his being, transformed as it is by grace, where God and he are alone together. Thus his spirit is necessarily subject to a plurality of acts by the very fact that it has to proceed outwards into the multiplicity of beings, and in this plurality has to seek for the unity of all things. It is this law of his being that sets him in the dimension of time and history (and it is this historical dimension in turn which allows scope for this interplay of many factors to be maintained in his life). What it implies for him is a 'richly variegated' adventure in the life of his mind and spirit, and at the same time, too, that ever-nagging pain which arises from never really quite reaching the point at which he has all in one and one in all. This truth, so simple as it is, yet exercising so overriding an influence upon man in all his dimensions, must be borne in mind if we are to grasp the meaning of the veneration of the Sacred Heart in its central significance and its ultimate implications.

Jesus Christ is the mediator. He is that unity in which God, who in his simplicity is all in one, has assumed the multiplicity of reality and its 'thirst for unity'. He did this when he assumed creaturehood (which is never one in all) and assumed it, moreover, in the mode of a spiritual being (which craves for unity). In assuming it he made it his own reality, which remains eternally his own (even in its multiplicity), and yet it is precisely in virtue of this fact that this reality of creaturehood which he has assumed, while still retaining its multiplicity, is redeemed, set free for and drawn abidingly into the indivisible unity of God (this unity, in spite of having taken this creaturely multiplicity into itself still remaining pure and unalloyed). The fact that the creature is not excluded right from the outset from unity as that which is meaningless is due to the prior fact that he *is*, he the incarnate Word of the Father, in whom the Father utters himself totally and indivisibly. Again it is because he *is* in this sense that this multiplicity does not signify something from which man can only flee. God himself has in fact been drawn into the diaspora which the creaturely mode of being represents. Because of this man does not need to lose him when he decides not to depart from this creaturely level, provided only that he takes this situation in which being is diffused and manifold for what it really is, namely as a situation in which this being has, in a true sense, been made one in (though not made one *with*) the incarnate Word of God. Thus the only way in which man can have all in one (he can only have this in the manner that befits the creature) is for him to have him who is both at once: all (the many) and one (the divine). The veneration of the Sacred Heart is intended to be the ultimate act of adoration, in which we adjure the unique and all-comprehending upholder of that reality and that unity that underlies the multiplicity in our religious life. It follows from this that he who has found Jesus Christ is *ipso facto* a venerator of the Sacred Heart in this sense. This is true even though he may not realise it, even though he may not call the Word 'heart'. Only he who understands this can, in all sincerity and truth, overcome the dilemma that either the ancients were not good Christians (on the grounds that they did not – explicitly – venerate the Sacred Heart) *or* the veneration of the Sacred Heart cannot be anything essential to Christianity (since in fact it has not existed right from the beginning of Christianity).

Now, however, this relationship with Jesus Christ has itself once more been subjected to the transforming effects of history. As it develops a whole range of different aspects come to be expressed. It has a history of its own, which advances irresistibly and cannot be reversed (however true it may be at the same time that it is a law of this process of historical development as such that it constantly returns afresh to the origins and sources whence it takes its rise). And for this reason the relationship with Jesus Christ as the unifying medium is itself made subject to the law of inevitable multiplicity. We call him by many names and praise him with many tongues. As the centuries unfold he grows in the spirit and heart of each of us (as in the spirit and heart of the Church herself). He must so grow. And if he grows, in this sense, then so far as the Church herself, her devotions and her theology, are concerned, it is quite inevitable that he should become, once more, in his own person, a vast cosmos of reality and truth, immeasurable and mysterious. And then what is left for the man who simply and humbly accepts his own limitations as a creature, the limitations entailed by the fact that he is in essence complex, and exists in the dimension of history? No other course whatever is still left open to him than to seek once more, on behalf of his own spirit and heart, on behalf of his whole Christian being, for a word to conjure up that unity, a kind of sacred epitomising formula such as will make it possible for him (at least in the here and now) to grasp as a unity that which has been presented to him piecemeal in the history of the Church, her devotion and her theology as the immeasurable fulness of the reality of Christ.

Such key-words do exist, with their power to adjure to epitomise and to unify. In them, in some sense (precisely insofar as this is possible for the creature, which as such can never be capable of initiating any act that is not basically complex and multiple) it has been found possible to gather up the all in the one and 'interiorise' it. Such key-words, present in the devotional life of the Church and in theology, can be modified. Any one of them, from being a single unifying key-word, which conjures up everything at one blow, can be broken down into a word signifying some particular aspect of the original whole. And it can never be said of any one word (at least without thereby falling into the pride of supposing that we can transcend our historical limitations) that it remains for all eternity a key-word with this special kind of epitomising power (probably *Logos* was once a word of this kind for John himself, in which, in a certain sense, his whole theology was 'epitomised'. Today, however, it has become precisely one key-word in theology among many others; other such words, which may once have had this force, are 'sophia', 'gnosis', 'Son of Man', 'Spirit' as applied to Christ). But woe betide that age which no longer possesses any word imbued with a quasi-magical force of this kind to epitomise all in one! Woe betide that age which no longer has any word which can convey to it the unity which has been achieved in the all through the effects of atonement upon it! In its thoughts and aspirations that age is deformed, confused and divided. Its message (however true it may remain) becomes a discordant babel, because its voices are directed outwards in all directions at once, and are devoid of any unity to bring them into harmony. Now it might be suggested that the words 'God' and 'Jesus Christ' do in fact constitute words precisely of this kind. And indeed, if we view them in the absolute, abstracting from the concrete historical circumstances in which they have been used and developed, and concentrating exclusively upon their essential content, it would be correct to say that precisely in themselves they could be words of this kind. But this would be precisely to overlook the concrete historical situation in which both we and these words (which we here take as representative examples) are placed. Viewed in the light of this they could never be the sort of words that epitomise the content of our faith, our devotion and our theology in all their multiplicity precisely because they themselves belong to the materials which have to be summed up in this way. For the first needs to be filled out with content and the second is so full of meanings and implications which are disunited and unco-ordinated among themselves that it needs to be unified.

Now let us ask ourselves whether there is anywhere in the contemporary Church at all where we can find such a key word as we have been describing, one that is capable of epitomising the fulness of our religion in this way (from what has been said it will be realised that we cannot simply 'discover' it on the grounds that there may be many such words which, in themselves, are capable of this. For this in turn precisely does not imply that we can choose any one we wish, seeing that the lot assigned to us humans in particular is characterised precisely by the factors of the historical, the contingent and the inescapable). The word we seek, then, is one which is truly evocative, and rouses a response in us. At the same time we must be able at least to guess of this word (even before we have used it enough to realise its full richness and depths) that its epitomising force is such as can penetrate to the very centre of our own being. And it is difficult to imagine that we shall be able to find any other word which has this evocative and epitomising force within it except the word 'heart'. Or can anyone suggest another such? Is there anyone who can say, 'only bend your ears in this direction. Here another word has been resounding all along, with its scope and unifying power. Is it not simply that you have hitherto failed to hear it?' The word we are seeking must, of course, be one which names Christ himself as the unifier. For it is in him alone that God is near (and the word of God really achieves a Christian tone and one that comes to our help in our state of elemental need). But it cannot be one that simply expresses this same Christ by means of a proper name. For if the word we seek had no further force beyond this, then, for the majority of the members of the Church in this age in which we live (for our present purposes we need not concern ourselves with other ages, nor do we need to maintain that what applies to the majority applies in an apodictic and absolute sense to all) this word itself would need some kind of unifying medium to gather up the whole complex range of distinct meanings which have come to be adduced from this word independently of one another in the course of the history of Christianity. Where then is another word, apart from this word, the 'Sacred Heart', which is capable of designating the Lord as him who brings the one and the all into unity, and which itself in turn unifies and brings into man's interior soul, the fulness of him whom it designates in this sense? There is no other such word. No other word has ever been uttered with this force, except the word 'Sacred Heart'. But this word has been uttered in the prayers of the faithful, sometimes whispered and sometimes cried out on the roof-tops (sometimes, alas, in a way that is certainly indiscreet to the point of being in terrible bad taste! But the love which is offered up in this is not such as can easily be measured by the standards of good taste and discretion), and the Church has taken this word up. She has stated that she herself knows no other word with this particular force. We might argue that this word is only one among many possible alternatives, and that tomorrow another word (educed from the fulness that is in Christ) will come to the fore, one that speaks to our hearts with a message of 'all-in-one', and at the same time, having summed up the fulness that is in Christ in this way, causes it to open up, once more, into its richness and multiplicity. Again, it might be argued that in the promulgations issued by the Church in this present day concerning the veneration of the Sacred Heart no account is taken of the fact indicated here that history has produced a whole list of such words. But all such arguments would do nothing to alter our actual situation. Certainly, as a matter of abstract generalisation, this may be one word among many. But in the concrete here and now *only* the word that stands for the heart of the Lord can be *that* word for which we seek, and which we can also fail to recognise and to hear, or even reject, even though it is there.

This word has the function of adjuring the heart, that which is innermost and unifying, the mystery which defies all analysis, the unspoken law which is more powerful than all man's ability to organise and coordinate, and all the techniques of organisation of which he can avail himself. It has the function of designating that point at which the mystery of man passes into the mystery of God. The infinite emptiness which lies at the innermost centre of man cries out to be filled with the infinite fulness of God. The heart that is adjured in this word is the heart that has been pierced, weighed down by elemental anxiety (*Angst*), drained to its last drop, overcome by death. What is designated in this word is that which signifies a love which is selfless and beyond all conception, the love which is victorious in failure, which triumphs when it has been deprived of its power, raises to life when it has been slain. It is the love that is God. The message proclaimed in this word is that where God is prayed to in the words 'My God why hast thou forsaken me?' there he is close at hand. The one spoken of here is one who exists fully on the physical plane, and yet is all in all, so that we can count his wounds and come to rest weeping tears of blessedness because we have no need to journey further once we have found God. Can it be denied that in this word we discover ourselves anew, our destiny in this present age, and what it means to be a Christian, all this being laid upon us as a burden and a grace at the same time, and committed to us as our mission and task? The special quality of a particular age is, in fact, for the most part not that which is most widely acknowledged (in other words yesterday's opinions which have become common and public), but that which is denied and yet, in spite of this, is laid upon us. But in this present age how could this be anything else than the necessity and the task of having to rediscover that heart anew, and at the same time to bear with our heart with all its loneliness, its darkness and dejection and its elemental anxiety (*Angst*) about God?

What else could we say by way of summing up the whole meaning of our Christian existence except this: that the eternal Word of God, issuing from the heart of the Father, has discovered our hearts, has endured them and keeps them for all eternity.

If what we have said is correct with regard to the epitomising and unifying force of this key word, which can be said to express the 'sum total' of our devotion (in the words of Pius XI and Pius XII), then two conclusions follow from this: first we must be reverent and therefore sparing in our use of this word, and second we must begin by learning the real significance of a key word of this kind, with its power to epitomise and to adjure.

We must be sparing in our use of it. Before we use it that which it is intended to epitomise and to unify must first be present. This word, therefore, is not to be numbered among the 'rudiments of Christian teaching' (Heb 6:1). For what is undertaken in these initial stages is a survey in all their breadth and fulness of those truths which are subsequently to be drawn together in anunity. And it is necessary to return again and again to this stage of the initial survey because without noticing it we lose sight again and again of those truths which we have already made our own. Again the word 'heart' would be reduced to an empty formula, utterly drained of the meaning and content it once had if we did not constantly renew our search of the scriptures, using our quiet hours to meditate upon, and preaching by word of mouth the truths which the Christian message contains. But in this we cannot always be speaking explicitly about the heart. This word which refers to the heart of Christ retains its force and its unique function only on condition that we have not already used it to excess in a spirit of exaggerated and unbalanced 'pietism' by employing it in all cases in which we have occasion to speak of Jesus Christ. This word should be uttered and invoked by us only in those cases in which we need to refer to the 'heart' of man precisely in the sense of that interior and hidden 'self' (cf. Rom 7:22; 1 Pet 3:4; Eph 3:16 ff.) that is in *him* (in virtue of his unfathomable fulness) and in *us* (in virtue of our emptiness and dissipation of spirit). This cannot be the case on every occasion, however important it may sometimes be (and as it actually was for the Lord himself, who spoke sparingly but at decisive points of our hearts and of his own: Mt 5:8; 11:29; 22:37, etc.).

We must understand the real significance of a word of this kind. For it is not a word merely in the sense of that which gives utterance to a 'concept'. In fact there is a point in every concept at which it becomes open to the infinite, transcends its own limitations, and achieves communication with the All. In fact every word (that is not simply a signal in the merely animal sense) contains undertones and resonances beyond the surface meaning which it is designed explicitly to communicate because it is always, as it were, floating upon a deeper level of meaning which cannot be communicated. But with the majority of words this openness to the incommunicable is not borne in upon us. For the most part they are intended to bring to our notice what can be firmly and clearly grasped in the form of a concept. In the case of the key words,[1] however, the special significance of these is precisely the fact that they are open, and that what they open up to is the inexpressible mystery of God (in our case that God who is the Absolute of inconceivability brought near to us in love). Certainly if these particular words cease to perform this function they can serve simply to express a concept. But precisely as key words in the sense intended here they have died (a more terrible death than the merely physical one). Now they do so die in our spirit when they are heard and uttered simply as concepts. For by taking them in this sense we are utterly failing to understand them in the sense which they are intended to bear for us. It is true that we say of the majority of words which occur in our religious parlance that they refer to a mystery. In uttering these words, however, we may altogether fail to conjure up this mystery, to

---

[1] On this concept and on the ideas which follow cf. K. Rahner, *Theological Investigations* III, 'Behold This Heart!': Preliminaries to a Theology of Devotion to the Sacred Heart', pp. 321–330; also 'Reflections on the Experience of Grace', pp. 86–90.

make it present to ourselves. We may restrict ourselves simply to the surface meaning of the word, discarding and neglecting those deeper levels of meaning which go beyond this, and precisely the mystery itself which lies concealed beneath it, and we may consign all this to the realm of that which we have simply failed to understand and to grasp. We may take this attitude to the word instead of allowing *it* to grasp *us* precisely as mystery, because we fail to grasp this level of significance in it. When we refuse to move outwards from the small circle of light represented by the literal meaning of the word into the wider sphere of sacred darkness that lies beyond then we kill the key word, depriving it of its force and reducing it to a mere word which can be used by the profane, the uninitiated and the loveless too (of whom even the ranks of the theologians can furnish abundant examples).

But how can we avoid depriving these key words of their force and killing them? How can we understand them as they must be understood if they are to retain their pristine force? From what has already been said it will be manifest that this cannot be achieved merely by conceptually enriching these words by 'filling' them with conceptual meaning or even with a conceptualised ('as distinct from a real and experiential') 'inconceivability' and 'infinitude'. In order to 'grasp' what has to be done here (this implies that we have not yet actually carried through what we have initially grasped as right, whereas in this context to 'grasp' something consists precisely in the recognition that here acting is the only right way of knowing) we have to bear this in mind: when we contemplate what has been uttered there descends upon us softly and, as it were, unnoticed, that mystery in which the life-force of that unique truth which is the immediate subject of our contemplation consists. But the actual mode in which this mystery is made present to us is not the direct mode in which a proposition is made present that is uttered and so made a subject of discussion. This mystery is made present not in conceptual terms but rather in being touched and stirred into life. What we are treating of here is not a 'feeling' or a movement of the affections in devotion which cannot be controlled, but rather that without which every concept would have to remain cut off in a state of isolation and incommunicability, in which it could no longer be understood. We are treating of that which belongs to the very essence of intellectual knowledge as such, and upholds it in being, of a reference to the inconceivable and inexpressible, which is itself beyond the power of the human intellect to grasp or to objectify, a reference such that the inconceivable and inexpressible itself is silently present in it. Certainly we can also speak of this reference which points us on to and opens us to the mystery itself (in fact we do precisely this!), but, taken as a distinct phenomenon in itself, this reference is not as such present 'conceptually' by being caught in an unusual kind of concept, for *per definitionem* it is originally and primarily such that it is precisely not present in this sense at all. It is present rather in the oblique and implicit mode in which the inconceivable is touched upon in the very act of conceiving of something in the true and ordinary sense. In itself this reference to the inconceivable could be present with sufficient force in all words (for all in fact draw their life-force from it), so that these too could be used with as powerful an effect as those key words which we have been discussing. And perhaps the language of Paradise was of this kind, such that the all-encompassing All reverberated in every word, touching men with its clarity and love. And all our words (in which, for the most part, this reference is suppressed and buried beneath the surface by our frantic and convulsive efforts to cling onto the 'idea clara et distincta') ought, ideally speaking, to experience and to undergo a return, concomitant with our own 'conversion', to that state in which they were brought together in a Paradisal symphony in which each one found its echo in the whole (in the unique Word of God). But even as it is, there are certain words which should approach more closely than the rest to this return to the pristine power of their origins as we ourselves make our personal return. And the word 'heart' is to be numbered among these. Only if we understand it in this sense have we understood it as it should be understood in very truth, if it is really to be something more than simply one among the many words which we use in our religious parlance, the words in which mere concepts of the realities referred to are expressed, but these realities themselves are not rendered present in the achievement, by the help of grace, of a transcendence that is real and effective.

We have already said that the term 'Sacred Heart' stands for that reality in which the unnameable mystery which we call God is made present to us as compassionate and self-bestowing proximity (instead of as one who withholds himself from us in silence and refuses us). This mystery is made present to us where we are in that which is the *fons et origo* of our earthly being, in the heart. And now we have sought to make a further point over and above this, that we must not merely speak of this heart but understand it too, in such a way that it really can be, for the individual, what it is in itself, that when we utter this word that which it expresses may take place in us; in a word, that when we utter it we may do so with 'understanding' that we may be 'at one' with it. If this word is really and effectively to remain a key word (and only so can it fulfil that epitomising and unifying function of which we have spoken at the outset of these remarks, without which there would be no need either of it or of any special cult of the Sacred Heart) then it must be understood in the manner indicated, i.e. not only as giving expression to a concept, but as containing in its innermost depths that abundance of grace and power which derives from the fact that it has an essential and immediate reference to that mystery in itself to which the word gives a name.

Anyone who finds it difficult to achieve an understanding of what we mean from what has just been said should attempt to approach the matter from a different point of view, and so to arrive at an understanding of it. In any religious concept the reference to God is in reality twofold: first, there is the conceptualisation and objectification of the reality referred to, and second, as that which makes this process possible at all, there is the achievement of transcendence precisely as such, in which we are carried beyond our earthly limitations to God, and so placed in contact with him in this sense as well. In any act of apprehending which takes place in the 'light of faith' and by the power of grace this twofold reference to God achieves a special potency. That which is objectified in conceptual terms is present as something that is given by external revelation in the *fides ex auditu* of the subject, but at the same time this same reality is also present in the state of being raised to supernatural heights of transcendence, a quality which does not merely make this transcendence a transcendence of being in general, but also imparts a basic orientation to the spiritual dynamism which is in man, which ultimately raises it to the *visio beata*, at the same time (as *gratia increata*) actually imparting the reality of what is believed to man. The transcendence which man achieves, spiritually and 'pneumatically' exalted in this way, does not constitute an object for investigation in itself, but neither does this mean that man is simply unconscious of it. It is not simply the mere mechanism of a spiritual or non-spiritual process. Man has a non-objectified awareness of it as that which is concomitant with his objectifying concept, as that which renders present, intimately and silently, that inexpressible 'something more' which accompanies any religious concept, and without which it cannot truly be such at all. Who can seriously dispute the fact that in a genuinely religious act this 'something more' really is present (as something of which man is concomitantly aware even if it cannot in any immediate sense be the object of his speculation)? No-one can dispute this who has achieved a sound grasp of what is meant in the Thomist metaphysic of knowledge by the *lumen intellectuale* and the *objectum formale* of the mind; no-one who in theology has achieved any understanding of that formal object which is present in every act that is raised to a supernatural level, and only in such an act, in virtue of the very fact that it has thus been raised to a supernatural plane of reality. No-one can deny it who takes seriously the teaching of scripture concerning the anointing by the Holy Spirit which teaches us all things, or concerning the 'sighs too deep for words' of the Spirit, which has been given to us as the Spirit of God which penetrates all things. But this 'something more', this silent openness to and reference to that which is meant, which is achieved in the very process of positing the act itself (and not simply in the object to which it is directed) can grow, can impress itself upon us more clearly and forcefully, and be received at a deeper and more 'existential' level. When we speak of a spiritual consolation which takes place at the highest point of the spirit in faith, hope and love, what we mean by this is this awareness of what is being referred to here, which is at once more exalted and deeper and, existentially speaking, 'more radical' than knowledge in the more direct sense. It is in this awareness that we should now utter the word 'Sacred Heart'. In the light of this awareness it must then become clearer to us that in a true sense all statements about religion (when they are really true and genuine) have to be made on the basis of this achieved awareness. Only in this way can we ensure that the word that stands for the Sacred Heart is not reduced to one among the many other words which we use in our everyday religious parlance. We can use this word only sparingly. We should use it only when we wish consciously to advert to, as a distinct entity in itself, and interiorly to unify with the rest of our religious knowledge, that 'something more' which is present in what we say when we speak of God's grace and compassion in Christ. And when we do use the 'word' 'Sacred Heart' in this sense, speaking of it hesitantly and softly, then we must speak it in such a way that the word thus sparingly used may be 'understood' in this especially exalted sense; this is the sense in which we shall learn to understand all the words of faith only when the eternal light shines upon us with all its brilliance unimpeded.

12

UNITY – LOVE – MYSTERY

OUR intention in the three considerations which follow is to attempt to discuss certain implications which are contained in the veneration of the Sacred Heart. At first it may appear that these points which we are discussing are at an extremely theoretical level. But it may perhaps be shown in the end that our reflections upon them here bring to light certain relevant factors, the significance and importance of which are not confined merely to the scientific and theological levels, but are above all religious. The first implication latent in this devotion is that of unity.

Unity

1. In reality the veneration of the Sacred Heart does not represent an attempt at concentrating the whole of Christian devotion and the whole fulness of what it means to be a Christian into this veneration of the heart of Christ, or of erecting this veneration into a structure capable of subsuming and integrating everything which Christian devotion contains within itself. This is something that certain devout but unenlightened and over-zealous practitioners of this devotion have already often attempted to do either explicitly or implicitly. It is false, and can only, in the long run, be damaging to Christianity as a whole and also to this devotion itself. Christianity is more than devotion to the Sacred Heart. But on the other hand it is nonetheless evident that this devotion is not simply one among many others on an equal footing, such as devotion to St Joseph or even to Our Lady, or even to realities which are, in some sense, still more sublime and more central in the world of our faith, which is still, so far as we are concerned, made up of many factors, as, for instance, the Blessed Sacrament itself. According to Pius XI and Pius XII devotion to the Sacred Heart can in some sense be called the 'summa religionis'. The object of this devotion constitutes the ultimate and innermost centre, the

ultimate reality from which everything else draws its light, in which everything else is, in a certain sense, united and held together. It constitutes a unity.

For the moment we mention the term 'heart', even in quite general terms, and even apart from the religious dimension in the true sense and the language pertaining to this, we are referring not to one factor among many others, nor even simply to all things in their diversity as drawn together into a subsequent unity. We are referring rather to an interior centre from which the diversification of human reality is unfolded, and in which this diversification, which also belongs to the very nature of man, remains united. It is constantly streaming out from this centre and flowing back into it. At the same time when it allows this multiplicity to flow from it. this centre reveals itself, while, when it draws everything back again into its unfathomable depths it becomes veiled. And in fact it is the same with the word 'heart' as used in the devotion of the Sacred Heart. When we use this term we are referring to, and calling upon, this one unifying centre of the complex reality of the Son of Man in all its unfathomable depths. We are referring to its ultimate meaning and its immeasurable mystery. Once we have understood the devotion to the Sacred Heart in this sense two points become clear: on the one hand it is neither intended to, nor capable of, embracing the whole of Christianity as developed in all its manifold aspects; on the other hand it is not in itself simply on the same level as any other object of devotion among the manifold realities towards which an act of Christian religion can and should be directed. In virtue of the incarnational structure of Christianity these realities must be manifold, even though any act of this kind is always aimed at God himself who is all in all, and at him alone. Thus it should surely be recognised that the problem of unity implicit in this devotion has not merely been posed as a genuine religious question with a significance that is 'existential' in these present times, but also, rightly understood, has been solved. It is this question and the answer to it that we now propose to spend a little time in considering.

Unity — a question that is age-old, obscure, painful and at the same time blessed! We wander through a complex and manifold world. Right from the outset, if we realise our true selves, we have constantly been exposed to this. We are never in the situation of possessing all in an One. And yet we can never be satisfied with any such One which is not at the same time All. We are ourselves made up of a whole range of complex factors. In our make-up there is spirit and flesh, an interior and an exterior, happiness and pain. We can never stop at any given point in our development. There is nothing that we can simply grasp and hold, and which at the same time stands revealed as the One and All, the sole factor of importance in our lives. And yet we still continue to seek for that unity which is not emptiness, not abstract, not the sort of unity which an abstract concept has, anunity which achieves the power to comprehend and embrace all things only at the expense of a disembodied emptiness with regard to its content. We seek for that unity which is fulness, because we neither can nor will be driven onwards into the indeterminate and the unknown. Also because even though reality as we know it is so diffuse and complex there is still so much unity in it, so much mutual interrelationship, mysterious harmony, mutual attraction of one thing to another, that it is quite impossible for us to do anything else than to search for this unity which consists in the fulness of all things, and this fulness of all things which comprises a unity — that unity which encompasses and covers all things. We do this because we *are* this act of seeking. Because even the encounter with the manifold and the complex as such, the act of consciously and deliberately distinguishing each individual thing as other from the rest — all this would never be possible if the very roots of our being were not constituted by the premonition of the unity that exists as an infinite goal and the all-embracing sense of the many which is ours in the power and light of our love for unity. But we, the finite, cannot hope to attain to this unity of inexpressible fulness by a process of transcending or compressing the diffusion and complexity in which reality is made present to us. We would fall into the darkness and silence of a lethal solitude if, wearied by this complexity, or despairing of it, we sought to attain the unity we desire in a manner which is neither possible nor fitting for a creature, striving to grasp at it in itself alone as it is beyond all multiplicity, and to hold it to ourselves by force.

The pain we experience, then, is one of tension. There is anunity that we seek, one which, in a certain sense, we have already grasped by anticipation, and one to which the very multiplicity all about us points us on. Yet this unity can never be possessed by itself alone. For just as we withdraw into this unity we must perforce turn back again and go forth into the multiplicity which belongs to the very mode of our existence. And the painful tension which this involves mounts to a climax of need precisely in our specifically religious acts. What a multiplicity and com-

plexity of religious practices is to be found in the life of the Church! How
numerous are her sacraments and her devotions also! How incalculable is
the host of her saints! While the process by which her teaching has been
explicitated in thousand upon thousand of individual doctrines is almost
bewildering! How manifold too are the methods and ways of the religious
life which are recommended, praised and even required by the Church.
The nature of Christianity is in itself simple, but it has been developed and
diffused into a whole of such complexity that it demands too much of the
individual to calculate or comprehend. And yet if our spirit is awake and
alive we cannot simply confine ourselves to a modesty and naïveté of
outlook that is *petit-bourgeois*, selecting this and that factor in Christianity which we may happen to have encountered, and being quite
comfortable and content to leave the rest to itself. At the same time we
cannot achieve an outlook that embraces the whole either, seeing it in its
sheer essential interior structure. And there is a further truth that is the
converse of this: again and again in the life of the Church and her Spirit
there suddenly flames up a mystical movement such as that of John of the
Cross which takes the form of an ardent longing for an ultimate unity in
which all the different ways of living Christianity, and all the complexities
are swept away, and all is resolved in a mysticism in which there are no
'ways', and which is dark and mysterious in character. This takes place in
all movements which embody the quest for simplicity and directness in
our way of living our religion, or which aim at the classic equilibrium and
concentration upon the one essential.

3. But how are we to find the unity in the midst of this incalculable
fulness? And how are we to find the fulness which this unity embraces?
How, above all, are we to achieve this in the living of our religion? We
invoke the experience of our own hearts and look to the heart of Christ. If
we accept the message of our own heart with faith and love, if we entrust
ourselves to that inconceivable heart and centre of all things which we call
the Sacred Heart, then we have all along been experiencing something of
the true solution to this problem. If there were no original unity prior to
all problems of how to reconcile unity with complexity and multiplicity of
content in a given whole, and if in that which we call our own heart we
were not already disposed to unity by God himself then any attempt at
such a reconciliation would be from the very outset futile. We would
either lose ourselves in the multiplicity or stick fast at the unity. But
because there is this heart created by God himself, because man already

possesses a unity bestowed upon him right from the outset, therefore he can proceed from this into the complexity and multiplicity without losing himself in it. He can gather up himself and the world together into a basic and radical unity without either losing himself or sticking fast in this sense — always provided that he commits himself to that unity of absolute fulness which we call God, always provided that this unity which is not man himself, yet without which he cannot exist, receives him by grace into proximity to itself, always provided too that (only one word more!) we have been drawn into the protecting love of Christ, which in his heart is real, close at hand, filled with blessings and single. And this is in fact the case. The unity by which we can really live is not the abstract or creaturely unity of the idea, or the unifying basis of our own nature, but rather the 'superessential' unity which by grace becomes more interior to us than the unity of our own being, and which, nevertheless, is not our own. It is a unity to which we have to commit ourselves because it has been bestowed upon us in grace. In this unity which is full of content, therefore, the conflict which takes place within our own being between diffusion and compression, extroversion and introversion — both taken in an extremely broad metaphysical sense — is reconciled without thereby disappearing altogether. But it is because this unity is so interior to our own being that it is a unity which has been bestowed in grace, which has been received, which must be 'blindly' presupposed, which is not at our disposal. It is a unity which we cannot discard in favour of any one specific individual factor which we choose to take as absolute, i.e. as an unifying centre in defiance of the facts regarding its true constitution.

All this has been put somewhat abstractly. Nevertheless it has a great significance for religion, and specifically for the practice of religion in one's life.

(a) This is because it has a message for us as the superessential unity bestowed upon us in Christ, never left to us to achieve for ourselves, but rather imposing itself upon us from without, and brought close to us in that reality which we call the Sacred Heart. And this is the message which it brings: Go out into the multiplicity and complexity which is yours by nature, and do not fear it. Have trust in the incalculable factors of your life with all its complexities with wisdom and foresight indeed, but with courage and trust as well. As an old mystic has put it, you cannot achieve total proficiency in a single exercise. Your heart must go out into the manifold even in the sphere of your religious practices. Do not be too ready to fear that you will lose yourself in this complexity. If you only take to yourself genuinely and whole-heartedly each individual factor, however small, as it comes (Goethe was wise enough to recognise this truth), then you will arrive at the whole, because it is precisely the whole that is inherent in every one of these individual factors, because it is a whole that is the outcome of that which constitutes the unity of them all as such and the mystery which lies at its heart is in turn constituted by the inner-most depths of the divine nature itself, which is also the superessential basis of your unity. Do not close in upon yourself too much. You must open yourself and so come to the fulness that you need. Otherwise it may happen that you stick fast within the confines of too much self-mastery, too tight a hold on yourself, too much self-examination. Go forth from the heart and centre of your own being in order that you may find your own heart. This in itself will be the unity underlying the multiplicity. The only way in which it can come home to itself is through the broad spontaneous adventure of living.

(b) But this unity which is bestowed upon us in the heart of Christ, and which has its real and effective symbol in that heart, also brings to us another message, which is the counterpart of the first: Return! Do not let yourself be poured away! Have the courage to return even if you seem to be the poorer for so doing, even if in doing so much seems to escape you, even if the heart and centre to which you return seems to be the dark and lifeless cavity of the grave, silent and empty, dead and death-dealing. Only if you have learnt this through practice, if you can be alone, if you have learnt to be silent, to renounce, to let things go, to be poor, only then can you also find the unity underlying the multiplicity. Only if this centre, this unity that draws all to itself which we call the heart, is actually pierced through and seems to be poured out into a terrible void in futile love for another, only then can you find that unity that can truly be called so; only then will it be bestowed upon you by God without any merit on your part.

(c) And now we seem to have returned to the position that we cannot bring the manifold and the complex into a unity until we have practised how to go forth in trust into the multiplicity, and how to gather up all into a unity in the centre of our hearts. In truth there is no formula to tell us how to harmonise and regulate this twofold movement outwards and inwards, the unity deriving from the single common basis, and the multi-plicity that issues from this same basis. There is no formula to enable us to achieve this unification, but nevertheless it has been achieved not by God, not as our work but as his grace, not in our hearts but in the heart of Christ. We know that our life must consist in putting both movements into practice, the outward and the inward. We must constantly be initiating the one movement for the sake of the other, in a continuous process of ingress and egress, without remaining fixed in either state. But the unity between these two outward and inward movements that we practise is something that we do not grasp in conceptual terms at all. It is hidden in God, in his providential control of things and in his love; it can be accepted by us only as unseen, as the divine mystery of our existence. We shall arrive; in all our wanderings we are aiming straight at the centre of the target, if only we are patient in our dealings with one another, because this is our life. If only we look to the unity which God himself bestows upon us, regarding it as the unity which is his alone to achieve and to control; it is a unity which remains hidden from us yet of which, at the same time, we are aware, recognising in faith, hope and love that it is the unity which love itself achieves and directs – which indeed love *is*. All this we recognise when we turn our eyes to the Sacred Heart.

Love

The second implicit factor which we wish to spend some little time in considering in these theological meditations of ours on the deeper meaning of the festival of the Sacred Heart is one that is in a true sense self-evident – that of love. The veneration of the Sacred Heart is, in fact, precisely a devotion to that love of God which has been made present to us in Christ Jesus our Lord, crucified and risen from the dead. For this reason it might be thought that of all the factors implicit in this devotion this one comes nearest to being explicit and on the surface, and therefore that no special effort of consideration and examination is needed in order to appreciate its significance. But this impression is dispelled the moment we advert to the fact that what is expressed in this word love is the mystery of reality as such, that in effect there is nothing less capable of comprehension than the reality which is designated by this overworked, hackneyed and degraded word, and which, according to scripture and tradition has to be so designated. Once we realise this then we find it easy to recognise that we need constantly to renew our efforts at finding an explanation in order to understand the element in this devotion which seems to be so completely obvious and clear to all.

1. First this devotion tells us that love is the very basis of our existence. When we speak of the heart then we are expressing that which is the centre, basis, origin and original unity prior to all multiplicity, which provides all existence with its goal, and constitutes a mutual interrelationship between all beings. And when we speak of the heart of Christ, then we are speaking of that particular origin and goal, that particular basis and centre, from which all that is complex and multiple draws its strength. It is that reality which on the one hand belongs wholly to God as the ultimate and absolute upholder of all things, and on the other has 'externalised' itself and indeed emptied itself in order to enter into the 'otherness' of non-divine being. As the outcome of this movement on God's part outwards from his own fulness into the empty void of the world, created beings have arisen and multiplicity has been initiated, and now these depend for their unity, their basic support and the power to achieve their goal upon this centre, itself now existing in a creaturely mode. And when we speak of this centre of the Sacred Heart then we are saying that this supreme Being, who upholds the reality of ourselves, the world we live in and our very existence, and who has himself assumed a 'this-worldly' mode, is he who also sustains the reality of love in all its unfathomable depths. Moreover, the mystery contained in this statement is one which absolutely beyond all human comprehension. Let us pause for a moment in our consideration of this truth. Withdrawing within the depths of our own hearts let us try to let the secret essence that pervades the world, nature and the history of these, as well as humanity and its history, silently distil itself there. Of course, we shall not come anywhere near to succeeding in this, but still let us try! Some intimation may, perhaps, be aroused in our hearts of the element of dumb self-obtuseness which is to be discerned in nature at the purely material level. It is so dead, so dominated by brute force, so alienated from itself! Our hearts may perhaps be impressed with something of the unrestrained prodigality of living nature, its cruelty, the life and death struggle taking place within it, the way in which life springs up rank and luxuriant from the decay of death; the seemingly meaningless phenomenon of constant fresh mutations of form springing up within it in an apparently endless succession, the way in which the interests of the individual are constantly and brutally subordinated to those of the species, the wild and lustful extravagance – so at least it seems – of the processes of generation, the reckless waste that there is in nature, the evolving processes within it which seem blind to their

own goal – all this may impress itself upon us. Then let us only turn to the history of mankind, the history of the mind and spirit which is almost powerless as it is forced to contemplate this cruel, blind and stupefying world of matter and of *bios*. Then we may open our hearts to some degree to all the anguish of guilt, of death, of futility, which mankind has added on its own account throughout a million years of human history, that history which has been so blind to its own goal, which has seemed to stagnate in a state of meaninglessness that is agonising. We might open our hearts to the miseries of slaves, of the dying, of those who have been duped, of children who have been tormented and violated. We may consider the loves that have been dishonoured, the ideals that have been betrayed, the trust that has been broken. And then our hearts may be so crushed with horror and despair, may feel that their own basic dignity has been dealt a mortal blow to the point where it feels that what little joy and love, faithfulness and blessedness is to be found in this sewer of world-history and human history does not make the sum total of the world and mankind better, but only more terrible still, because there seems to be just enough meaning in the world to make us able to feel the prevailing meaninglessness in all its deathly pain. And when we experience all this then let us look to the Sacred Heart pierced by the lance and say to ourselves: 'The basis of all reality is love.' Let us say to ourselves: 'It is from this source alone that there streams out all this incomprehensible reality, with its multiplicity, its contradictions, its agonies, its endless journeys to unknown goals, together with its blind alleys, its struggles and deaths, its darkness, its total incomprehensibility.' Let us not forget that when we speak of the Sacred Heart then we are not merely saying: 'Somewhere in the world there is a heart which has felt love and has suffered.' We are not merely making a statement at the 'categorical' and 'this-worldly' level about one particular heart among others. On the contrary this statement of ours is on the 'transcendental' plane, if we may so express it. For what we are asserting is that each and all of the beings in the world stem from this one source, and this one *fons et origo* which comprehends all things, makes room for all things, judges all things and illumines all things, this original unity, we say, is love. And in making this statement about the heart of the Lord we are almost saying more – if we may be permitted so to express it – than if we simply said that there is a God who is in himself light, blessed simplicity and love. For in making this statement we are not merely saying that above this darkness of incomprehensibility there

exists this luminous and blessed unity which possesses itself in love. We
are saying that this blessed and luminous upholder of all things in being
has, by his creative act, not merely allowed all this dark chaos of the world
to spring up from him in all its recalcitrant multiplicity, but that he has
taken this anguished and loveless incomprehensibility to his own heart,
has himself assumed it as his own reality, has allowed his own heart to
fall into the dark abyss of the world, has inserted his own heart into the
lethal void of non-divine being, to exist there as the true source of all this
reality that is in the world apart from God. When we hold fast to this
truth unto death, standing firm despite all disappointments, clinging to it
even as we fall into the abyss of death, that state in which our own hearts
are pierced through and drained of their life-blood, then we are made
blessed – otherwise not. It is not so easy to understand the truth that
underlies the veneration of the Sacred Heart.

2. Love, then, is the well-spring, the sole and unique source of all that
reality which we experience with such incomprehension. And if this is the
case then it follows *ipso facto* that love itself is every bit as mysterious as
that which issues from it, every bit as mysterious as that infinite fulness
must necessarily be which is the origin of all that constitutes the world and
being. In the devotion to the Sacred Heart, therefore, there is an act of
veneration of, and an act of formal invocation addressed to, a mystery. But
this invocatory formula is not really one in the true sense at all because in it
man does not exercise any power of his own, but, if he grasps its significance aright, i.e. if he is himself grasped by it, is rather made subject to the
power of another. Let us never forget, when we speak of love, that – if we
like to formulate the matter in somewhat metaphysical terms – spirit, the
state of being that is self-cognizant, freedom, love and everything which
follows from such concepts are 'transcendental' concepts, i.e. they stand
for realities which cannot be explained in terms of other realities. The
knowledge of them cannot be progressively built up from some other and
better known entity. They are not deducible from anything else. Rather
they must be understood right from the very first, from the first moment
that we decide to speak of them and to bring the awareness of them home
to ourselves or to others. Concepts of this kind, therefore, are also
inexhaustible concepts. They cannot, in any true sense, be limited or
circumscribed. Once we have attained to them in some way or at some
point they initiate an infinite movement, only gradually filling themselves
out with their true meaning, which increases immeasurably in depth

through the experience of life, through the grace of God and finally through the immediacy of our relationship with God. In all this these transcendental concepts continue to exist precisely as mere concepts and as a mere 'transcendentalising' experience of our own personal orientation to the infinite mystery. But the process continues until they so to say break out of these limitations and become something more than mere concepts and a mere experience. They do this in virtue of the content implanted in them right from the very first by grace, that content in which their ultimate significance consists, and which is nothing less than the ineffable reality of God himself, and of his world as permeated with himself. And in this way this reality is made present to us no longer in terms of the concepts appropriate to it but directly and in itself. Now among 'concepts' of this sort, in which we are grasped and overpowered in the very act of grasping them, i.e. allowing ourselves to be grasped by them, is to be numbered love – love, that is to say, not merely existing as an abstract concept made explicit in words, but love as it is in itself, even though initially we have only an incipient understanding of it, experiencing it and grasping it merely as promise. The only way in which we can be totally seized and encompassed by this love is for it to unite us with everything, for us to identify ourselves with everything by 'understanding' it, taking the world wholly to our hearts in all its incalculable greatness, all its inconceivable terrors and sufferings; finally for us to ensure that nothing pertaining to this world and its history remains any longer 'alien' to us, that there is nothing that still remains outside our existence, dead to us because we have failed to understand it. And if we understand love as the absolute and integrating power of a process latent in existence that is moving towards the unification of that which is multiple and complex in blessedness, then how inexpressibly far from their own true consummation our lives must seem to us! How very little we can already have understood and actually have achieved of a love of this kind! Considered as that in which our own ultimate fulness will be achieved, love will still be a mystary, because it is only if it is united with the incomprehensibility of God himself. Only if we direct our gaze to the heart of Christ, therefore, do we know what love is: the mystery of the world, the overcoming of the terrors which are in the world, that which unifies and embraces, that which transforms, that which liberates and is tender, that which is only realized in its fulness when the one who loves makes a total surrender of everything pertaining to the movement of his own personal history towards its fulfilment. This is achieved when this love of his is pierced through and silently pours out its heart's blood into the futility of the world, and thereby conquers it. It is this that is described and conjured up in the supreme canticle to love of St Paul: patient and kind, without envy, not puffed up, not pretentious, not passionately attached to its own pre-judices, not vexed, not vindictive, devoid of envy, rejoicing in the truth, always ready gently to excuse, believing all things, hoping all things and enduring all things. There is really no word capable of describing this love, because there is nothing else like it which we could use as an external standard in order to define it; also because it is, in itself, the unifying and absolutely original essence of all reality, and therefore there is nothing apart from it except emptiness and nothingness. For it has been written: 'But God is love', and in these two words man finds two different ways of expressing the single infinite mystery of his own existence.

3. One reflection of this unfathomable love still remains to be men-tioned in its own right, that of joy. We Christians must be the blessed ones, those who smile, those from whom the light of their redemption radiates out, those who have been redeemed, those who have been liber-ated, those who know that the kingdom of God and the fruits of the Spirit signify, amongst other things, that joy which is the wondrous radiance of love itself. What a pity that we should so often be the joyless ones, the morose, those who go forward groaning beneath the burden of the law, the yoke and burden of which seem anything but sweet and light to us! What a pity that we should proceed as those who are under an unbearable strain, those who either have a bad conscience on account of the dis-crepancy in their lives between the letter of the law on the one hand and the actual shape their life assumes on the other, or else recompence them-selves for their adherence to the letter of the law by indulging in a loveless zeal and an attitude of harsh bigotry towards others! If only we had love we would actually be filled with joy because love alone makes bearable that law which it alone can interpret and apply in the glorious freedom of being children of God, far from all servility to the letter of the law; and yet at the same time love does not misuse this freedom or pervert it into an egoism which seems to be attractive but is in reality slavery. If only we had love, that love which takes away pain, and in which we could fear-lessly suffer our hearts to be pierced through, then we would be joyful with that joy which proceeds from God and streams from the Sacred Heart pierced by the lance. Then we would have the joy of those who

overcome, then our witness would be credible, then others would be able to recognise in us that we did indeed proclaim the *euangelion*, the good tidings which sound so different from the talk that goes on in the streets of the world, for this is intended to abolish pain, incomprehensibility and death. Then we would be those whose joy no man can take away, those to whom that joy is given which is at the same time the truth of death and of renunciation. But in order to be able to have this joy we must love. We must commit ourselves to the mysterious adventure of love, which only he who looks upon the heart of Christ can guess at.

Mystery

The third point which we wish to consider from among the factors implicit in the veneration of the Sacred Heart is that of mystery. Here some repetition of what has already been said is inevitable. This, however, will do no harm. True religion really begins at that point at which we have the courage to face up to that which is always the same, precisely to that mystery which comprehends all things and envelops all things. In the nature of the case this is necessarily one and single. It is the basis and the end of all religion, adoration and love, gathering up all things in love within its own unity. It cannot therefore be matter for blame that we are speaking once more of points which have already engaged our attention.

1. What has the heart to do with mystery? This is the first question that might be asked. The original and primary connotation of heart is unity, is source. The term 'heart' stands for that which expresses itself and yet is always in possession of itself. Heart conjures up the idea of that which is prior to all else, and yet which can only be understood in that which it suffers to spring up and come to bloom, to develop and unfold from within it. Heart connotes the origin of things, which must lead on to that which is beyond itself in order to realise its own nature, and at the same time that which, in all its self-expression and self-discovery, remains the eternally fresh and unquenchable source which is never spent, never becomes empty, and therefore remains ever surprising, ever new — in brief the mystery that is eternally youthful. Whatever aspect we have in mind when we speak of heart, it can only be termed a mystery in a derivative sense. We can only call it so when we have already assigned its causes, found a way of expressing it to ourselves, been able to point to that which went before it. And then *ipso facto* it is no longer simply the source without origins which is eternally inexhaustible and in that sense an absolute

mystery. And yet for all this we can only call something 'heart' in the true sense if it has some element in it precisely of this unattainability, which belongs to that which is eternally inexhaustible and without origin, something of the quality of fatherhood, in that it belongs inalienably to the particular individual and can never be transferred to another. We can only apply the term 'heart' to something in the true sense insofar as it has these qualities in it. For this very reason the Fathers have in fact long since pointed out that the Word issued from the heart of the Father. In fact when we use the term 'heart' we mean something original which is inexhaustible in itself, and never drained of its contents, so that when we look into it our gaze can never penetrate to an empty void within. It is something that realises its own nature in the unlimited fruitfulness of its thoughts and deeds, the manner in which it is expressed and presented to the outside world. And yet at the same time in all this its depths are never plumbed. It is never ultimately laid bare or reduced to its constituent elements. In brief it is, and remains, mystery because it is everything and, in a true sense — in that it is altogether itself and to the extent that it is heart — has no norm beyond itself by which it can be defined and regulated. It is not for nothing that we speak of the heart's secrets. It is not for nothing that we say of the all-knowing God that he alone knows the heart of man. It is not for nothing that we praise knowledge in its most exalted form by saying that it is the heart's own message, and it is no random choice of words that leads us to speak of the 'depths' of the heart. The heart would never be understood in its own unique truth if it were not conceived of as a mystery *par excellence*.

2. When, therefore, we look to this heart that is the Lord's, we are looking at the sign of that mystery which dominates and encompasses our whole life. There would be no heart if the heart of the Lord were not already there as that which is prior to all others, that which remains for ever mysterious, if it were not for this mystery that lies at the very roots of reality as such. And to that extent this heart points us on to the mystery of God himself. It is not only the human heart of God's eternal Logos, who is the inconceivable mystery of God himself precisely because God is *the* mystery *par excellence*. It is a symbol of mystery as such, and therefore, too, of the mystery of the eternal Godhead. We theologians do in fact say, in some corner or other of our system of dogmatics (only swiftly to forget it once more!), that God still continues to be he who is inconceivable even in the immediacy of the beatific vision. But for the most part

we interpret this statement to ourselves merely as a statement of the fact
that this vision, since it pertains to finite creatures, must still, in spite of its
immediacy, be itself finite and so imperfect. For the most part we fail to
understand that when we speak of the inconceivability of God even in the
immediacy of the beatific vision we are speaking precisely of the true and
proper content of this vision and that inner reality at its centre which
constitutes it as blessed, because God is only seen as God when he is
viewed in his inconceivability, because everything that we grasp about
him (in virtue of the fact that we are grasped by him) only appears as
divine in the true sense that is proper to it when it extends outwards and
onwards into that blessed obscurity which alone constitutes the true day,
when in the very act of grasping the divine and being grasped by it, it is
experienced as the inconceivable, and this inconceivability is not that in
God which we leave aside in our contemplation of him, but rather the
very object of our awe, the very quality which we call blessed and surrender ourselves to in love. But for the most part we forget all this, and as
theologians we are actually in grave danger of supposing that theology is
an unveiling of God in the sense of a breaking down of his inconceivability
(even if we recognise that we can only achieve this to a limited extent).
We like to feel ourselves to be those admitted to God's secret counsel,
distinguished from other people in virtue of the fact that we have grasped
more about God, whereas in reality the true theologians are those who
have understood better than other men that God is inconceivable. For
the most part we call to mind the mystery of God only when we have
become confused in our own processes of reasoning, instead of understanding theology as an initiation into the mystery of God and as the
systematic breaking down of all our over-hasty conceptions of God, so
that he rises more and more above us who are finite and limited. Rises
above us, I say. No! — vanishes altogether, rather, standing revealed as
the one true God for whom no image of God can ever be a substitute, as
the God who is close to us in love precisely as he who is inconceivable,
and who has so generously bestowed himself upon us in Jesus Christ and
in his Spirit. The heart of the Lord points us on to this supreme mystery
of the divine. As the sum total of our religion, the message of this heart to
us is: the ultimate basis of our whole existence is mystery. Mystery is not
merely a contributing factor in our existence as pilgrims here below, it is
the final and definitive factor. This mystery precisely in itself, and in its
inconceivability, is what is ultimately true and real in our existence. When

the ultimate and definitive truth shines out unveiled, and is no longer
viewed in reflected images and likenesses, then this *aletheia*, which will
then have been disclosed, will be the nearness of the mystery itself. This
will not be by-passed. On the contrary it will have been made quite
impossible to by-pass or evade it. The concept does not yield place to an
empty transparency in that which we perceive, but rather to the state of
being seized and possessed by truth. And blessedness consists not in the
fact that what we see in the beatific vision is forcibly divested of its mystery.
On the contrary it consists in the mystery itself as such. The mystery
itself is beatitude because man, provided he accepts his true nature in all
humility and love, achieves a blessed and loving harmony with the fact
that God is all in all and is the Mystery *par excellence*. And this state of
being encompassed by the mystery is even here below the ultimate fulfilment of his existence. Properly speaking, nothing is surer or more
obvious to us than the state of silent questioning which extends beyond
all that we can call in question and all that we can dominate and control,
the state of being faced with questions that are too much for us, and
accepting this in humility and love. It is this alone that makes man wise.
Man knows nothing in the ultimate depths of his own nature more
precisely than this: that his knowledge (both at the everyday level and in
scientific disciplines) is only a tiny island in a boundless ocean of that
which he has never experienced. He knows, therefore, that the existential
question confronting every individual who has knowledge in his own
particular concrete circumstances is the question of which he loves most,
the tiny island of so-called-knowledge or the ocean of infinite mystery;
whether he concedes that in a true sense the mystery is the sole factor
which is self-evident and self-explanatory, or whether, according to him,
the tiny light with which he illumines this little island of his (this little
torch he calls science) is his eternal light which is destined to illumine him
forever — Oh what a hell it would be if it were so! The meaning of existence, or the elemental question which it represents for us, is this: whether
we learn not merely to regard the mystery as imposing limitations and
restrictions upon our being and life, but rather to achieve that positive
relationship with the mystery as such in which we accept it, believe in it,
love it and adore it, and so achieve blessing. He who does not love the
mystery does not know God. His gaze constantly wanders from him, the
real and true God, and he adores the image of him that has been made
according to our measure and standard instead of God's own. When we

direct our gaze to the heart of Christ this can teach us how lovingly to surrender our whole being to the mystery which endures, which from its own depths upholds us in being, which is the love that is beyond all conception, which bears us and, by withdrawing us from the acts of our own self-will and so from ourselves, draws us to our own true blessedness.

3. In yet another quite special respect the Sacred Heart points us on to the mystery of our own existence. God is the mystery *par excellence* not merely *in himself,* but also inasmuch as he freely disposes of us as he wills. This is true inasmuch as the exercise of our own personal freedom in the activities of our lives, the innermost and ultimate decision of our whole existence which derives from this freedom of ours is in its turn encompassed, maintained and determined by the freedom of God. And this divine freedom is beyond us and beyond our powers of cognition, hidden in the silent depths of God himself, so that we are ourselves in turn hidden from ourselves precisely at that point at which we are most of all ourselves, in the autonomous and wholly inalienable decision of our own personal freedom. We are aware of ourselves, we are thrown upon ourselves and left to ourselves. There is a point in the radiant centre of our existence, even if it is one that is not susceptible of subsequent speculation upon our part, at which we and our own self-knowledge are identical, one and the same. And precisely this point is one which cannot be subjected to our own reflexive thought. We cannot clearly objectify it or define it in any explicit terms. Nor can it be shared with others, and again we cannot check or control it. And so we are ourselves a mystery which remains hidden in the mystery of God. The teaching of the Church herself is relevant here, when she reacts against the doubts of the new age and the strivings for self-knowledge which also constituted a potent force in the Protestant doctrine of the certainty of salvation. The Church is reacting here against the attempts at achieving a self-possession that is conscious and absolute. And she tells us that on the contrary we do not know with absolute certainty whether we are in God's grace, and further whether we have attained final salvation. Certainly this is a factor which does not carry much positive weight in the average Christian life of our times, in which there is so little understanding for those experiences of fear and hesitation and incessant questioning which belong to an Augustine, an Ignatius of Loyola, a Francis of Sales and many others, and also to Luther and Calvin and other representatives of the spirit of the Reformation with regard to the question of salvation: Am I one of the elect?

Shall I find salvation? Does God love me with that true, powerful and
effective love which signifies and assures salvation for me, sustaining
the elemental assent which of my freedom I yield up to God? When
man is brought face to face with himself in his innermost depths he arrives
in the ultimate state in which he feels himself existentially threatened,
troubled, uncertain, overwhelmed by questions which have to be
answered, yet which are beyond his powers to answer, those questions,
namely, entailed in the basic uncertainty as to what the answer is to the
question of the individual's own salvation. And then man notices that he
himself is, in his ultimate depths, a mystery, and still remains a mystery
even though it constitutes the heart and centre of his being with all its
limitations. He notices that as a mystery in this sense he is delivered up to
God, the Mystery *par excellence*, and that he can only do one thing: no
longer restrict himself to the faint light of his own reasoning powers and
so direct his efforts towards his own salvation rather than to God himself
(as though we could achieve a greater certainty of this on our own without
God than by letting ourselves fall into the mystery of his predestination),
but on the contrary surrender himself to God unconditionally and unreservedly with a love by which he really loves him more even than his own
salvation and his own personal assurance of this salvation. But how shall
we find it in ourselves to let go of ourselves in this way, and in a true sense
no longer to cling onto ourselves, to the innermost heart and centre of our
own being at the last, but rather to surrender it to God? That which is
most wholly proper and personal to man himself is his salvation. It is
with this that he identifies himself in the most radical manner by the
ultimate and definitive decision which he takes of his own freedom. Now
there is only one point at which he can surrender this totally and unreservedly without thereby being annihilated and without falling into the
despair of the damned, and that point is God, whom he experiences as
compassion. It is not that he can distinguish and separate out different
elements in this forgiving and redeeming compassion of God or in the
radical nature of his incomprehensibility and sovereignty, and thereby
seize this grace of his own individual salvation to himself as something
that he has gained control of by his own powers. No, man must surrender
himself totally and without reserve to God in the act which we call faith
and hope. But he can only do this if he surrenders himself to God as the
love in which he can and must believe, and for which he can and must
hope as that which has been freely bestowed upon him. But this act,

considered as the outcome of conscious and deliberate reasoning, is only possible for him through Jesus Christ the crucified and risen Lord, through his heart, this heart that has been pierced through, the heart which has itself been subjected to the immeasurable depths of deprivation in death and to a state in which it seemed to be abandoned by God, that heart which surrendered itself to the judgment of God upon the world, this act, I say, is possible only in the presence of that heart which — this is the miracle of grace that is new and quite unique in each individual case — gives us the courage to forget ourselves and to believe in his love as a love which has been bestowed on me in particular (or, to put it more precisely), to hope in it in that act of hope which is more than faith in a merely general sense, and which already in itself leads on to love. We gaze upon the heart of the Lord and the question upon which an eternity depends fills the innermost centre of our being, our heart and our life: Do you love me? Do you love me in such a way that this love truly, powerfully and unconquerably creates an eternity of blessedness that is *my* eternal life? To this question there is no answer such as would finally put an end to the mystery, or which man could give of his own powers. This question leads on to a mystery which has been brought close to us in this heart of the Lord. But if through this question we are led into the heart of the Lord because it is asked in faith, hope and love, then it is not answered but rather overtaken and overcome by the mystery which is love, by the mystery of God himself which cannot be questioned.

God, eternal mystery, nameless infinitude, unfathomable source of blessings, you who encompass all things and are encompassed by none, you have uttered your own eternal Word into your creation and into our lives in order that your eternal mystery may itself become for us the protection that is your inexpressible nearness to us, and may also become the centre of the world itself. We contemplate this Word of yours that you have uttered. We look upon him who is the heart of the world. We look upon the heart of the Son which we have pierced. All the incomprehensibility of ourselves and our lives lies hidden in this heart. All the elemental fear of human existence is forever contained by it. Everything that is sublime and holy finds its way back to this as its source. Everything finds its true nature there, and realises itself as love. Everything is drawn into the mystery that is the blessedness of love.

PART FOUR

Prospects

13

THE FUTURE OF THE RELIGIOUS BOOK

WHEN a theologian is asked whether he believes that there is any future for the religious book he will certainly begin by replying 'Obviously there is'. But if (in the particular case) after this initial answer he begins to ponder the question he may perhaps become somewhat less sure. He asks himself whether he has not answered too hastily, prompted in this by his own subjective interests in the matter. And then, by way of drawing distinctions, he will say that since he is convinced that religion itself has an eternal validity he was in fact basically right in his answer when he foresaw a future for the religious book as well. But this is still very far from saying *what form* the religious book of the future will assume. The reason why this cannot be foretold is that even the concrete form assumed by religion itself, in spite of the fact that it is, in essence, indestructible, is extremely changeable and is in this very day, presumably undergoing changes which are extremely swift and extremely radical.

Can it be foreseen what *guise* the religious book will appear in, and will indeed have to appear in, given that it has a future at all?

Of course even in the future religious books will still differ greatly among themselves, and this does not merely apply to their subject matter. It applies to the readers too, for even in the future these will be extremely varied in respect of age, sex, social milieu, experience of life; moreover their particular needs will also be different, as also will be the questions which their particular historical situation makes them feel to be of special concern to them. This is obvious and there is no need to dwell upon it any further at this point, although it may seem that religious authors and publishers often forget whole groups of the population who would read religious books if there were any available suited to their particular needs (for instance in Germany we have fashion magazines of a purely secular kind – such as *Für Sie* which carry a good page on religion and morals suitably written, and read very readily and with great sympathy because it is 'addressed' in a realistic and effective way to the type of reader concerned, and adapted to the particular needs of this type).

But these considerations apart, can we point to certain specific qualities which are characteristic of the religious writing of the future, given that there is in fact to be such a future at all? (In the answer we find to this question it may turn out that properly speaking these qualities have all along been necessary for the religious book in the true sense, but this will make no difference to the present argument.) The first characteristic which must be demanded of it is that it shall be freed from any 'ideology'. By this we mean that in it the religious element must not appear as some strange and unrealistic superstructure of theory superimposed upon that reality which man experiences both interiorly and exteriorly as an inevitable part of his life, as something that is really and effectively present in it, and which he constantly experiences anew. This kind of religious literature must appeal to man's genuine experience (this means, of course, the whole of that experience, not just a part of it). It must express this to him better than he can express it for himself. It must bring him to a realization of himself, and not simply to 'good thoughts'. In this religious literature the question that must constantly and relentlessly be raised is 'Where and how in the reader is that reality already present which this book is intended to bring to his notice?' There is a constant danger for the Christian here. He can always present the content of the faith in a form in which it has been fitted into an alien ideology, justifying himself in this by reminding his readers that it is, after all, 'revealed', that is, that it comes to humanity *ab externo* and from the 'sources' of revelation, and that it needs to be adapted and retranslated, etc. But in truth revelation represents precisely the destruction of the ideological façade behind which man hides and 'suppresses' the reality of God and of himself. Revelation tells him precisely what he really is. It is the total and exhaustive interpretation of what he really experiences himself to be. We have only to understand that there is an experience of grace, that God has already come to us in the Spirit prior to his coming to us in the word in order to realise that we have no need to speak of the reality of the faith as though it were another (and happier) world added onto this present one in which we are imprisoned, and existing alongside it. For this reason it can do no harm if the religious book of the future begins with matters which seem to be in the foreground, for it is these that constitute the realities of life. It must begin, then, with human activities, with work, love, death, and all the well-worn and familiar matters with which human life is filled, with the 'spirit of unbelief' which makes hearts sceptical and fearful of giving way to 'illusions', for it appears to such hearts that faith only holds out illusions to man. It is precisely to the extent that the religious book sets itself to burrow down beneath the surface of the 'superficialities' of life, which are obviously present in it, to the factors below the surface (and only so can it be a religious book in any true and effective sense) that it has to begin precisely with these 'superficialities', for it is only through them that we can make our way into the deeper truths. For this reason the religious book of the future must guard against losing its true character by branching out too hastily into speculative theology. It is precisely in these last few decades that (in contrast to earlier ones) an excessively 'refined' theology has evinced itself in such books, which has had a subtle way of turning loose the whole of speculative theology (which in itself is necessary) into the field of devotion (even such a writer as Dom Marmion and similar ascetical authors seem to me to have incurred this danger to some extent). It seems that we can only produce anything or make anything attractive if we turn to those men who live a cloistered way of life in a protected environment, cut off from the world, an environment which must necessarily be, to a large extent, remote from real life. From this point of view, so it seems to me, even the biblical approach to devotion can no longer be considered altogether so suitable in the religious book of the future. Certainly the bible always remains the foundation book of Christianity, precisely because it is genuine in itself and free from ideological prejudices. But for all this, regarded realistically, it has, so far as we are concerned, receded so far back in history from us that it is no longer possible for a religious book to be a florilegium of passages from scripture with a few words of commentary attached to each. Scripture is indeed too remote, historically speaking, from *our* lives, and we must learn to recognise this realistically, and not be so full of pious enthusiasm as to use it exaggeratedly and without discretion. In all cases in which it is not scientific exegesis that is being aimed at the religious author should quietly spare the reader the long journey (whenever and wherever it is in fact long) from the letter of scripture to the reality signified by it. He should speak directly of this reality itself. And then it is always open to him, in appropriate cases, to say at the end of his investigation 'and this is already to be found in such-and-such a passage of scripture'.

A further consequence of this, however paradoxical it may at first seem, is that the religious book of the future will have to be concerned with the genuine basic themes of theology, and not with secondary details of dogmatics, morals and ascetics. Indeed it must itself constitute an original theology in its own right, with a subject matter that is of central importance. It has to be addressed to a man who is forced to live in an extremely 'worldly' world, one who has much else to do besides reading religious books, one for whom life does not begin to be interesting only when he enters the realm of the explicitly religious (as perhaps it did for certain poor devils in earlier centuries whose lot was one of drudgery). It must be addressed to a man who has to live the Christian life not as a particular 'calling' which is apart from the rest of his life, but rather as the brightness, the power and the ultimate mystery of his own life. How can such a man effectively bring home to himself the reality of God not as something that is evident or manifest to him, but rather as the inconceivable mystery of existence? How can he make real his encounter with Christ in such a way that Christ 'is present' to him in his everyday life? What is the term 'prayer' really intended to signify? How can we come to terms with love, with our everyday lives and with our deaths? And so on. (However, though there are not many themes, there is one that is inexhaustible for this purpose: simply the single inescapable mystery of human existence.) These are the real themes for the religious book. Thus it will probably come about that the religious book becomes theological in a real and effective sense, while the theological book becomes no less really religious. For only when the pristine unity between them is regained does the religious book become worthy of belief. It cannot presuppose the world of faith as something already given (as earlier ascetical literature did) in order to go on from there to draw out the devotional implications of it for the practice of everyday life. It must, in a certain sense, constantly be making its own original attempts to create this world afresh. For this there is need of a 'new theology' (however unpleasant the associations may be which have come to be attached to this phrase), and conversely theology (considered as a science) will be fully employed if it sets itself to achieve this task, if it is aimed at stating in an effective manner what was really meant by the traditional formulae, why they appeal to an experience which is ultimately existential (this being made possible by grace), and bring one to a confrontation with one's self. Perhaps, therefore, the living theology of the future will have very little 'scientific' about it (i.e. it will not suppose that it can only be true to its own nature if it concerns itself with historical or speculative matters – art for art's sake – these in turn only being of interest to the scientific theologians themselves). Meanwhile the religious literature will be very 'theological' (i.e. facing up to the ultimate and basic questions in a new, honest and radical way). Would it be a pity if the theological and the religious book of the future were almost indistinguishable one from another? In this particular field can the situation not be precisely the opposite of what it is in other sciences? In these other sciences the gulf between the 'specialist' and the 'layman' becomes perforce ever greater, and rightly so: the 'popular understanding' is a sign of scientific inexactitude. But in the realm of theology and religion the cleavage between these two ought perhaps to become ever smaller, and we could even go so far as to regard this diminution as a criterion for the genuineness of both kinds of literature (the theological and the religious). To the extent that a given statement does not adequately express the innermost centre of existence it is also, by theological standards, not scientific (taking all this *cum grano salis*). In any case the chief task of the religious literature of the future will be to serve as a pointer to the first origins of every genuine exercise of religion. It will not be to work out a complicated apparatus of religious asceticism for which these origins represent axioms and mere presuppositions, which are taken for granted as self-evident.

Accordingly the religious literature of the future will be gentle and discreet in its pronouncements. It will itself undertake the task of unmasking pseudo-religious attitudes, and will no longer leave this task to sociology, depth psychology and the scepticism of contemporary atheism. It must also be able to be read by the new man with the mentality of a contemporary practitioner of the natural sciences and a technician of the modern age – the more so since we are all, to some extent, brought under these influences. In the post-individualistic phase of human history this literature must not give the impression of being an opiate, catering for needs which are ultimately unimportant and designed to soothe the pains of the 'sensitive soul' of the introvert. This literature will have in mind the man who regards himself as confronted by a task to perform in this world. It will not be intended as a substitute for medicine, including psychological medicine, or for depth psychology. Rather it will presuppose these. It will regard moral problems as beginning only at that point at which these really are initiated. It will never speak of God as though it knew all about him and had succeeded in expressing the whole truth of him in theological statements and moral maxims. It will openly recognise and accept the interior 'complexity' of man. It will not be too hasty or indiscreet in seeking to bring everything in man under the aegis of religion. It will prove its genuineness by letting the world be worldly and, *precisely in so doing*, making it comprehensible as that which genuine religion presupposes.

But the religious book will also have the courage to demand of man that he shall recognise and accept that he is infinitely more than merely a man. He must recognise the blessedness of the pain that is accepted, in which the finite becomes interior to the infinite love in its incomprehensibility.

How should the religious book not have a future? It will be transformed and will endure. It will achieve this even if it takes the form of an unending variation upon a single basic theme: 'My God, my God, why have you forsaken me?' Even then it will endure and will lead us to that point in our human existence at which this existence is thrown headlong into the redeeming mystery.

LIST OF SOURCES OF VOLUMES 7 & 8

CHRISTIAN LIVING FORMERLY AND TODAY

Preliminary draft for an address which the author delivered on several occasions during the months of October, November and December 1966 in certain major cities of Germany (Cologne, Frankfurt, Koblenz and Essen). First published in *Gul* 39 (1966) Vol 5.

BEING OPEN TO GOD AS EVER GREATER

Originally an unwritten address delivered at a conference for Jesuit interns at Rottmanshöhe in 1959. A tape-recording of this was taken and subsequently edited, and the typescript of this served as the basis for a version of this conference which was duplicated and disseminated in this way. A final radical revision and expansion was made when it was published in *Gul* 39 (1966), 183–201.

INTELLECTUAL HONESTY AND CHRISTIAN FAITH

An address delivered at the invitation of the Society of Catholic High Schools at the university of Vienna (on 14 March 1966). This address was repeated on the occasion of the General Students' Day of the Societies of New Students on 31 May 1966 in Darmstadt, on 4 July 1966 for the Catholic Students' Society of the university of Saarland in Saarbrücken, and on 17 July 1966 at the invitation of the Catholic Students' Society at the university in Bochum. It was originally published in *Stimmen der Zeit* 91 (1966), 401–417.

DO NOT STIFLE THE SPIRIT

A festal address delivered on the occasion of the Austrian Catholic Day on 1 June 1962 in the great aula of the university of Salzburg. Published in full for the first time in *Löscht den Geist nicht aus. Probleme und Imperative des Österreichischen Katholikentages 1962*, edited by the

Praesidium of Catholic Action of Austria (Innsbruck 1963), 16–25. For the reprinted version appearing in this volume the address delivered at that time (immediately *before* the beginning of the Council!) was again revised afresh, but only certain inessential points were corrected (cf. p. 87, n. 1).

THE CHRISTIAN IN HIS WORLD

Inaugural lecture at the Nordic 'Catholic Day' on the occasion of the 1100th anniversary of the death of St Ansgar, held in Hamburg on 18 June 1965. Published for the first time in *Stimmen der Zeit* 90 (1965), 481–489.

'I BELIEVE IN THE CHURCH'

This study originally appeared in *Wort und Wahrheit* 9 (1954), 329–339. In the form in which it was then presented the article was concerned with the question of how to understand the dogma promulgated in 1950 of the physical assumption of the Mother of God into heaven (hence the subtitle: 'The New Marian Dogma and the Individual'). For the purposes envisaged in including it in the present volume the essay has been adapted and once more revised, and this reference to the dogma of the Assumption has been eliminated.

CHRISTMAS THE FESTIVAL OF ETERNAL YOUTH

Christmas address delivered over the Bavarian radio on 25 December 1964. The manuscript of this address was distributed in duplicated form, and subsequently revised once more for printing in *Gul* 38 (1965), pp. 401–404.

HOLY NIGHT

Hitherto unpublished in this form.

PEACE ON EARTH

Hitherto unpublished.

SEE WHAT A MAN!

First published in *Gul* 28 (1955), 1–3.

THE SCANDAL OF DEATH

Address delivered in the course of a Good Friday transmission over the Bavarian radio on 8 April 1966. The duplicated typescript was subsequently revised for printing in this volume. A record of it has also been produced by the Christophorus-Verlag, Freiburg-i-Br.

'HE DESCENDED INTO HELL'

This study has previously appeared under the title, 'Karsamstag' in *Gul* 30 (1957), 81–84. Considerable alterations have been made to the whole study.

HIDDEN VICTORY

Three short addresses designed to follow one upon another on the occasion of a Good Friday service (The Liturgy of the Word) over the Bavarian radio on 9 April 1966. In its present form it is a reprinting of a slightly altered version, also produced as a record by the Christophorus-Verlag, Freiburg-i-Br. (Cf. above, 'The Scandal of Death').

EXPERIENCING EASTER

Written as a meditation on the 15th Station of the Cross, and published in a book written by Frau A. Röper, *Die Vierzehn Stationen im Leben des N.N.* (Kevelaer, 1965), 120–132. Stylistic corrections have been introduced here.

ENCOUNTERS WITH THE RISEN CHRIST

First published in *Gul* 28 (1955), 81–86.

HE WILL COME AGAIN

Published for the first time under the title 'Er wird so wiederkommen wie ihr ihn habt zum Himmel auffahren sehen', *Gul* 32 (1959), 81–83.

THE FESTIVAL OF THE FUTURE OF THE WORLD

A meditation given on the eve of the Ascension 1961 in the Collegium Canisianum at Innsbruck. First published under the title, 'Christi Himmelfahrt' in *Korrespondenzblatt des Collegium Canisianum* 96 (1961–62), 68–8.

THE CHURCH AS THE SUBJECT OF THE SENDING OF THE SPIRIT

First published in *Gul* 29 (1956), 94–98 (title: 'Die Kirche als Ort der Geistsendung').

THE SPIRIT THAT IS OVER ALL LIFE

Meditation delivered on the occasion of Pentecost, 1960 in the Collegium Canisianum. First printed under the title, 'Gedanken an Pfingsten' in the *Korrespondenzblatt des Collegium Canisianum* 94 (1960), 34–40.

SUNDAY, THE DAY OF THE LORD

Address delivered in the course of a 'Holy Hour' of the Pax Romana held at the Eucharistic World Congress of 1960 in Munich on 6 August 1960. Published in *Statio Orbis. Eucharistischer Weltkongress 1960 in München*, Vol II (Munich 1961), pp. 195–197. The version reprinted in the present volume is based upon a somewhat altered version which the author published in the periodical *Der grosse Entschluss* 20 (1965), 246–248.

THE EUCHARIST AND OUR DAILY LIVES

First published in *Der grosse Entschluss* 17 (1962), 391–396; 440–443.

ON TRUTHFULNESS

An address delivered at the Conference of Youth Workers held at Passau, 1960. First printed in *Katechetische Blätter* 85 (1960), 413–416; 468–474; 511–520.

PARRESIA (BOLDNESS)

First printed in *Gul* 31 (1958), 1–6.

THE WORKS OF MERCY AND THEIR REWARD

Hitherto unpublished in German. A translation of the text into French appeared in '*L'Evangile de la Misericorde*', *Hommage au Dr. Albert Schweitzer*. (On the occasion of his 90th birthday), ed. by Alphonse Goettmann. (Editions du Cerf. Paris 1965), 345–353.

PROVING ONE'S SELF IN TIME OF SICKNESS

First published in *Gul* 29 (1956), 64–67 (originally under the title 'Reflexionen zur Zeit der Krankheit').

ON CHRISTIAN DYING

Published in *Wort und Wahrheit* 14 (1959), pp. 653–657 under the title, 'Zum Tode verurteilt? Über das Sterben im christlichen Verständnis'.

WHY AND HOW CAN WE VENERATE THE SAINTS?

Original version in *Gul* 37 (1964), 325–340. The text reprinted here has been revised.

ALL SAINTS

Published in *Gul* 29 (1956), pp. 323–326.

IDEAS FOR A THEOLOGY OF CHILDHOOD

Lecture delivered at the Second International Convention of the SOS Children's Villages at the SOS Children's Village of Hinterbühl near Vienna on 1 October 1962. First published as a continuous whole in *Gul* 36 (1963), 104–114.

THE SACRAMENTAL BASIS FOR THE ROLE OF THE LAYMAN IN
   THE CHURCH

First published in *Gul* 33 (1960), 119–132.

THE POSITION OF WOMAN IN THE NEW SITUATION IN WHICH THE CHURCH FINDS HERSELF

An address delivered at the Convention of the Union of German Catholic Women on 20/21 June 1964 at Munich. Printed in *Die Frau im Aufbruch der Kirche*, O. Brachfeld, K. Horn, U. Ranke-Heinemann, E. Gössmann, K. Rahner ed. (Munich 1964), 120–145.

ON THE SITUATION OF THE CATHOLIC INTELLECTUAL

A lecture delivered on 21 May 1966 at Frankfurt a.M. under the title of 'Aufgabe und Varantwortung des Hochschullehrers in der Sicht des Konzilskonstitution "Die Kirche in der Welt von Heute"' (at the invitation of the Rabanus-Maurus-Akademie). The version printed here has been revised and in part expanded.

THE TASK OF THE WRITER IN RELATION TO CHRISTIAN LIVING

Published under the title 'Über den Buchautor' in the Festal Almanac of the publishing house of Otto Müller (on the occasion of its silver jubilee) entitled *Werke und Jahre* (Salzburg 1962), 66–86. (Here given in an emended version.)

PRAYER FOR CREATIVE THINKERS

Originally composed for the fifth Austrian 'Formation of Youth' Week, held in Tirol (23 May 1954). Published in *Der grosse Entschluss* 10 (1954), 9–10.

ON THE EVANGELICAL COUNSELS

First published in *Gul* 37 (1964), 17–37.

THE THEOLOGY OF POVERTY

First delivered as a lecture in the course of a conference of religious orders, published in *Gul* 33 (1960), 262–290. Previous title: 'Die Armut des Ordenslebens in einer veränderten Welt'.

THE THEOLOGICAL MEANING OF THE VENERATION OF THE SACRED HEART

A contribution to the *Festschrift des theologischen Konviktes Innsbruck 1858 bis 1958* under the title 'Vom Ziel unseres Strebens unter dem Symbol des Herzens Jesu' (Innsbruck 1958), 102–109.

UNITY – LOVE – MYSTERY

Meditations held at the Triduum of the Sacred Heart 1962 in the Collegium Canisianum at Innsbruck. Published in the *Korrespondenzblatt des Collegium Canisianum* 97 (1962), 4–15.

THE FUTURE OF THE RELIGIOUS BOOK

Not hitherto published in German. A contribution to the Christmas message of Messrs Paul Brand, publishers, Hilversum – Antwerp, *Toekomst van het religieuze boek* (Hilversum 1965), 12–17 (together with other contributions by L. Rinser, H. J. Schultz, J. B. Metz).

Note: No reference has been made to the numerous reprintings in German-speaking countries. Translations are mentioned only if the relevant study was first published in a foreign language.

INDEX OF PERSONS

SUBJECT INDEX

Apostolate:
of scientist 108 *sqq.*
of creative thinker 132
witness of consumer ascesis 208 *sqq.*

Atheism:
real possibility of collective and cosmic A. 79 *sqq.*

Authorship:
and Christian living 112 *sqq.*
author as such stands under the summons of Christ in grace and activity has special Christian relevance 112 *sqq.*, 129
every human act of writing is a free act and so involves responsibility 115 *sqq.*
when dealing with Man enters Christian dimension 117 *sqq.*
intrinsic connection between really great Christianity and really great writing 119 *sqq.*
A. can justifiably be Christian in various ways 121 *sqq.*
possibility of being Christian by open restriction of self to limited field 122 *sqq.*
Christian value of A. which leads to form of an open question 123 *sqq.*
writer who is full, though unacknowledged Christian 125 *sq.*
the professedly non-Catholic writer who fails to realise his position is a Catholic one 126 *sq.*
professedly Catholic author 127 *sqq.*
any author wholly and always susceptible 129
future of religious book 251 *sqq.*
necessity of future religious book to be free from ideology 252 *sq.*

necessity of future religious book to deal with basic themes of theology 254
necessity of bridging gap between theological and religious literature 254 *sqq.*

Baptism:
as entry into church seen to be basic to understanding of layman 55 *sqq.*
distinction between baptised and justified 58 *sq.*, 113

Charisms:
in Church 133 sq., 178

Christ:
question of veneration of saints and his unique mediatorship 10, 218
significance of humanity of C. for our relationship with God 11 *sqq.*, 57, 217 *sqq.*
proximity of Silent God in C. 14 *sq.*
the 'presence' of the Historical Lord 15 *sq.*
all childhood derives name and origin from that of Logos 49 *sq.*
situation of Catholic intellectual 94 *sqq.*, 131 *sq.*
poverty in teaching of Jesus 181 *sqq.*
theological meaning of veneration of the Sacred Heart 217 *sqq.*
unity aspect of veneration of Sacred Heart 229 *sqq.*
love aspect of veneration of Sacred Heart 235 *sqq.*
'mystery' aspect of veneration of Sacred Heart 241 *sqq.*

Christianity:
patterns of C. 3 *sqq.*, 230